For
Hugo and Ella
and
other children of the 21st century

# Contents

# Foreword

'Blessed are the flexible for they shall not be bent out of shape.'
(Anon)

The 'All Our Futures' report was published in 1999. The report was commissioned by the government following the 1997 publication of the White Paper 'Excellence in Schools' and alongside the revisions to the National Curriculum, including the advent of the National Literacy and Numeracy Strategies (DfES 1998 and 1999 respectively). Its messages were long overdue to most teachers of early years and primary age children as this was the first time in over a decade – since the advent of the National Curriculum – that creativity was reinstated in the political agenda. Not only was the focus on creativity welcome but the messages the report contained were forthright and transparent:

> Creativity is possible in all areas of human activity, including the arts, sciences, at work, at play and in all other areas of daily life. All people have creative abilities and we all have them differently ... Creative education involves a balance between teaching knowledge and skills, and encouraging innovation. (NACCCE 1999: 6/7)

This alone – and there is much, much more – makes Anna Craft's book an imperative read for all those engaged in early years and primary education.

Many teachers and others, for example parents, have conceived of creativity as mainly associated with 'the arts' and because these were given very low priority in the National Curriculum and in subsequent school inspections, children's opportunities to be creative became inevitably very restricted. However, as many writers, including Anna, have pointed out, creativity is – and must be thought of – as far more than 'the arts'. It is a way of thinking and doing and knowing – even of being. Albert Einstein is reported as having once said, 'Imagination is more important than knowledge'. As early years educators – given that the age of children who concern us most are at their most creative, imaginative and playful – we must learn to express and articulate on behalf of children, the very qualities which we are trying to engender and develop through a creative curriculum. We must learn to sponsor creativity to promote the highest levels of thinking, originality, innovation, resourcefulness, individuality, vision, initiative and self-expression, as well as artistry.

As Anna Craft points out in this well-conceived and skilfully written book, there are many aspects to young children's creativity which extend well beyond much of what appears in either the National Curriculum or the Curriculum Guidance for the Foundation Stage (CGFS) (DfEE 2000) despite the latter having a specific curricular element called 'Creative Development'. Creativity is a key, cross-curricular thinking skill which has huge implications for our future society, whether in relation to generating a multi-role (rather than a jobs-for-life) society, coping with the speed of change or engendering what Anna calls a 'lifewide resourcefulness'. This book responds to what the writer calls a 'culture of individualism' and its potential for ensuring that people are able to challenge and think beyond existing traditions. It offers a scholarly discussion based on a sound and well-expressed analysis of the disciplinary background to various reports and research findings.

'Little c creativity' as explained in this book is more than 'just' a curriculum. It is about the capacity to route-find in life, to take action and to evaluate what is effective or successful. All children are capable of 'little c creativity' and all teachers ought to be capable of referencing their pedagogical approaches towards providing children with meaningful learning experiences that have 'little c' potential. A few talented children and adults will reach genius level – 'high c creativity' – but the majority need opportunities to use 'little c' thinking and skills and to work and play with teachers who recognise the relationship between teaching creatively and teaching for creativity and inspiring children into a 'can-do' approach to life and learning. There is no 'ceiling' on development of creativity – or any other skills and understanding. The challenge presented by the author to Professor Howard Gardner's multiple intelligences (1983, 1993, 1999) is very welcome as there were no stated criteria by which Gardner selected the particular intelligences with which he is associated and there are dangers that such concepts will limit thinking about learners' capabilities. While 'little c creativity' requires intelligence per se it also requires what Anna calls 'possibility thinking', that is, considering alternative futures, different possibilities and thinking, which shapes the future as well as the present. While the notion of multiple intelligences is predicated upon excellent performance in certain cognitive domains, 'little c creativity' is looser and more egalitarian, having innovation at its core.

The results of *not* developing 'little c creativity' are awesome, not least an impaired capacity to cope with basic challenges and the lack of ability to pose important and relevant questions. The onus therefore rests on early years practitioners to ensure that children are made aware of new possibilities and to foster divergence as well as convergence in relation to problem-solving potential. This is no easy task with a prescribed curriculum, even one which is broad. As with the CGFS – early years practitioners need their very own brand of 'little c' creativity to work with the challenges they face in ensuring that young children develop imagination, initiative, self-expression, self-creation and know-how as much as knowing 'what', particularly at Key Stage 1. Reading this book, it is clear that the writer shares other early childhood educators' concerns that the prescription under which many practitioners work hinders professional thinking and practitioners' own brand of 'little c creativity', so vital if the discontinuities and inconsistencies between the curriculum espoused for 3–5 year olds and that designed appropriate for 5–7 year olds are to be overcome. Practitioners need to regain their artistry in teaching, for in the past decade or so this has increasingly taken a back seat to conformity and a technical construction of teaching and schooling. We need to put lifewide education back into schooling to deal with the demands of the modern world which will require continued and expansive creative thinking from its present and future adult citizens. The author is convincing in making a strong case for this.

Of over-riding interest to me is the close but perhaps tenuous link between play and creativity for, whilst it has to be recognised that not all play is creative, imagination and 'what if' kinds of thinking promoted in, for example, socio-dramatic play are bound up with creativity in its broadest sense. We know that the 'best' play to enhance cognitive (and metacognitive) development is that which not only questions the content of what is happening but emphasises the application of skills and knowledge through play and allows children to play with, for example, language and thought processes. It is the kind of 'advanced' play through which children raise their own challenges and take ownership and control over their own learning, perhaps nowhere more epitomised than in the Reggio Emilia approach which has gained heightened recognition internationally at a time when many countries are actually tightening their curricular approaches to early education. More importantly, play can take children beyond any barriers to thinking through its focus on pretence and endless possibilities (Moyles and Adams, 2001). Play also stimulates certain dispositions towards learning which can foster creativity in ways denied by more formalised means of learning.

It is good to see that in this book, Anna Craft is clear that one cannot be creative consistently across time or actions, and that some people find it easier to access their 'little c creativity' potential than others. But in the context of her concept of 'lifewide learning' – which I find so much more powerful and culturally inspiring than lifelong learning – it is clear that most of us ought to be freed more often than many of us currently are to engage in making connections, taking chances, coping with paradox, giving and receiving criticism of what we do and think, and generally freeing our minds to embrace our 'little c creativity' and heightened playfulness. Young children as well as adults need thinking time in order to develop confidence and competence. This is simply not happening in contexts where 'pace' is the order of the day (as in the National Literacy Strategy – see Moyles, *et al.*, 2002) and creativity of all kinds is lost in the rush to meet targets and produce outcomes. This is not to say that 'little c creativity' lacks outcomes; far from it. As Anna suggests, being imaginative assumes an outcome; otherwise, how would we know that imagination exists! It assumes change, difference and novelty, all of which are observable.

Early years practitioners and academics will find that, in reading Anna Craft's stimulating book, they are challenged to use their own 'little c creativity' to think beyond the constraints of what is currently provided and to imagine a world where young children are freed to use all cognitive and metacognitive means at their disposal to become lifewide learners. Readers will be rewarded by gaining knowledge not only from the writer's broad theoretical sweep, merely hinted at in this Foreword, but through the book's rich stories of young children and practitioners using their own brand of 'little c creativity' to extend and enhance education from a child-centred stance. We can only dream of the impact on our future society of a curriculum based on developing creativity as outlined by Anna Craft – and hope that, for our children, that day comes soon.

Professor Janet Moyles
March 2002
Anglia Polytechnic University, Chelmsford

## References

Department for Education and Employment (DfEE) and Qualifications and Curriculum Authority (QCA) (2000) *Curriculum Guidance for the Foundation Stage*. London: DfES/QCA.

Department for Education and Employment (1998) *The National Literacy Strategy: Framework for Teaching.* London: DfEE

Department for Education and Employment (1998) *The National Numeracy Strategy.* London: DfEE

Gardner, H. (1983) *Frames of Mind: The Theory of Multiple Intelligences.* London: William Heinemann Ltd

Gardner, H. (1993) *Multiple Intelligences: The Theory in Practice.* New York: Harper Collins.

Gardner, H. (1999) *Intelligence Reframed: Multiple Intelligences for the 21st Century.* New York: BasicBooks

Moyles, J. Hargreaves, L. Merry, R. Paterson, A. and Esarte-Sarries, V. (2002) *Interactive Teaching in the Primary School: Digging Deeper into Meanings.* Buckingham: Open University Press.

Moyles, J. and Adams, S. (2001) *Statements of Entitlement to Play (StEPs): A Framework for Playful Teaching.* Buckingham: Open University Press.

National Advisory Committee on creative and Cultural Education (NACCCE) (1999) *All Our Futures: Creativity, Culture and Education.* London: Department for Education and Employment.

# Acknowledgements

I am grateful to the many people who have contributed to my thinking in this book, either directly or indirectly. These include countless children and early years practitioners in many settings, Bob Jeffrey at the Open University, Professor John White at London University Institute of Education, Bernadette Duffy at the Thomas Coram Early Excellence Centre, Kevin McCarthy of Re:membering Education, Lesley James, Geoff Botting and Michaela Crimmin at the Royal Society of Arts, Kate Williamson and Lesley Morris at The Design Council, and numerous colleagues in the Open University Centre for Creativity and in the Creativity in Education Special Interest Group within the British Educational Research Association, both of which have evolved in the last twelve months from our research group at the Open University. Additionally, as this book took shape, my own two infants, Hugo and Ella, in their interactions with other children, provided me with innumerable home-based opportunities to observe and analyse practices which support children's creativity in the early years.

My thanks are also due to Joanna Attard, Kelly Hulbert, Angela Killick, Lorraine Ares de Parya and Michelle Petzer for their inspiration and support. From a different perspective, I am grateful to my own parents, Professor Maurice Craft and Alma Craft, for their ongoing mentoring and advice. Finally, a continued thank you to my partner, Simon, for his understanding, encouragement, inspiration and support.

Anna Craft
The Open University
January 2002

# INTRODUCTION

## Lifewide creativity in context

This book has been written in the hope of broadening the discourse on the role and scope of creativity in the education of children aged 2½ to 8. Conceived of at a time when the notion of creativity was becoming 'universalized', i.e. coming to be seen as relevant, current and appropriate in a wide variety of contexts in education, the economy and in policy making, this book conceptualizes an approach to creativity which is not tied to particular teaching subjects or activities (Jeffrey and Craft, 2001). It argues that creativity is relevant across life – the term I have come to use is 'lifewide' (Craft, 2001) – as well as lifelong.

The book draws primarily on philosophy, but also on psychology and sociology, offering a conceptual account of the notion of lifewide, or as I sketch it throughout this book 'little c creativity' (first discussed in Craft, 2000); and it presents an argument for fostering it, in the early years, supported by vignettes and case studies from early years education settings. It represents a departure from dominant approaches to exploring creativity in all three disciplines in its focus on the everyday. This Introduction briefly sets the ideas in this book in the context of the earlier literature. It draws on part of a literature review carried out for the Qualifications and Curriculum Authority during 2000, which provided an early foundation to the two three-year curriculum projects it ran, both of which focused on creativity in different parts of the curriculum for children aged 5 and above.

### Early studies of creativity: psychoanalytic, cognitive, behaviourist and humanistic

Theories and ideas about creativity have a long history. Given the distinctively human capacity to develop new ideas and original products, this is perhaps unsurprising, as some have suggested (Ryhammar and Brolin, 1999). The Greek, Judaic, Christian, and Muslim traditions all contain the notion of 'inspiration' or 'getting an idea', founded on the belief that a higher power produces it (*ibid.*, p. 260). However, the focus underwent a major shift during the Romantic era in Europe when the *source* of inspiration started to be seen as the human being, accompanied by the artistic expression of ideas. During this era, originality, insight, creative genius, and subjectivity of feeling were highly valued. From the end of the nineteenth century, the question of what fostered creativity began to be investigated, particularly in psychology, although, as Hudson points out, it was not until the mid-twentieth century that creativity began to be associated with science as well as with art – and that he attributes to the general position of scientists in society, who by that time had shifted from being perceived as technicians to being seen as 'cultural heroes', and also to the need for America to develop its armaments industry (Hudson, 1966, p. 120).

The first systematic study was undertaken by Galton (1869). His focus was 'genius' and what followed was a hundred or so studies on this theme, defined as achievement acknowledged in the wider public arena. This line of investigation remained prevalent way into the 1920s. The early years of the twentieth century also saw a move towards the empirical investigation of creativity within the new discipline of psychology by some of the influential thinkers of that era, as indicated below. There were four major traditions in which this took place:

- *Psychoanalytic.* This included Freud's discussion of creativity as the sublimation of drives (Freud, 1908, 1910, and 1916) and Winnicott's work on development which makes creativity central and intrinsic to human nature (Clancier and Kalmanovitch, 1987, Winnicott, 1971). Freud's discussions of creativity are embedded in his pyschoanalytic framework for interpreting daydreams and play, and creativity is seen as the sublimation of drives, or of wish-fulfilment. It has also been suggested (Clancier and Kalmanovitch, 1987, p. 89) that Freud saw creative activity in adult artists as equivalent to the child at play. Winnicott was the first clinician to have noticed the significance of the transitional object for the young child, providing continuity from familiar surroundings to those which were less so (this being a 'natural' developmental progression). He observed that an imaginative life is often entwined with the transitional object, this being one aspect of what he called transitional phenomena. In this way, to Winnicott, creativity was closely linked to play and necessary to a child's development.
- *Cognitive.* This grew on the foundation of Galton's work and included Mednick's exploration of the associative process

(Mednick 1962, 1964, drawing on Spearman, 1931), and also Guilford's exploration of the divergent production of ideas and products (1950, 1964, 1967). Mednick (1962) put forward the theory that the more creative the person, the more consistent their responses to associative connections between apparently unrelated matters. Later, Mednick and Mednick (1964) explored how creativity was affected by offering multiple stimuli and encouraging associative exploration of these, although this work was not completed. Guilford explored divergent-production abilities, reporting on the research available to him at that time, concluding that fluency, flexibility, and originality were significant factors in creative behaviour (1967). Cognitive work on creativity also included studies of creativity as a problem-solving capacity, building on the thinking of, for example, Wallas (1926). Other work in the cognitive tradition saw creativity as an aspect of intelligence (drawing on, for example, Binet and Henri, 1896). However, the evidence on whether there is any correlation between general intelligence and creativity was contradictory; work by Barron, 1963, Cline, Richards and Abe, 1962, Torrance and Gowan, 1963, and many others suggesting a link between general intelligence and creativity, and work by Getzels and Jackson suggesting no such link (1962). One explanation given for the contradictory evidence was that creative thinkers were less likely to conform to the expectations of any test environment (Hudson, 1968).

- *Behaviourist*. This third tradition in cognitive psychology included work by the 'father' of behaviourism, Skinner (1968, 1971, 1974). Skinner's conceptualization of creativity was that it occurred as a chance mutation in the repertoire of behaviours.
- *Humanistic*. Theorists here included Rogers (1970), and Maslow (1971, 1987), whose discussions focused on the self-realizing person acting in harmony with their inner needs and potentialities. Rogers, whose thinking influenced work in therapy and counselling, identified three inner conditions for creativity. First was extensionality (or being open to experience), second was having an internal locus of evaluation in relation to one's own performance, and thirdly the ability to play (or to toy with elements and concepts). Maslow conceptualized creativity as 'self-actualization' (Maslow, 1971), a perspective built upon in my own discussion of 'little c creativity', in this book and elsewhere (Craft, 2000). For Maslow, self-actualizing people share a range of characteristics which he regards as desirable in that he conceives of self-actualization as psychologically healthy.

The characteristics he cites include being creative, being problem- rather than self-focused, having autonomy in attitude whilst being accepting of self and others, having an ethical framework and also operating to a democratic framework (Maslow, 1987).

Some creativity theorists were influenced by more than one tradition or line of work (Rhyammer and Brolin, 1999). Overall, though, the early decades of the twentieth century were influenced to a greater degree by *philosophical* speculation than by empirical investigations, because of the methodological approaches of at least two of the four branches described above. These approaches to the study of creativity continue to provide theoretical frameworks for investigators, although with different emphases at different points in time.

The 1950s brought a particularly rich and influential period of research in creativity. At this time, the emphasis was on the psychological determinants of genius and giftedness, and creativity was being seen by now as a 'generalized' phenomenon rather than tied in to a particular area of knowledge only. Empirical enquiries formed the methodological basis for much of the investigative work, usually involving large-scale studies. Many would argue that this era of research was launched by Guilford's (1950) examination of the limitations of intelligence tests and his investigation of 'divergent thinking'. There followed many studies which attempted to test and measure creativity, to pin down its characteristics and to foster it through specific teaching approaches, both within education and beyond. An influential figure in the classroom was Torrance (1962) who developed many experiments and tests for creativity. Others explored the impact of courses designed to encourage creativity, many based on the work of Osborn, which used brainstorming and a special question-asking technique (Osborn, 1963). These studies (by, for example, Meadow and Parnes, 1959, Parnes, 1962, Parnes and Meadow, 1959) demonstrated that courses designed to improve creativity appeared to increase originality but not necessarily fluency (i.e. the 'flow' of ideas). Parnes and Meadow (1960) claimed that the effects of creativity courses were long-lasting (from eight months to four years). There were also claims that there were some 'transfer effects' showing that students of such courses improved in confidence and self-reliance more generally.

## Lines of study since the 1950s: personality, cognition and how to stimulate creativity

The 1950s research led to three major lines of development: work in personality, cognition, and how to stimulate creativity. These lines have drawn on all four methodological traditions outlined above.

### Personality

The first line of study, 'personality', included a focus on prominent creative persons, and the early work was done by Barron (1955), who suggested that personality rather than the original act itself would be a more appropriate focal point for study. Much work was later carried out by the Institute of Personality Assessment and Research, at Berkeley and led by the work of MacKinnon, (1962a, 1962b, 1969, 1975), Getzels and Csikszentmihalyi (1976), and Simonton (1984). It also included a second focus, the study of much narrower personality traits or dispositions, which are correlated either positively or negatively with creativity. For example, it was suggested that dogmatism, conformism, narcissism, frustration, resilience, elation and hypomania all affect tolerance for creativity. These studies of personality traits or dispositions are surveyed and summarized by Shaw and Runco (1994) and Eisenman (1997). In parallel with these studies, others, such as Bruner, developed work on personality 'conditions' that affect creativity, some of which he described as paradoxes: passion and decorum, freedom to be dominated by the object, deferral and immediacy, the internal drama, and the complexity of abilities may contribute to creativity (Bruner, 1962).

From this particular strand of creativity research, the creative person can, it seems, be described as having the following characteristics (summarized by Brolin, 1992):

- strong motivation
- endurance
- intellectual curiosity
- deep commitment
- independence in thought and action
- strong desire for self-realization
- strong sense of self
- strong self-confidence
- openness to impressions from both within and without
- attracted to complexity and obscurity
- high sensitivity
- high capacity for emotional involvement in their investigations

Some authors have also suggested that willingness to take risks is a critical attribute of the highly creative individual (McLelland, 1963, p. 184 and Roe, 1963, p. 170).

Although these personality studies have provided important information about creative people, they have been criticized for a number of reasons, most significantly that they have been too narrow, focused on eminent and/or productive persons, and that consequently the qualities identified appear to be both contradictory and superficial. In addition, as the criteria for the selection of subjects and for defining what is creative vary from study to study, it is difficult to compare one with another. Eysenck, on the other hand, has recently argued that studies of creative individuals have demonstrated surprising agreement over the years (Eysenck, 1997).

## Cognition

So much for personality-based creativity research. The second major approach since the 1950s has been continued work in cognition. Since the 1950s, two major lines of cognitively oriented creativity investigation have emerged, namely psychometrics and experimental psychodynamics.

### Psychometrics

Psychometric approaches to creativity were begun by Guilford, who developed a tool for measuring the extent of divergent thinking, which he later refined into the concept of 'divergent production' (Guilford, 1967). Later variations of Guilford's work include the Torrance Tests of Creative Thinking (Torrance, 1966, 1974). These permeated school contexts, particularly in the United States where tests of creative thinking have been used to assess pupils' creative thinking. This approach was influenced heavily by Mooney's (1963) 'four elements' view of creativity, which defined it as encompassing specific aspects of the environment (place) of creation, the product as an outcome of creativity, the process of creation, and the person doing the creating. The Torrance Tests have however, been criticized for measuring intelligence-related factors rather than creativity as such, and for being affected too easily by external circumstances. In addition, it has been suggested that the test procedure simply measures 'creativity on request' as opposed to creativity in daily life. On the other hand, it has been suggested recently that the tests have proved to be useful in estimating the potential for creative thought (Bachelor and Michael, 1997), and some have suggested that they may have a future (Kirschenbaum, 1998; Plucker and Runco, 1998). In addition, some aspects of the work done in psychometrics, such as that undertaken by

Hudson (1966), focused on the interrelationship between divergent and convergent thinking in creativity, rather than the pure measurement of creative responses.

## Psychodynamics
Psychodynamics was the second line of enquiry within cognitive psychology. During the 1970s and 1980s, work was undertaken on personality, perception and creativity. These studies, which were focused on specific groups such as architects, students, children and young people, artists and university teachers, have suggested that the creative person:

- has the ability to arrive at alternative views of reality
- has good communication/a good connection between logic and imagination
- has the courage to go against social conventions
- has a belief in their own ideas
- is emotionally involved in the work of creation
  (Smith and Carlsson, 1990; Schoon, 1992; Andersson and Rhyammar, 1998).

Another major development during the 1980s and 1990s in personal and cognitive research has been the shift of emphasis away from measurable, outcomes-based and product-linked approaches such as those developed by Torrance in the 1960s and 1970s, including tests of creative ability (op. cit.). More typical of the more recent era are investigations which have focused on understanding the creative mind in terms of intelligence (Gardner, 1993), and attempts to explore implicit theories of creativity held by 'experts' within specific fields of knowledge (Sternberg, 1988; Speil and von Korff, 1998).

## How to stimulate creativity
The third of the three lines in creativity research since the 1950s has focused on ways to stimulate creativity. During the last fifty years, there has been a strong concern that education should emphasize the development of creativity. Implicit in this is the assumption that creativity can be so influenced. Indeed, there is some evidence that certain kinds of classroom settings do increase learner creativity; Haddon and Lytton (1968) for example, reported a study of children at the top end of primary school that demonstrated a higher learner creativity in informal classroom settings, which are more likely to encourage adventurous thinking in children. Lytton later made a range of recommendations for strategies which might stimulate creative thinking in children, in particular encouraging positive attitudes

towards self-initiated learning and exploration, and encouraging curiosity (Lytton, 1971). Interestingly, Lytton's explanation for the interest at that time in fostering creativity in schools was to see it as a response and counter-balance to 'the threatening mechanization of man and society' (*op. cit.* p. 113), a contrasting state of affairs to today's highly technological global world. Returning to the stimulating of creativity, a range of attempts to encourage learner creativity have been developed since the 1950s, as well as policy reviews such as the Plowden Report (CACE, 1967), which associated creativity with play, and later the NACCCE Report, which saw creativity as cross-curricular (NACCCE, 1999); but there is, as Ryhammar and Brolin (1999) point out, a serious lack of systematic, controlled evaluations of such programmes and policy statements. It is also the case that the methods and criteria for evaluating these are underpinned by differing theories of creativity. In addition, whether looking at the work of cognitive psychologists, psychodynamicists, humanists, or behaviourists, the question of how far it is possible to transfer creative thinking into new contexts, remains unclear.

## Studies since the 1980s: creativity and social systems

By contrast with all these earlier developments, the main direction of research into creativity in the 1980s and 1990s has been to contextualize it in a social psychological framework which recognizes the important role of social structures in fostering individual creativity (Rhyammar and Brolin, 1999). This has been described as a fourth, coherent area of study – creativity and social systems (Jeffrey and Craft, 2001) – in addition to personality, cognition, and how to stimulate creativity.

Some significant theories have been put forward in which creativity is seen from a systems perspective, where various elements of the overall social and cognitive context are seen as highly relevant to the activity of creating (Csikszentmihalyi, 1998; Sternberg, 1988; Sternberg and Lubart, 1991a, 1991b, 1995).

Also, three major studies have been undertaken – one in Europe (Ekvall, 1991, 1996) and two in the USA (Amabile, 1988; Isaksen, 1995) – that have explored the organizational climates which serve to stimulate creativity. The overall results from these three programmes have suggested that in a creative climate, the participants in the organization:

- feel challenged by their goals, operations and tasks
- feel able to take initiatives and to find relevant information
- feel able to interact with others

- feel that new ideas are met with support and encouragement
- feel able to put forward new ideas and views
- experience much debate within a prestige-free and open environment
- feel uncertainty is tolerated and thus risk-taking is encouraged

In addition, Amabile's (1988) model suggests that individual creativity may be affected by even very minor aspects of the immediate social environment. For example, creativity may be impeded where rewards are determined in advance, where there is undue time pressure, over-supervision, competition, or where choices are restricted in terms of approach or working materials, or where evaluation is expected. The work of Worth (2000) suggests that the family context in early life makes an important difference. The role of the context or school subject domain has been increasingly emphasized since the early 1990s.

During the 1990s, under the influence of the perspective from social psychology, research into creativity in education became more comprehensive, and began to focus more on the creativity of ordinary people. At the same time, the methodology for investigating creativity in education also shifted, within a general trend, from large-scale studies aiming to measure creativity, toward ethnographic, qualitative approaches to research focusing on the actual site of operations and practice, as well as toward philosophical discussions around the nature of creativity.

In education in the United Kingdom, for example, Beetlestone (1998) focused on creativity in the early years' classroom; Woods (1995) and Woods and Jeffrey (1996) explored teacher creativity; Jeffrey (2001a, 2001b) examined pupil perspectives on creative teaching and learning; and Craft (1996) wrote on how to nourish the creative teacher. Beetlestone documented from a large variety of early years contexts practical strategies for embedding the fostering of creativity within the early years curriculum. Woods and Jeffrey worked through in-depth case studies to document ways in which a small group of teachers operate creatively in the face of a wider context which arguably suppresses the creativity of the teaching profession. Jeffrey explored, through ethnographic work, pupils' perceptions of creative teaching. Craft explored in depth the perspectives of eighteen educators involved in a holistic postgraduate course specifically designed to nurture their own creativity (Craft, 1996).

There are, of course, some overlaps in these periods; for example, from the applied education context, Fryer (1996) undertook a large-scale survey (rather than a qualitative approach), investigating teachers' attitudes towards creativity in their daily professional work. And paralleling the developments in psychology, within philosophy there was a shift away from regarding creativity as being tied up with product-outcomes, and toward being connected with imaginativeness (Elliott, 1971).

## The focus and scope of this book

So much for a very brief overview of the research context, and it will be clear that whilst there is a significant amount of literature concerning the nature of creativity, there is relatively little *empirical* research into the development and assessment of pupils' creativity. There are also important areas which are unresolved; for example, whether being creative in one subject/domain can be transferred to another subject/domain. Some of these under-represented areas are discussed in Part 3.

In this book creativity is positioned differently from the ways in which it has been represented in curriculum policy for children in the early years since the 1960s. Although it draws on shifts in focus in the late twentieth century, such as the move to take more account of social context, the book is essentially a conceptual study of the creativity of the individual child in the context of the twenty-first century, of postmodern global society.

The book is organized in three parts. Part 1, The Early Years and Primary Curriculum, seeks to set the curriculum context and to argue a rationale for a particular form of creativity, i.e. personal effectiveness or 'little c creativity', in the early years curriculum, contrasting it with other approaches to creativity. Part 2, Exploring and Evaluating Little c Creativity, continues the conceptualization of little c creativity, exploring the roles played in it by intelligence, imagination, and self-creation, self-expression ... and possibility thinking. This section concludes with a critical discussion of the concept of little c creativity, exploring some of the dilemmas that the concept poses.

Finally, Part 3, Applying Little c Creativity in Early Years Education, turns to the practicalities of implementing the notion of little c creativity. It does this first in terms of the curriculum, then in terms of teaching and assessment, and then in terms of the educator's engagement with their own creativity and that of others. The final chapter of the book poses some wide-ranging questions at a systemic/societal level, in relation to fostering this kind of creativity in education.

Overall, the book argues for an alternative formulation – as it were, a 'third way' or 'third wave' – for conceptualizing creativity in the early years, arguing that as we enter a critical phase for our planet and our species, little c creativity will be increasingly important for the children who will inherit both our achievements and our mistakes. Howard Gardner has said in one of his recent books: 'We seek ... individuals who will be admirable not only as ... creators but also as human beings' (Gardner, 1999, p. 248). So this book proposes lifewide, or little c creativity as a third wave, which is firmly set in a *humane ethical context*, and in illustrating what this might mean, examples are given that are drawn from field work in a range of early years settings (playgroups, nurseries, reception and primary classes, the home), as well as from everyday life.

## References
Amabile, T. (1988) 'A model of creativity and innovation in organizations', in B. M. Staw and L. L. Cunnings (eds) *Research in Organizational Behavior.* Greenwich, CT: JAI.

Andersson, A. L. and Ryhammer (1998) 'Psychoanalytic models of the mind, creative functioning and percept-genetic reconstruction'. *Psychoanalysis and Contemporary Thought,* **21**, 359–382.

Bachelor, P. A. and Michael, W. B. (1997) 'The structure-of-intellect model revisited', in M. A. Runco (ed.) *The Creativity Research Handbook,* vol. 1. Cresskill, NJ: Hampton Press.

Barron, F. (1955) 'The dispoition toward originality'. *Journal of Abnormal and Social Psychology,* **51**, 478–85.

Barron, F. (1963) *Creativity and Psychological Health.* New York: Von Nostrand.

Beetlestone, F. (1998) *Learning in the Early Years: Creative Development.* Leamington Spa: Scholastic.

Binet, A. and Henri, V. (1896) '*La psychologie, individuelle*'. *Année Psychologie,* **2**, 411– 65.

Brolin, C. (1992) 'Kreativitet, och kritiskt tandande. Redsckap for framtidsberedskap' [Creativity and critical thinking. Tools for preparedness for the future]. *Krut,* **53**, 64–71.

Bruner, J. (1962) 'The Conditions of Creativity', in H. Gruber (ed.) *Contemporary Approaches to Creative Thinking.* New York: Atherton Press.

Central Advisory Committee for England (CACE) (1967) *Children and Their Primary Schools (The Plowden Report).* London: HMSO.

Clancier, A. and Kalmanovitch, J. (1987) *Winnicott and Paradox: from birth to creation.* London and New York: Tavistock Publications.

Cline, V. B., Richards, J. M. Jr. and Abe, C. (1962) 'The validity of a battery of creativity tests in a high school sample'. *Educational Psychology Measurement,* **47** 184–9.

Craft, A. (1996) 'Nourishing educator creativity: A holistic approach to CPD'. *British Journal of In-service Education,* **22**(3), 309–22.

Craft, A. (2000) *Creativity Across the Primary Curriculum.* London: Routledge.

Craft, A. (2001) 'Third Wave Creativity? Lessons in the early years'. Paper presented as part of '*Creativity, in Education*' *symposium* at British Educational Research Association (BERA) Annual Conference, Leeds University, September 2002.

Csikszentmihalyi, M. (1998) 'Society, culture and person: a systems view of creativity', in R. J. Sternberg (ed.) *The Nature of Creativity,* pp. 325–39. Cambridge: Cambridge University Press.

Eisenmann, R. (1997) 'Mental illness, deviance and creativity', in M. A. Runco (ed.) *The Creative Research Handbook,* vol. 1. Cresskill, NJ: Hampton Press.

Ekvall, G. (1991) 'The organizational culture of idea management: a creative climate for the management of ideas', in J. Henry and D. Walker (eds) *Managing Innovation.* London: Sage.

Ekvall, G. (1996) 'Organizational climate for creativity and innovation'. *European Work and Organizational Psychology*, **5**, 105–23.

Elliott, R. K. (1971) 'Versions of Creativity'. *Proceedings of the Philosophy of Education Society of Great Britain*, **5**(2), 139–52.

Eysenck, H. J. (1997) 'Creativity and personality', in M. A. Runco (ed.) *The Creativity Research Handbook*, vol. 1. Cresskill, NJ: Hampton Press.

Freud, S. ([1908] 1959) 'Creative writers and day-dreaming', in J. Strachey (ed.) *Standard Edition of the Complete Psychological Works of Sigmund Freud*, vol. 9, pp. 143–53. London: Hogarth Press.

Freud, S. (1910) 'Five Lectures on Psycho-Analysis'. *Amer. F. Psycholol.*, **21**.

Freud, S. ([1910] 1957) 'Leonardo da Vinci and a memory of his childhood' in J. Strachey (ed.) *Standard Edition of the Complete Psychological Works of Sigmund Freud*, vol. 11. London: Hogarth Press.

Freud, S. ([1916] 1971) *The Complete Introductory Lectures on Psychoanalysis*. Oxford: George Allen & Unwin.

Fryer, M. (1996) *Creative Teaching and Learning*. London: Paul Chapman Publishing Ltd.

Galton, F. (1869) *Hereditary Genius: An inquiry into its laws and consequences*. London: Macmillan.

Gardner, H. (1993) *Multiple Intelligences: The theory in practice*. New York: HarperCollins.

Gardner, H. (1999), *Intelligence Reframed: Multiple Intelligences for the 21st Century*, New York: Basic Books

Getzels, J. W. and Jackson, P. W. (1962) *Creativity and Intelligence*. London: Wiley.

Getzels, J. W. and Csikszentmihalyi, M. (1976) *The Creative Vision: A longitudinal study of problem-solving in art*. New York: Wiley.

Guilford, J. P. (1950) 'Creativity'. *American Psychologist*, **5**, 444–45.

Guilford, J. P. (1964) 'Intelligence, creativity, and learning', in R. W. Russell (ed.) *Frontiers of Psychology*, pp. 125–47. Chicago: Scott Foresman.

Guilford, J. P. (1967) *The Nature of Human Intelligence*. New York, NY: McGraw Hill Book Company.

Haddon, F. A. and Lytton, H. (1968) 'Teaching approach and the development of divergent thinking abilities in primary schools'. *British Journal of Educational Psychology*, **38**, 171–80.

Hudson, L. (1966) *Contrary Imaginations*. London: Methuen.

Isaksen, S. G. (1995) 'Some recent developments on assessing the climate for creativity and change', paper presented at the 'International Conference on Climate for Creativity and Change', Centre for Studies in Creativity, Buffalo.

Jeffrey, B. (2001a) 'Primary Pupils' Perspectives and Creative Learning'. *Encyclopedia*, **9**, Spring, 133–52.

Jeffrey, B. (2001b) 'Maintaining primary school students' engagement in a post-reform context' (unpublished working paper)

Jeffrey, B. and Craft, A. (2001) 'The universalization of creativity', in A. Craft, B. Jeffrey, and M. Leibling (eds) *Creativity in Education*. London: Continuum.

Hudson, L. (1968) *Frames of Mind. Ability, Perception and Self-Perception in the Arts and Sciences*. London: Methuen.

Kirschenbaum, R. J. (1998) 'The Creativity Classification System: An assessment theory'. *Roepler Review*, **21**(1), 20–6.

Lytton, H. (1971) *Creativity and Education*. London: Routledge and Kegan Paul.

MacKinnon, D. W. (1962a) 'The personality correlates of creativity: a study of American architects'. *Proceedings of the Fourteenth International Congress on Applied Psychology*, Munksgarrd.

MacKinnon, D. W. (1962b) 'The nature and nurture of creative talent'. *American Psychologist*, **17**, 484–95.

MacKinnon, D. W. (1969) 'What makes a person creative?' in B. C. Rosen, H. J. Crockett and C. Z. Nunn (eds) *Achievement in American Society*. Cambridge, MA: Schenkman Publishing Company, Inc.

MacKinnon, D. W. (1975) 'IPAR's contribution to the conceptualization and study of creativity', in C. W. Taylor and J. W. Getzels (eds) *Perspectives in Creativity*. Chicago, IL: Aldine.

McLelland, D. C. (1963) 'The calculated risk: an aspect of scientific performance', in C. W. Taylor and F. Barron (eds) *Scientific Creativity: Its Recognition and Development*. London: Wiley

Maslow, A. H. (1971) *The Farther Reaches of Human Nature*. Harmondsworth: Penguin.

Maslow, A. H. ([1954] 1987) *Motivation and Personality*. New York and Cambridge: Harper & Row.

Meadow, A. and Parnes, S. J. (1959) 'Evaluation of training in creative problem-solving'. *Journal of Applied Psychology*, **43**, 189–94.

Mednick, S. A. (1962) 'The associative basis of the creative process'. *Psychological Review*, **69**, 220–32.

Mednick, S. A. and Mednick, T. (1964) 'An associative interpretation of the creative process', in C. W. Taylor (ed.) *Widening Horizons in Creativity*. New York: Wiley.

Mooney, R. L. (1963) 'A conceptual model for integrating four approaches to the identification of creative talent', in C. W. Taylor and F. Barron (eds) *Scientific Creativity*, pp. 331–40. New York: Wiley.

National Advisory Committee on Creative and Cultural Education (NACCCE) (1999) *All Our Futures: Creativity, Culture and Education*. London: Department for Education and Employment.

Osborn, A. F. (1963) *Applied Imagination*. New York: Scribner.

Parnes, S. J. (1962) 'Can creativity be increased?' in S. J. Parnes and F. J. Harding (eds) *A Source Book for Creative Thinking*. New York: Scribner.

Parnes, S. J. and Meadow, A. (1959) 'Effects of brainstorming instructions on creative problem-solving by trained and untrained subjects'. *Journal of Educational Psychology*, **50**, 171–6.

Parnes, S. J. and Meadow, A. (1960) 'Evaluation of persistence of effects produced by a creative problem-solving course'. *Psychological Reporter*, **70**, 357–61.

Plucker, J. A. and Runco, M. A. (1998) 'The death of creativity measurement has been greatly exaggerated: current issues, recent advances, and future directions in creativity assessment'. *Roeper Review*, **21**(1), 36–9.

Roe, A. (1963) 'Psychological approaches to creativity in science', in M. A. Coler (ed) *Essays on Creativity in the Sciences*. New York: New York University Press.

Rogers, C. R. (1970) 'Towards a theory of creativity', in P. E. Vernon (ed.) *Creativity*. Harmondsworth: Penguin.

Ryhammar, L. and Brolin, C. (1999) 'Creativity Research: historical considerations and main lines of development'. *Scandinavian Journal of Educational Research*, **43**(3), 259–73.

Schoon, I. (1992) *Creative Achievement in Architecture: a psychological study*. Leiden: DSWO Press.

Shaw, M. P. and Runco, M. A. (eds) (1994) *Creativity and Affect*. Norwood, NJ: Ablex.

Simonton, D. K. (1984) *Genius, Creativity and Leadership: historiometric enquiries*. Cambridge, MA: Harvard University Press.

Skinner, B. F. (1968) *The Technology of Teaching*. New York: Meredith Corporation.

Skinner, B. F. (1971) *Beyond Freedom and Dignity*. London: Jonathan Cape.

Skinner, B. F. (1974) *About Behaviourism*. London: Jonathan Cape Ltd.

Smith, G. J. W. and Carlsson, I. (1990) 'The creative process. A functional model based on empirical studies from early childhood to middle age'. *Psychological Issues monograph 57*. New York, NY: International Universities Press.

Spearman, C. (1931) *Creative Mind*. New York, NY: Appleton.

Spiel, C. and von Korff (1998) 'Implicit theories of creativity: the conceptions of politicians, scientists, artists and school teachers'. *Journal of High Ability Studies*, **9**(1), 43–58.

Sternberg, R. J. (1988) 'A three-facet model of creativity', in R. J. Sternberg (ed.) *The Nature of Creativity*. Cambridge: Cambridge University Press.

Sternberg, R. J. and Lubart, T. L. (1991a) 'An investment theory of creativity and its development'. *Human Development*, **34**, 1–31.

Sternberg, R. J. and Lubart, T. L. (1991b) 'Creating creative minds'. *Phi Delta Kappan*, April, 608–14.

Sternberg, R. J. and Lubart, T. L. (1995) *Defying the Crowd. Cultivating Creativity in a Culture of Conformity*. New York: The Free Press.

Stoycheva, K. (1996) 'The School: A place for children's creativity?' Paper Presented at the Fifth 'ECHA (European Council for High Ability) Conference', Vienna, Austria, October 19–22, 1996.

Torrance, E. P. (1962) *Guiding Creative Talent*. Englewood Cliffs, New Jersey: Prentice-Hall.

Torrance, E. P. (1966) *Torrance Tests of Creativity*. Princeton: Personnel Press.

Torrance, E. P. and Gowan, J. C. (1963) *The Reliability of the Minnesota Tests of Creative Thinking*. Minnesota: Bureau of Educational Research, University of Minnesota.

Torrance, E. P. (1974) *Torrance Tests of Creative Thinking*. Lexington, MA: Ginn & Company (Xerox Corporation).

Wallas, G. (1926) *The Art of Thought*. New York, NY: Hartcourt Brace.

Winnicott, D. W. (1971) *Playing and Reality*. New York: Routledge.

Woods, P. (1995) *Creative Teachers in Primary Schools*. Buckingham: The Open University Press.

Woods, P. and Jeffrey, B. (1996) *Teachable Moments: The Art of Teaching in Primary Schools*. Buckingham: Open University Press.

Worth, P. (2000) 'Localised Creativity: A Lifespan Perspective.' Unpublished PhD Thesis, Milton Keynes: The Open University Institute of Educational Technology.

# PART ONE
# The Early Years and Primary Curriculum

This first part of the book, The Early Years and Primary Curriculum, offers an analysis of the curriculum policies and practices which have dominated creativity in the early years of education since the mid-twentieth century.

The first chapter explores two early 'waves' of conceptualizing creativity in the early years and primary curriculum: Plowden, in the 1960s, and then a range of initiatives in the 1990s. Contrasting these two 'waves' of activity, it sets the scene for the second chapter, which asks what it is that young children need to learn in the current social, economic and technological context. Chapter 2 proposes 'personal effectiveness', or little c creativity as an important part of what is needed in the early years and primary curriculum. Chapter 3 contrasts 'little c' and 'big c' creativity, suggesting that they occupy different ends of a spectrum.

Together, the three chapters in Part 1 offer a foundation for the analysis of little c creativity in Part 2, and the practical chapters in Part 3.

# CHAPTER 1

# Curriculum context

*This chapter sets the context for the book, exploring the two recent periods in which creativity has been engaged with at policy level, for the early years of education. It looks first at the Plowden Report published in the 1960s, and its influence on creativity, and then at various policies introduced during the late 1990s.*

## Introduction

In England, there have been two recent periods in which creativity has been recognized as a desirable aim for inclusion in the curriculum, particularly in primary education. The first was in the 1960s with the publication of the Plowden Report, and the second during the late 1990s.

The first period linked creativity to a particular, child-centred, discovery-based pedagogical approach and to the arts. But it was just such a 'free' approach to creativity that formed part of a celebrated critique of child-centred education practices (edited by Cox and Dyson, 1971), known as *The Black Papers*. This critique, arguably, laid the way for the introduction of a subject-content based national curriculum at the end of the 1980s. In addition, some thought that many schools were implementing the Plowden ideas incompetently (Alexander, 1995).

However, since the mid 1990s, there has been a growing recognition from policy-makers and commentators alike that learner creativity is an extremely important aim for education. The economic imperative to foster creativity in business has helped to raise the profile and credentials of creativity in education more generally.

During a recent review of the National Curriculum, the Secretary of State for Education and Employment set up a number of advisory groups to provide input into the debate. One of these groups was the National Advisory Committee for Creative and Cultural Education

(NACCCE) which submitted its final report in 1999. The report contained a wide range of recommendations that called for further work and investigations into creativity and cultural education.

The focus of this book is creativity in the curriculum in England for children aged 2½ to 8, overlapping with, but distinct from, the concerns of both Plowden and NACCCE. This chapter begins by exploring The Plowden Report (CACE, 1967), which not only had a major general influence on the curriculum for this age range, but also crystallized thinking about creativity in education for the generation which followed it. It goes on to consider how various critiques of Plowden can be seen as having helped to lay the ground for the National Curriculum, introduced in 1989, and the Early Learning Goals for under-5's (applicable in pre-school environments and also in the first year, now called the 'Foundation Stage' – formerly Reception – at school), introduced in the late-1990s. The way in which Plowden conceptualized creativity is scrutinized and contrasted with approaches to creativity embedded in the newer curricula and in the NACCCE Report (1999).

## The Plowden Report

The Plowden Report drew on a large body of so-called liberal thinking on the education of children. This included work by Dewey, Froebel, Piaget, Rousseau, Pestalozzi, Montessori, McMillan, and Isaacs. Each of these writers developed a distinct position on children's learning, and ways in which it should be fostered. It is not a prime focus of this chapter to examine any of these writers' ideas individually but rather to consider critically the outcomes in Plowden. In other words, this chapter is concerned with how their ideas were brought together within the Report itself.

The recommendations of the Plowden committee in this were wide-ranging, including proposals for the organization of primary and secondary education, as well as the provision of nursery education for pre-school children (children under the age of 5), also staffing, the training of staff, and buildings and equipment. For pre-school and school education, primary and secondary, the committee drew together what it considered to be good pedagogical practice and made recommendations for the curriculum that encompassed not simply what was learned, but also how. For the purposes of the discussion in this chapter, curriculum is taken, in the same way, to include both curriculum content and how this is learned.

The Plowden recommendations highlighted the importance of

children learning by discovery and of children being permitted to take an active role in both the definition of their curriculum and the exploration of it. The trend towards active and individualized learning was endorsed, as was learning through first-hand experience of the natural, social, and constructed world beyond the classroom (although the roles of knowledge and skills were also acknowledged as was the significance in education of what they described as 'learning by description' (para. 553, p. 202). A central role was given to play, which was seen as providing 'the roots of drama, expressive movement and art' (para. 525, p. 193). Teachers were encouraged to enter the play world of the child, observing carefully what the children were learning and intervening to extend learning at appropriate times. Play was seen as a vehicle for fostering imagination, as this quotation suggests: 'Their imagination seizes on particular facets of objects and leads them to invent as well as to create' (para. 525, p. 193). Play was also seen as providing a 'natural' stepping stone to other parts of the curriculum: for example, they claimed that 'Play can lead naturally to reading and writing' (para. 536, p. 197).

The Plowden Report influenced early primary education at the levels of both policy and practice. It brought together a range of constructivist theories of learning, which in turn both encouraged and endorsed a variety of child-centred practice, which included the nature of curriculum, the physical layout and resourcing of the classroom, and general classroom management. It thus had a major influence on pedagogy, *appearing* to 'revolutionize' it by endorsing a child-focused pedagogy far removed from an earlier, far more formal, curriculum-centred one. It has been argued by many, however, to have been a revolution more in appearance than reality, setting up a false dichotomy between progressive and traditional approaches to teaching and learning. The empirical study by the Oracle team (Galton *et al.*, 1980) was the first to highlight the false division. That study found that although, superficially, primary school children appeared to be working in a much more informal way (for example, seated in groups around tables rather than in rows), in fact they were usually working on individual tasks as in the traditional approach. A subsequent study by Bennett *et al.*, (1984) suggested that although in many classrooms a child-focused environment appeared to be in operation, in practice much work was not well-matched to individual learning needs; they found that most teachers in their study were not effective in accurately diagnosing children's learning needs. High attainers were regularly underestimated and low attainers regularly overestimated.

In addition the Plowden Report was severely critiqued immediately after its publication for weaknesses in its philosophical position as well as in the practices it embraced. To take the philosophical critique first, I want to look briefly at eleven fundamental philosophical problems within the report.

First, one of the most significant beliefs which appeared to be underlying Plowden was that of *the necessity of concrete experience for knowledge and understanding*. This was disputed by Bantock, one of the Black Paper writers (1971). He argued that the necessity of concrete experience for knowledge and understanding is a fallacy because it is tautological. In other words, he suggests, the child can only make sense of what he knows how to make sense of. As he writes, 'it is no good setting children free in a field and asking them to "experience" nature; they can only experience what they can already recognize' (Bantock, 1971, p. 107). The belief is, in other words, circular. Dearden (1976) developed this point, noting that also 'forms of understanding such as mathematics and science of cultural achievements . . . all of this cannot be rediscovered by a confrontation with objects' and, further, he points out that 'discoveries do have to be discoveries and not just exciting areas, models, confusion or blankness' (p. 82).

Of course, it could be argued that the role of the teacher is to facilitate the child in making sense of new experiences and thus developing an understanding of existing bodies of knowledge. Indeed, although Plowden did not devote much time to the teacher's role, it did not, either, deny the pivotal significance and sensitivity of the teacher's position in balancing individual access, interest, and learning with curriculum structure and the needs of the larger group, as the following quote suggests, taken from a section concerned with pupil choice over parts of the class timetable:

> The teacher must constantly ensure a balance within the day or week both for the class and for individuals. He must see that time is profitably spent and give guidance on its use. In the last resort, the teacher's relationship with his pupils, his openness to their suggestions and their trust in him are far more important than the nominal degree of freedom in the timetable (para. 537).

Having said this, Plowden was rather ambiguous on the extent to which children needed to acquire any particular body of knowledge, indeed the report recommended a flexible approach to curriculum which left the content of learning ultimately open to the individual teacher to determine through an integrated, or project, approach. This was because the Plowden philosophy was one of differentiation of experience; different individuals and classes would have specific interests and needs at any point in time which would vary from one another and thus Plowden argued, 'Any practice which predetermines the pattern and imposes it upon all is to be condemned' (para. 538). By not addressing the problem of knowledge Plowden is wide open to the critique launched by Bantock and others – for how is a learner to develop sensitivity to a domain of learning without having first been exposed to it? Recent empirical work in science and technology (for example, McCormick *et al.*, 1993) emphasizes the interaction between pupils' knowledge of a domain and their sensitivity to possibilities within it and suggests that the Plowden position, learning by direct experience in the environment first followed by consolidation, was over simplistic.

The second area of critique of Plowden emerges from the discussion above. It is *the ambiguity of the term, 'discovery learning'.* This appears to be an acknowledged by the Plowden committee itself. For although 'the sense of personal discovery influences the intensity of a child's experience, the vividness of his memory and the probability of effective transfer of learning ... at the same time it is true that trivial ideas and inefficient methods may be "discovered" ' (para. 549). Indeed Plowden also at knowledges that 'time does not allow children to find their way by discovery to all they have to learn' (para. 549) – and the Committee notes that 'we certainly do not deny the value of "learning by description" or the need for practice of skills and consolidation of knowledge' (para. 553). Thus, not only are the methods of discovery learning (the extent to which learning is child-centred or teacher-directed) unclear, but so also is the extent of its relevance.

The third area of critique confirms *the problem of defining a child's needs.* Plowden adopted a notion of maturation underlying a child's needs, based on Piaget's developmental theory, and emphasized the teacher's role in 'diagnosing children's needs and potentialities' (para. 874). However, what constitutes a child's needs is problematic. Inevitably, needs are embedded in culture and may be confused, in the case of young children, with 'wants', as Dearden (1968) has pointed out: 'child-centred theorists ... are sometimes apt to take one thing as the criterion of needing. The child in infant classroom wants to play with sand, *ergo* he needs to' (p. 17). As he points out, to operate a curriculum based on a child's needs in this way is in effect to follow the child's interests, but not necessarily his or her needs. In addition, he notes that organizing a curriculum based around a child's so-called needs does not solve what he calls 'the problem of motivation' (p. 14), precisely because a child's needs are not necessarily equivalent to their wants. In other words, satisfying what a child wants may not be what they need and may not give them the satisfaction they seek.

Dearden suggests that a further fundamental problem with defining a child's needs is that such a 'diagnosis' is inevitably caught up in a value-judgement about what is desirable. What is seen to be desirable is, then, a matter of debate, and not absolute.

It could be said that the way Plowden proposed a child's needs was to imply they were what Griffin (1986) has called 'basic' (i.e. that a child requires certain things to survive simply by virtue of being human). However, whereas we need, for example, food, to survive (and thus this is a basic need), a more accurate description of the needs Plowden refers to would be what Griffin calls 'instrumental' needs (i.e. that the needs arise because of the ends chosen). Instrumental needs are inevitably based on value-judgements about the worth of specific ends.

Moreover, the construction of a curriculum based on children's needs does not reflect, as Hirst and Peters (1970) argue, the breadth of ways in which any curriculum actually arises empirically. They ask, 'Does not a curriculum arise as much from the demands of society and the history of man's attempt to understand and appreciate the world as it does from children's needs and interests?' (p. 31). Indeed, Hirst and Peters suggest that the progressive approach to education actually assumes a 'traditional' curriculum content, but that what lies behind their approach to learning was the idea of the self-directed learner. Other problems to do with self-direction are examined in point eight, below.

Fourth, it has been argued that, *the Piagetian, and, possibly Dewey-esque notion underpinning Plowden, that the child's 'essential nature' unfolds by laws of growth merely by the child's exploration of a diverse physical environment, is over-simplistic and misinformed*. One perspective on this position is that the social in human development is completely ignored, a theme which has been the subject of a great deal of empirical research in social psychology, particularly from the mid-1980s onwards. From philosophy of education, the under-emphasis on the social in Piaget's theory has been challenged by Hamlyn (1990) who suggests that 'the interrelationships between the individual and the environment which are involved in knowledge of that environment *presuppose* a social existence' (p. 135). For the social context *is part* of the environment. Another perspective is that the notion of maturation dictating a child's readiness to take on new learning confuses simple physical maturity (i.e. growth) with what Dearden calls 'educational' growth (1968, p. 27). He points out that whereas physical growth is an empirical fact, educational recommendations are 'the ethical choices of particular individuals, groups or cultures' (*ibid.* p. 27), although they are made to look as if they are empirical necessities.

Fifth, the whole notion of *development* that underpins the Plowden Report is, it has been argued, problematic. The Plowden Report appears to rest on this view, expressed some fifty years earlier by the educational reformer Holmes (1911). His thesis was that a teacher's role is to provide the conditions for a child to develop its inborn instincts (the dramatic, artistic, musical, inquisitive, communicative, and constructive), which will evolve from their biological origins without much reference to social context and outside influence. However, it could be argued that expectations of development are culturally defined rather than absolute and universal. Indeed, as the philosopher Dearden points out (1968), the ethic of developmentalism, as one which values the individual child, is 'not an ethically disinterested science ... but a system of normative guidance for achieving a particular chosen ideal of 'maturity' (*ibid.*, p. 28). Peters (1969) makes the same point, saying: 'Talk of "development", like talk of children's "needs", is too often a way of dressing up our value-judgments in semi-scientific clothes' (p. 8). In addition, the very idea of 'developmentalism' has its own logical problems, as White (1998) has noted. First, the comparison of the person to the seed which contains a blueprint for the adult plant, is inappropriate, he argues, in that desires and capacities differentiate and change, but cannot be said to 'unfold'. For, he says, 'the changes wrought in ... capacities are cultural products: people are socialized into them' (p. 8). He also suggests that the concept of developmentalism implies an end-state, or a mental ceiling; a concept which many teachers and psychologists have argued against.

The concept of a child's *readiness to learn*, which stems from developmental accounts of learning and which is deeply embedded in the Plowden report, forms another, sixth, area of critique. It was the criticism widely made of the methodology of child-centred learning. The notion, famously expressed by Rousseau (1911), that the child should be left undisturbed until their faculties had developed can be seen as naïve. For the teacher's role and the role of experience and environment are undefined and inexplicit, begging the questions, 'Are we [to await] a spontaneous act of the child's maturation processes signalled to a patiently attendant teacher? Or can "readiness" – and should it – be induced?' (Bantock, 1971, p. 104). Dearden (1968) suggests that the use of the term 'readiness' in Plowden is confused, in that there are at least three kinds of readiness, none of which is spelled out in the report. Dearden proposes these as 'physiological readiness' (p. 30); 'conceptual necessity' (p. 30) (i.e. the necessity of understanding something fundamental before being able to build on it, such as, for example, having some understanding of written language before being able to be said to be 'reading'); and third, readiness in terms of the child's own interest in learning in the said topic area. The concept, says Dearden, begs other questions, such as readiness for what; the extent to which the conditions of readiness are absolute or purely desirable as seen by specific teachers; the extent to which any kind of readiness can be actively brought about or waited for; and, if the conditions for readiness are not necessary but simply desirable, on what basis these can be justified.

Seven, Plowden placed the development of the child at the centre of the educational process, and implied in this that *what was natural (to the child) was also good*. It has been argued that this is a logical fallacy, in that what is natural is not necessarily good. As Dearden (1967) writes: 'What is natural might also be good, but it cannot follow simply from its being natural that therefore it is good. In reality, much that seems to be natural (spontaneous and untaught) would normally be judged to be bad, such as spite, selfishness, aggressiveness, boastfulness, jealousy.'

An eighth argument concerns *the concept of self-direction*, epitomized in the well-quoted phrase of the Plowden report, that 'the child is the agent of his own learning' (para. 527), as discussed by Peters (1969). The principle of self-direction incorporates within it, amongst other assumptions, the function of autonomy as a moral principle – itself not clearly defined. Evidently, as Peters argues, autonomy is important in a pluralist society; but to develop autonomy, children need to develop knowledge and skills which involve specialized study. If all children need to acquire knowledge and develop skills in a range of areas of study, this would appear to contradict the notion of encouraging individuality, both in the sense of all children having access to the same curriculum and also in the pedagogical arrangements which would support this state of affairs. Further, Peters suggests that it is in fact only logically possible for the child to be autonomous if they have a clear idea of what following the rules means, and what the framework is from which they are to deviate and become independent. Peters also suggests that we know little about what actually promotes autonomy (and indeed 'creativeness' as he calls it). For he suggests, 'It may well be a very bad way of developing this to give children too many opportunities for uninformed "choices" too young' (*ibid.*, p. 11).

From a slightly different perspective, The Black Paper writers emphasized the need for rules and boundaries, saying that children need 'self-discipline ... freedom within defined limits ... the security resulting from a realization of cause and effect, from having decisions imposed and being able to enjoy the peace and security that comes from an ordered life' (Johnson, 1971, p. 99).

The fear of *over-extension of individual autonomy* is another, ninth, area of criticism. Johnson expresses the fear that over-extending freedom, trusting the child to explore and develop without a curriculum and pedagogy which provided clear, adult-delineated boundaries, could lead into some kind of social breakdown. This was one thread of critique that can be seen as having led ultimately to the introduction of the National Curriculum at the end of the 1980s, and later, in the late 1990s, the National Literacy Strategy and the National Numeracy Strategy.

Johnson also commented that child-centred approaches such as that espoused by Plowden, formed part of a welfare state which, by its very existence, he suggested, undermined attitudes of personal responsibility. The combination of Plowden and the welfare state, he suggested, led to 'a world where [children] follow their own inclinations and where there are virtually no rules' (Johnson, 1971, p. 99). In defence of Plowden, however, the report makes it quite clear that there is a balance to be drawn by teachers between guidance and freedom. Even Rousseau, on whom the report draws, recommends a balance between culturally defined norms and the lack of them.

However, *the tension between the interests of the individual and of society* forms another, tenth, area of critique. The tension between interests of the individual and society is not resolved in either the Plowden report or in practice. It is unclear whether the stress lies in fitting the children for the society into which they will grow up (as Dearden notes, 'children unavoidably are our future adults', 1976, p. 55), or as making the school a place in which children learn to be, first and foremost, children, rather than adults of the future (Plowden, 1967). The liberal theme, of education's role being to enable individuals' 'self-realization', which forms one of the approaches in tension, is not, of course, new. It can be seen as having its foundations in British idealism in the late 1800s. It came into focus through the writings of Holmes (1911), mentioned earlier, a reformer of elementary education and one of the first to promote a vision of primary education as enabling self-realization – the highest ideal in his view of human life. Holmes' notion of 'self-realization', however, contrasted with the 'idealist' thinking of his time which saw individuals as parts of wholes, in that his concept of self-realization was highly individualist and not necessarily connected with the social context. It has been described as having been pivotal in the construction of a 'progressive' theory of education which was strongly individualist and thus as 'utterly anti-idealistic' (Gordon and White, 1979). The individualist approach to learning was also developed by another idealist, Dewey (1916), who came to describe his own notion of 'self-realization' as 'growth'. Unlike Holmes, however, he argued that to realize oneself was 'to promote the well-being of one's community' (Gordon and White, 1979, p. 198), thus suggesting that society has some stake in education. Holmes and Dewey can be seen as representing different ends of a spectrum, at one end of which (Holmes's) the aim is to foster individuals qua individuals, and at the other (Dewey's), the aim is to foster individuals and in so doing to contribute to the development of the wider society. Perhaps at a point more extreme even than Holmes's, is Percy Nunn's (1920). A 'New Realist', he became an inspirational leader in educational thought, proposing self-expression and the realization of individuality and self-expression as the highest aim of education, via a pedagogy that allowed the child to grow without interference, and in which biology or evolution drives learning. Just as the tensions between these three perspectives is not resolved between Holmes, Dewey, and Nunn, despite being more or less contemporaries of one another, neither are they resolved in the Plowden Report. The central difficulty is the one of explaining how value-judgements are made and evaluated by the individual without some reference to the wider social context.

Finally, it was argued by some of the Black Paper writers *that the Plowden Report misrepresented the nature of human beings*, in that children are not naturally 'good' (Black Paper 1) and that child-centred learning ('the new fashionable anarchy' – Black Paper 1) 'flies in the face of human nature, for it holds that children and students will work from natural inclination rather than the desire for reward' (*ibid.*). It is evident that these views are rooted in an achievement-for-rewards orientated perspective, where achievement is equated with happiness, as this quote suggests: 'hard work, leading to success, is the right of every child. To let children think that they need to only be interested in things, requiring no effort, is asking for trouble later on' (Pinn, 1969, p. 103); a view which, despite contradicting the values of the child-centred paradigm, which brands as meaningless the reward system, can nevertheless be argued to be a reflection of the way in which our society actually functions.

Such then, were some of the fundamental philosophical criticisms of Plowden, made by the Black Paper writers. There was also much criticism focused on practice, and I will briefly rehearse some of these here. For example, Johnson (1971) and Pinn (1969) both argued that *the emphasis on acquiring and perfecting basic skills under the progressive approach was not only inefficient, in that some children never perfect their skills, but is also undesirable and unfair*. As these commentators observed, the lack of structure and the emphasis on 'readiness' meant that basic skills were acquired more slowly. As a consequence, children were denied the freedom to extend their own horizons, which these skills, particularly literacy, offer.

*The use of Piaget's theories to back up and justify methodology* was challenged by Bantock (1971) as being mistaken. His argument was that although Piaget identified stages of development and then recommended the importance of concrete experience, never-theless he offered no blueprint for formal instruction. This criticism must, however, be questioned; for intrinsic to the theory of develop-ment Piaget outlines is the central notion of spontaneous and child-directed concrete experience of the environment which, it would appear, has direct and self-evident application to and implications for, education.

*The inefficiency of the learning by discovery process*, particularly if it is the only form of learning, was another area of criticism. It was argued that in fact the learning by discovery process, being slower, frustrates those children 'who yearn to be *told* the answers to the questions they are asking because the answers will enable them to rush on to the next step in their eager intellectual inquiry' (Bantock, 1971, p. 114). The ridiculousness of the notion of each child being able to, as it were, 'discover the wheel' all over again with little guidance from an adult is exposed by Dearden (1976), who argues that not only is what to discover culturally defined, but also that 'an opportunity to discover is also an opportunity to fail to discover, which is likely to make learning by discovery slower and less certain than learning from intelligent instruction and explanation' (p. 82).

*The integrated approach to knowledge* which Plowden recommended, through the use of project work, came under heavy criticism also; one of its weaknesses being, some argued, that it denied children access to significant cultural capital. As Peters (1969) argued: 'surely one of the great achievements of our civilization is to have gradually separated out and got clearer about the types of concepts and truth-like criteria involved in different forms of thought' (p. 14). The relationship between forms of thought, or as Peters came to call them, 'forms of knowledge' and the subjects of the school curriculum, is beyond the scope of this book, but this particular critique might be seen to have contributed to the eventual move toward the subject-centred National Curriculum in the late 1980s.

From the extreme Right of the political spectrum came the criticism *that schools operating the child-centred approach advocated by Plowden would fail to provide a stable framework for children, many of whom do not have a stable home situation.* Johnson asserts, 'the child from the inadequate home, more than any other, needs security and ordered home-life, sensible discipline and quiet' (1971, p. 100). Behind this argument, however, is the assumption that the school using individual learning techniques lacks 'security ... sensible discipline and quiet' (*ibid.*) when there is no logical or empirical reason to assume this is necessarily so any more than within the traditional approach.

A further extreme Right criticism came from Bantock (1971), who suggested that *discovery learning would promote short-term interest and concentration*. Again, there is no logical or empirical connection between these two states of affairs. This is not to say that short-term interests might not be a potential problem to be aware of within the discovery learning approach, but it may also be a 'problem' within the traditional approach, too. Children's attention span would, it could be argued, be mediated by a range of factors, including their relationship with their teacher and their interest in the subject matter, their home background and family circumstances, their gender, class and ethnic background, the mesh between their mother tongue and the language of the classroom, and so on. In other words, it seems that the school (and the discovery approach) may not logically or empirically be held totally responsible for the existence of a short attention span in children.

There were also critiques which focused more on the role of the teacher, and these were perhaps more significant in underpinning the thinking behind the changes which later occurred at a policy level, concerning the curriculum. For it was said that *the Plowden approach demanded far more of teachers in understanding the principles of child development, the areas of the curriculum and how they may relate to the child*. It also meant their being able to evaluate the progress of individual children within multifarious activities, both in the classroom and outside it. As Pinn put it, 'This type of teaching requires extremely competent teachers, to keep records of each child's progress, and to ensure that each child is getting the help he requires' (1969, p. 102).

*The shift of teaching style* involved for many teachers, in adopting Plowdenesque approaches, led in some cases to extreme discomfort and some disasters. The celebrated William Tyndale events between 1973 and 1975 were one example of the disastrous effects in one school of trying to force teachers to change their style. As Crawford writes (1969, p. 100), 'It is just possible that some teachers and some children do not react happily to such an environment.'

*The failure of teachers to 'diagnose children's problems'* (O'Connor, cited in Bennett *et al.*, 1984) is another major criticism born of empirical investigations into the actual pedagogical practices of teachers professing to follow Plowden. Reasons given in the literature for this failure included lack of pre-planned content in the curriculum, and the incompatibility of ensuring balance and progression in the curriculum when the scope of individual choice is enlarged (Lloyd, in Walton, 1971). A further reason was the sheer difficulty of meeting the individual needs of a large number of children when all were encouraged, at least to an extent, to follow their own interests within a relatively unstructured learning environment. This last point was in fact recognized within the Plowden Report, but was also observed in the empirical work carried out by Bennett *et al.* (1984).

Finally, some criticisms of the Plowden Report centred on the implications of discovery learning for curriculum content: the notion that the 'medium' may become the 'message', that is, that the principles behind the organizational forms and concrete experiences may not necessarily emerge. (The notion of the medium becoming the message was discussed in visual images and text by McLuhan *et. al.*, 1967).

It must be noted that although the Plowden Report had widespread influence and sparked a vast amount of discussion regarding progressive and traditional approaches to learning, many classrooms did not in fact take up the report's specific recommendations. The consequence was that the culture of primary education may have stemmed from Plowden, but did not represent anything like all primary school practice, as Galton *et al.* (1980, 1999) showed in their empirical investigation.


## Plowden and creativity

Plowden made a significant contribution to the way in which creativity in early school education was subsequently understood. The report suggested that a child's creativity was both benign and that it lay at the heart of all teaching and learning arrangements. What Plowden had to say about creativity was primarily associated with play. Justifying the provision of a varied physical environment for learning, the report suggests that the child's 'imagination seizes on particular facets of objects and leads them to invent as well as to create' (para. 525). It formed, then, an early attempt to suggest how to stimulate creativity. It chimed with what some creativity researchers were suggesting about the sorts of environments likely to either suppress or stimulate creativity (for example, Hudson suggested that 'conventional education is hostile to creativity, progressive education is not', 1966, p. 133). It can also be seen as having provided an early foundation for the move in creativity research towards an emphasis on social systems rather than personality or cognition or psychodynamics (see Introduction for an historical overview of creativity research). Being concerned with the curriculum and learning more broadly, however, the Plowden Report did not make direct reference to any of the substantial literature in psychology on creativity.

But the Plowden perspective on creativity is subject to all the same criticisms as were outlined above in respect of the report in general. In addition, there are several problems arising from Plowden specifically associated with the fostering of creativity.

First, there is *the problem of the role of knowledge*. If a child is to identify possibilities, or to exercise imagination in any context, this must perhaps be done with knowledge, for without it a child cannot logically go beyond what is 'given'. This argument will be further developed in Chapter 7 on Possibility Thinking. The difficulty with Plowden is that it implies that a child may be let loose to discover and learn without any prior knowledge, which, as Bantock argues (1971), is not logically possible.

Second, *there is some lack of context implied in the rationale for 'self-expression'* which seems to underpin the Plowden philosophy. The Plowden Report appears to conceive of the child's growth and expression in a moral and ethical vacuum. This lack of social context reflects the earlier thinking of some of those whose influence can be seen in the Plowden report; for example, the social Darwinism of Nunn's (1920) 'New Realist' approach, which claimed the goal of education to be the highest possible realization of the individual. For Nunn, this meant fully developing the individual's powers of self-expression, that is giving shape to the individuality held biologically within oneself. It also reflects the thinking of the slightly earlier idealist writer, Holmes (1911), who in developing his concept of 'self-realization' as the primary role of elementary education, played down the wider social context in which the 'self' resides. Denying the role of the social in, at the least, providing a context in which values are 'normed' has come under criticism. For example, Dearden (1976) wrote of Holmes: 'Edmond Holmes resoundingly declared "let the end of the process of growth be what it may; our business is to grow". But Hitler grew.' It could be argued that the idea that early education might foster children in having ideas and expressing them, should be set in a moral and ethical context within the classroom; indeed, I have argued this elsewhere (Craft, 2000).

Third, Plowden suggests that play provides the foundation for a variety of other forms of knowledge and expression: 'In play are the roots of drama, expressive movement and art' (para. 525). While not wishing to take issue with this particular claim, I would argue that *it appears to connect play creativity within the arts only and not with creativity across the whole curriculum* (although Plowden does make much of the social foundations which both spawn play activities and to which children adjust through their play activities). The Plowden approach is not dissimilar to Herbert Read's thesis, that 'art should be the basis of education' (Read, 1943, p. 1). There is a further problem also which is that *play and creativity are not the same as one another*. Not all play is creative; this I explore in Chapter 10.

In the Plowden Report, creativity thus became associated with a range of other approaches which included discovery learning, child-centred pedagogy, an integrated curriculum, the embracing of self-referencing and the apparent move away from an emphasis on social norms for evaluative purposes. Because of the conceptual and practical problems with the progressive movement, it was later argued that the fostering of creativity was perceived as a rather loose notion (NACCCE, 1999, p. 13), and it was thus pushed to the back of policy makers' priorities in curriculum development. But although there are these conceptual problems with the way in which creativity was conceived and presented in the Plowden Report, it nevertheless provided a landmark in envisioning a role for creativity in the curriculum.

### Developing policy on creativity in education since Plowden

Later in the twentieth century, as the foundations of what was to become the National Curriculum were laid, the Plowden concept of creativity was left behind. Nothing was put in its place initially, for the focus was on the formulation in 1989 of a curriculum with a high propositional knowledge content. Later, after the first revision of the National Curriculum in 1995, the attention of curriculum policy makers turned increasingly to thinking and other life skills involved in children's learning, in preparation for the next revision which was put in place in 2000. This latter now appeared to give some attention, at policy level, to the fostering of creativity, which mirrored the resurgence of interest in psychology and education research (following a great deal of interest and investment in the foundation disciplines of education in the 1950s and 1960s, there had been a dying-away until approximately the 1990s). The revival of research interest can be seen, Jeffrey and Craft argue (2001), as drawing in the role of social interaction in a way that previous studies had not done. The role of the social in creativity research and thinking is explored further in Chapter 5.

Four different aspects of policy change may thus be discerned in recent years. First, the Early Years Early Learning Goals, developed initially by the School Curriculum and Assessment Authority as 'Desirable Learning Outcomes' and completed as 'Early Learning Goals' later by the Qualifications and Curriculum Authority (QCA) in the late 1990s, included a major area of experience for under-fives as being 'creative development'. A perhaps significant aspect of this was the identification in 2000 of the Reception Year (four to five year olds) as the Foundation Stage. Whereas in the first two versions of the National Curriculum, children from the age of five were subject to the National Curriculum (meaning that Reception teachers had to plan two separate curricula, one for four year olds and the other for five year olds), there was a powerful departure in September 2000. From that time, Reception children were offered a curriculum based on the Early Learning Goals only, and this specifically included Creative Development.

Second, the commissioning of the National Advisory Committee on Creative and Cultural Education (NACCCE), which reported in 1999, acknowledged the fostering of pupil creativity as a necessary outcome from school learning for pupils of all ages. The Committee gave advice on what would need to be done at a range of levels including policy level, to foster the development of pupil creativity within school education.

Third, the Qualifications and Curriculum Authority (QCA) and Department for Education and Employment (DfEE) published in 1999 a handbook for the National Curriculum in primary schools (QCA/DfEE 1999a). The Handbook notes that embedded within the National Curriculum for Key Stages 1 and 2 are six 'key skills', one of which is named 'creative thinking skills'. Teachers are to plan their curricular opportunities to encompass the development of such skills.

Fourth, a range of other initiatives were set up from the start of new century. For example, in 2000, QCA set up a curriculum project, examining the nature of creativity across the curriculum in primary and secondary schools. Then, in mid-2001, the independent think-tank Demos, in conjunction with The Design Council, launched a 'Creativity Manifesto', based heavily on the Demos publication by Seltzer and Bentley (1999), *The Creative Age*, and entitled *What Learning Needs* (Jupp *et al.*, 2001). The partnership included an interactive website, 'CreativeNet', which encouraged educators to consider how creativity could be fostered in education and work contexts. In late 2001, the Department for Culture, Media and Sport launched its plans for a pilot phase of the Creative Partnerships project, bringing together arts-based organizations and education. There were many other examples too. Since this fourth category is diverse and many projects are as yet unpublished, they will be omitted from the discussion which follows – the focus being instead on Creative Development, the National Curriculum and the NACCCE Report.

**Creative Development**
To take 'Creative Development', one of the six Early Learning Goals identified as learning goals of children between the ages of three and five, the codifying of this part of the early years curriculum meshed

closely with the existing norms and discourse about early education. For 'Creative Development' encompasses art, craft and design, and various forms of dramatic play and creative expression, all of which have traditionally formed a core part of early years provision. It emphasizes the role of imagination and the importance of children developing a range of ways of expressing their ideas and communicating their feelings. Both the use of imagination and 'being in relationship' have been described as core to creativity (Craft, 2000).

Although many welcomed the codifying of creativity in some form within the early learning curriculum, nevertheless several problems with 'Creative Development' as described in the Early Learning Goals may be detected. First, it could be said that formulating creative development in this way implies that creativity involves specific parts of the curriculum and certain forms of learning only. Yet, problem finding and solving, using imagination and posing 'what if?' questions could (and do) occur within a whole range of domains.

Second, conceiving of creativity as something which may be 'developed' also opens it to the criticisms of developmentalism, discussed above. Thus, there is an implication that there is a ceiling, or a static end-state. The curriculum guidance published by the Qualifications and Curriculum in 2000 offers what it calls developmental 'stepping stones' for each of the Early Learning Goals including Creative Development, exemplifying what to expect from and provide for, children from the age of three to the age of five. There is an implication that, given the appropriate immediate learning environment, children will 'develop'.

Third, it has been argued (Craft, 1999) that the implication is that play and creativity are in fact the same, when quite evidently they are not. Play may be, but is not necessarily, creative. For example, 'Snakes and Ladders', being dependent upon a mix of chance and a set structure, is not creative; but 'Hide and Seek' may well be, demanding the consideration of options and possibilities for hiding places and seeking strategies. Creativity, then, is not necessary to all play. And, to be fair, the Desirable Learning Outcome, 'Creative Development', does not suggest that creativity is necessary to all play. However, at least one early publication which offered practical ideas of how to translate the policy into teaching and learning activities, appeared to conflate the concept of play with the concept of creativity (Beetlestone, 1998). This was done by proposing a range of role-play ideas for fostering imaginative play, transforming parts of the classroom into, for example, a travel agent's, a fire station, a hairdresser's, and an office. It has been argued that the inclusion of imaginative play within creative development in curriculum policy, and its translation into practice in the way that Beetlestone has done, represents a conflation of the two concepts (Craft, 2000). But, it should be noted that Beetlestone's approach is in contrast to that of the early curriculum guidance released with the initial policy (SCAA, 1997), which clearly distinguishes between play and creative development, the latter being about the exploration of sound, colour, texture, and so on. It also emphasizes children's emotional response to the arts and the development of listening and observation skills as well as children's ability to communicate feelings and ideas of their own. Although the development of imagination is also a part of creative development, it is not framed in terms of play alone.

### The NACCCE Report

The NACCCE Report attempted to provide a theoretical framework for creativity in education, to underpin its recommendations for the development of practice. It linked the fostering of pupil creativity with the development of culture, in that original ideas and action are developed in a shifting cultural context. It proposed in other words that pupils' creativity is expressed in terms of the knowledge and understanding developed within society in a range of domains, taught in the school curriculum. It also suggested that the fostering of pupil creativity would contribute to the cultural development of society. It acknowledged that creativity rarely occurs without some form of interrogation of what has gone before or is occurring synchronously.

The Report distinguished between different definitions of creativity, namely the 'sectoral' definition, representing creativity in the creative arts, and the 'elite' definition, representing the 'high' creativity of the gifted few. The Committee, however, proposed a third, 'democratic', definition as the one perhaps most appropriate to education, suggesting that 'all people are capable of creative achievement in some area of activity, provided the conditions are right and they have acquired the relevant knowledge and skills' (para. 25). It is towards the fleshing out of this concept that most of the creativity part of the report is devoted.

This third notion, of 'democratic creativity', is a concept which has some connection with Plowden, in at least two ways. First, the NACCCE approach values pupils' self-expression as a part of the fostering of their creativity, as did Plowden. Second, it is a 'universalist' or 'democratic' approach, in the same way that Plowden was; in other words, both reports are underpinned by the assumption that all people are capable of creativity.

But the NACCCE 'democratic creativity' definition *contrasts* with the Plowden approach in a number of ways also. First, it places the acquisition of knowledge and skills as the necessary foundation to creativity. In this sense the NACCCE report reflects the wider curriculum and learning debates, which emphasize the 'situating' of knowledge and skill; it also reflects the creativity literature in psychology, which towards the end of the twentieth century came to emphasize knowledge and competence in the domain as necessary to learning. This latter shift in the creativity literature is documented in the Introduction. Second, as NACCCE was focused exclusively on creativity, it naturally had a great deal more to say on it than the Plowden Report. NACCCE made a wide range of recommendations at the levels of both policy and practice, and devoted a chapter to the development of the construct of creativity, drawing on psychology, philosophy and education studies to do so. Thirdly, it distinguished between teaching creatively and teaching for creativity, suggesting that the former is a necessary precondition for the latter.

The NACCCE definition of creativity was 'Imaginative activity fashioned so as to produce outcomes that are both original and of value' (para. 29). Each of these terms was carefully defined. Chapter 9 will examine critically the contribution which the NACCCE definition and recommendations have made to the curriculum. In Chapter 10, I will be considering critically some of the pedagogical claims made by the NACCCE Report.

## The National Curriculum

The *National Curriculum Handbooks* for primary and secondary schools, propose a role for creativity in the aims of the school curriculum, saying that 'the curriculum should enable pupils to think creatively … It should give them the opportunity to become creative …' (QCA, 1999a, p. 11; 1999b, p. 11). Creativity is defined in the *National Curriculum Handbooks* as a cross-curricular thinking skill. This reflects the notion proposed by some that creativity is not the preserve of the arts alone but that it arises in all domains of human endeavour. Yet, identifying creativity as a skill could be seen as an oversimplification; to operate creatively in any knowledge domain must necessarily presuppose an understanding of that domain, and thus creativity cannot be seen as a knowledge-free, transferable skill, a position that will be developed throughout this thesis. On the other hand, the National Curriculum, even in its revised form, is very knowledge-heavy, and thus the curriculum framework itself does provide the knowledge-base within which creativity is to operate.

Identifying creativity as cross-curricular in the National Curriculum also raises the question of whether creativity manifested in different domains is a transferable skill or a domain-specific one. I want to suggest that since, at its core, creativity is driven by the same central process, that of seeing possibilities, it is indeed the same skill, which is manifest differently across the various domains of application, but also that knowledge of the domain of application is essential to its development. This common foundation is significant in the actualization of 'lifewide' creativity (Craft, 2001). I will be returning to these issues in Chapters 7, 8 and 9, which focus on possibility thinking, evaluating little c creativity, and exploring little c creativity in the curriculum, respectively.

These steps toward the development of policy, practice and theory in creativity in education perhaps reflect a wider burgeoning of interest beyond education at the start of the twenty-first century. The Introduction traced the major research studies, situated in their theoretical perspectives, and this increase in interest might be seen as reflecting broader social economic and technological imperatives (Craft, 1997, 1998, 2000).

Although the recent policy developments have occurred almost simultaneously, a notable feature of them, it could be argued, is their lack of coherence as a set of measures, both in focus and the way that creativity is defined. Whereas the notion of 'Creative Development' and the National Curriculum look at creativity in the curriculum for different age-stages, the NACCE Report was focused on creativity across learning much more broadly, linking creativity with culture. Within creative development, creativity is linked with other early learning processes, such as play, art, and design. The National Curriculum proposes creativity as a skill to be applied across the curriculum but does not explore in any detail what this means, and the NACCCE Report makes an attempt at a 'democratic' definition of creativity. A further contrast between them is that although the NACCCE Report's thinking on creativity is far more in-depth than that in the Early Learning Outcomes or in the National Curriculum, it is nevertheless the only one of the three which is not statutory, but is guidance only. This fact suggests that the placing of creativity more centrally in the school curriculum has not yet occurred, despite a growing recognition of the need to ensure that creativity is fostered in learners and teachers.

## CONCLUSION

This chapter has been concerned to consider critically the landmark which Plowden represented in the identification of creativity as a desirable outcome of early primary education, and it has sought to reflect critically on what has occurred in policy since. I have suggested that the recent developments in policy contrast

> with Plowden and are clearly a development on from the earlier thinking and policy. The various recent initiatives, however, are, I have suggested, discontinuous and inconsistent with one another.

In the next chapter, I want to ask what it is that young children need to learn in the current social, economic and technological context, and to propose 'personal effectiveness', or 'little c creativity' – lifewide (Craft, 2001) – as an important part of what is required.

## References

Alexander, R. (1995) *Versions of Primary Education*. London: Routledge.

Bantock, G. H. (1971) 'Discovery methods', in C. B. Cox and A. E. Dyson. (eds) *The Black Papers on Education*. London: Davis-Poynter Limited.

Beetlestone, F. (1998) *Creative Children, Imaginative Teaching*. Buckingham: Open University Press.

Bennett, N., Desforges, C., Cockburn, A. and Wilkinson, B. (1984), *The Quality of Pupil Learning Experiences* London: Lawrence Erlbaum Associates.

Central Advisory Committee for England (CACE) (1967) *Children and Their Primary Schools* (*The Plowden Report*), Volume 1: London: HMSO.

Central Advisory Committee for England (CACE) (1967) *Children and Their Primary Schools* (*The Plowden Report*), Volume 2: Research and Surveys. London: HMSO.

Craft, A. (1997) 'Identity and creativity: educating for post-modernism?' *Teacher Development: An International Journal of Teachers' Professional Development*, **1**(1), 83–96.

Craft, A. (1998) 'UK educator perspectives on creativity', *Journal of Creative Behavior*, **32**(4), 244–57.

Craft, A. (1999) 'Creative development in the early years: implications of policy for practice'. *The Curriculum Journal*, 10(1), 135–50.

Craft, A. (2000) *Creativity Across the Primary Curriculum*. London: Routledge.

Craft, A. (2001) 'Third Wave Creativity? Lessons in the early years'. Paper presented as part of 'Creativity in Education' symposium at British Educational Research Association (BERA) Annual Conference, Leeds University, September 2002.

Crawford, G. W. J. (1969) 'The Primary School: A Balanced View', in C. B. Cox and A. E. Dyson (eds) *Black Paper Two: The Crisis in Education*. London: Critical Quarterly Society.

Dearden, R. F. (1968) *The Philosophy of Primary Education*. London: Routledge & Kegan Paul.

Dearden, R. F. (1976) *Problems in Primary Education*. London: Routledge & Kegan Paul.

Dewey, J. ([1916] 1954) *Democracy and Education*. New York: Macmillan and Company.

Galton, M., Simon, B. and Croll, P. (1980) *Inside the Primary School*. London: Routledge & Kegan Paul.

Galton, M., Hargreaves, L., Comber, C., Pell, T. and Wall, D. (1999) *Inside the Primary Classroom: 20 Years On*. London: Routledge.

Gordon, P. and White, J. (1979) *Philosophers as Educational Reformers*. London: Routledge & Kegan Paul.

Griffin, J. (1986) *Well-Being, Its Meaning, Measurement and Moral Importance*. Oxford: Clarendon Press.

Hamlyn, D. W. (1990) *In and Out of the Black Box*. Oxford: Blackwell.

Hirst, P. H. and Peters, R. S. (1970) *The Logic of Education* London: Routledge & Kegan Paul.

Holmes, E. G. A. (1911) *What Is and What Might Be*. London: Constable.

Hudson, L. (1966) *Contrary Imaginations* London: Methuen.

Jeffrey, R. and Craft, A. (2001) 'The universalization of creativity', in A. Craft, R. Jeffrey and M. Leibling (eds) *Creativity in Education*. London: Continuum.

Johnson, C. M. (1971) 'Freedom in Junior Schools', in C. B. Cox and A. E. Dyson (eds) *The Black Papers on Education*. London: Davis-Poynter Limited.

Jupp, R., Fairly, C. and Bentley, T. (2001) *What Learning Needs*. London: Design Council & DEMOS.

McCormick, R., Hennessy, S. and Murphy, P. (1993) *Problem-solving Processes in Technology Education: A Pilot Study*. Milton Keynes: School of Education, The Open University.

McLuhan, M., Fiore, Q. and Agel, J. (1967) *The Medium Is the Massage*. New York: Bantam Books and Random House, London: Penguin Press.

National Advisory Committee on Creative and Cultural Education (NACCCE) (1999) *All Our Futures: Creativity, Culture and Education*. London: Department for Education and Employment.

Nunn, T. P. (1920) *Education: Its Data and First Principles*. London: Arnold.

Peters, R. S. (1969) *Perspectives on Plowden*. London: Routledge & Kegan Paul.

Pinn, D. M. (1969) 'What Kind of Primary School?', in C. B. Cox and A. E. Dyson (eds) *Black Paper Two: The Crisis in Education*. London: Critical Quarterly Society.

QCA and DfEE (2000) *Curriculum Guidance for the Foundation Stage*. London: DfEE/QCA.

QCA and DfEE (1999a) *The National Curriculum Handbook for Primary Teachers in England*, London: DfEE/QCA.

QCA and DfEE (1999b) *The National Curriculum Handbook for Secondary Teachers in England*. London: DfEE/QCA.

Read, H. (1943) *Education Through Art*. London: Faber.

Rousseau, J. J. ([1762] 1911) *Emile*, trans. Barbara Foxley. London: J.M. Dent.

SCAA (1997) *Looking at Children's Learning: Desirable Outcomes for Children's Learning on Entering Compulsory Education*. London: School Curriculum and Assessment Authority.

Seltzer, K. and Bentley, T. (1999) *The Creative Age: Knowledge and Skills for the New Economy*. London: Demos.

Walton, J. (ed.) (1971) *The Integrated Day in Theory and Practice*. London: Ward Lock Educational.

White, J. (1998) *Do Howard Gardner's Multiple Intelligences Add Up?* London: University of London Institute of Education.

# CHAPTER 2

# A rationale for little c creativity

*This chapter provides a rationale for the particular focus of this book, which is the investigation of the case for ordinary creativity as a desirable learning outcome of learning in the education of young children, aged three to eight. It proposes 'personal effectiveness', or 'little c creativity', as way of conceptualizing creativity.*

## Introduction

In the last Chapter, I considered critically the recent curriculum guidance on creative development for children aged three to five in the form of the Early Learning Goals, and also for children aged five to eight in the form of the National Curriculum, contrasting these developments with the earlier influences of the pivotal Plowden Report. One of the issues which should have become apparent in this discussion was the discontinuity between the two curricula: the one for the under-fives and the other for five-year-olds and over. For whilst the Early Learning Goals identify Creative Development as a curriculum area in its own right, the National Curriculum describes 'creativity' as being a cross-curricular skill. Aside from the questions around whether creativity can be seen as domain specific or as a so-called 'transferable' skill, which will be discussed in Chapter 9, there are a number of discontinuities between the two curricula.

First, it is not at all clear that 'Creative Development' as defined in the early learning curriculum is the same as 'creativity' as defined in the National Curriculum, either in terms of content or form. Creative Development encompasses the content areas of 'art, music, dance, role play and imaginative play' (QCA/DfEE, 2000, p. 116) and in terms of form is one of six Early Learning Goals. It appears to involve some notion of progression, as discussed in Chapter 1; and indeed, the QCA/DfEE curriculum guidance (QCA/DfEE, 2000) is presented in such a form as to demonstrate how this progression is evidenced in pupil activities.

By contrast, creativity in the National Curriculum is embedded in the cross-curricular part of the curriculum within 'thinking skills', in the form of 'creative thinking skills', which are supposed to be applied across all subjects. By way of content these are proposed as enabling pupils to 'generate and extend ideas, to suggest hypotheses, to apply imagination and to look for alternative innovative outcomes' (QCA/ DfEE, 1999a, p. 22). Thus, in the National Curriculum, creative thinking skills provide a part of 'knowing how' (*ibid.* p. 22) which balances the weight of propositional knowledge in the curriculum for children aged five to sixteen. Progression is not worked out in any of the National Curriculum documents, although aspects of creativity can be found embedded here and there in curriculum areas (where progression is worked out purely in terms of the subject domain).

Second, whereas many aspects of play are officially endorsed within the desirable outcome of creative development in the early years curriculum, this is not so in the National Curriculum. The invention by QCA and DfEE in 2000 of the 'foundation stage' (formerly known as Nursery and Reception) where children are subject only to the early learning goals, has helped to smooth this discontinuity, and to bring some of the imaginative and other play resources (such as the home corner, blocks, figures and puppets) back in to the Reception class. However, the discontinuity has simply been pushed back to Year 1 where 5-to 6-year-olds are subject to the more formal National Curriculum with its lack of emphasis on play, and educators are still faced with the challenge of how to help children make the transition from one to the other. As I have argued elsewhere (Craft, 2000), the question of how far children should be enabled to explore the ten National Curriculum subjects through play remains a real problem for infant teachers, particularly as the National Literacy and Numeracy Strategies increase the time-share and emphasis on formal learning/ instruction in the infant classroom.

Thirdly, and most significantly from the point of view of the argument presented here, neither of the above situates creativity in relation to qualities of persons demanded by life at the start of the twenty-first century, although the National Curriculum comes closer to this than the early learning goals do.

In the next part of this chapter, I want then to make the case for creativity forming part of the curriculum for young children. I will do this against the background of the existing curriculum and also the external context.

## Curriculum context

Recent years have seen a great deal of activity and interest in the nature of the curriculum for the early years of education. The National Curriculum for children in Year 1 upward has been revised several times since its inception in 1989. This, together with the formation of an early years curriculum for children aged three to six up to and including the first year of school (this whole span now known as the Foundation Stage), has codified the content and some of the processes of early learning in an unprecedented way. One interpretation of the general direction being taken during the process of developing these curricula for young children is that it has moved young children's learning firmly in the direction of formalized, 'basic' skills and knowledge, and away from a 'child-focused' curriculum.

The introduction of the Early Learning Goals in 2000 involved the codifying of six areas of learning, offering the basis for curriculum planning for children's learning. They encompass:

- personal, social and emotional development
- communication, language and literacy
- mathematical development
- knowledge and understanding of the world
- physical development
- creative development

Some have argued that the desirable learning outcomes around which the early learning goals are constructed are over-formalized, that they exert an inappropriate downward pressure from the priorities of school-aged children on those who are pre-school age, and that they under-emphasize the role of play and unstructured learning in the early years (Drummond, 1999; Schmidt, 1998; Pascal and Bertram, 1999).

Similar observations may be made in respect of the National Curriculum, for the emphasis on formality has been one of its features. For children aged 6 and over in state education (i.e. those who are subject to the National Curriculum), claims for the centrality of the 'basics', i.e. numeracy and literacy, have led to the development of the National Literacy Strategy and the National Numeracy Strategy. These may be described as prescriptive formulae for curriculum and pedagogy in these two areas, demanding the allocation of specific time and resources on these topics. This emphasis on literacy and numeracy adds formality to an already heavily content-orientated curriculum, with specified knowledge, understanding and skill across the ten foundation subjects.

The introduction of the Foundation Stage means that in any school with an infant department, children in the Foundation Stage follow the six broad areas of learning specified as Early Learning Goals, a curriculum quite different to that of children aged six and over (who follow the National Curriculum).

There are, as the discussion above highlights, inevitable curriculum and other discontinuities in the very fact of having the two different curricula, although there are also continuities, and the Foundation Stage *is* designed to provide a stepping stone toward the National Curriculum. Clearly, there is a wide range of potential (and existing) content areas for the foundation stage and next-steps in children's learning, in offering children access to the knowledge domains of their current society as well as skills and attitudes appropriate to the twenty-first century. The twenty-first century is itself a context different in many ways from that of the late twentieth century when current curriculum policy was formed, and it is this external context which I examine briefly, next.

### The external context for early education

Uncertainty is a given in industrialized societies in today's world as documented by many sociological commentators (Apple and Whitty, 1999; Blake *et al.* 1998; Carlson and Apple, 1998; Giddens, 1990, 1991, 1998; Usher and Edwards, 1994). Patterns of life which may have been more predictable in earlier times are now much less so. This is the case in social structures, where families, communities and individuals mesh much less predictably than in earlier times (Kellner, 1992; Smart, 1993).

It is also the case in the economy, both local and global. Here a range of factors including the pace of change, reduced market certainties, the mixing of previously public sector enterprises with the private sector, the interconnectedness of individual countries, regions, localities, and even individuals with the global economy, and changing demographics across different countries, mean that the face and shape of the marketplace is changing rapidly. It is certainly the case that some aspects of economic change have fostered a degree of a uniformity in the marketplace, where national and multi-national business conglomerates operate both production and retail parts of the economy, thus going beyond local culture and custom (Ritzer, 1993). However, alongside the apparent uniformities, where for example one now expects to see the same chain stores evident in the high street of all small towns, nevertheless the pace of change is such that individuals working within the economy cannot expect jobs for life or even to be able to use specific skills for life (Smith and Spurling, 1999). And as consumers, individuals find themselves faced by a plethora of short shelf-life choices.

The accelerating spiral of change in technology is another element which both responds to and feeds change. Information and communication technology in particular pervades all aspects of life, and computers now underpin the social fabric. An increasing proportion of the population now own a personal computer, which potentially provides access to a rapidly shifting information system which is worldwide and instantaneous, and offers the power to connect with others in a very fast developing 'e-marketplace' for ideas and transactions of all kinds.

The very speed of change has itself introduced the need to exercise choice in a wide range of settings and at many levels, from the individual through to the collective.

The influential sociologist, Giddens (1998), summarizes some of the controversies that arose in the latter part of the twentieth century through which uncertainty is played out. Describing these as dilemmas that any social democratic process (including its educational policies) must address, Giddens cites globalization (defining it and its implications), individualism (exploring how modern societies are becoming more individualistic), left and right (the evaluation of the claim that these terms no longer have meaning in politics), political agency (to what extent is politics moving away from a democratic framework), and ecological problems (and how they should engage with social democratic politics) (Giddens, 1998, p. 27–8). Some of these are further discussed by Giddens and Hutton (2000) in debating potential explanations of, and consequences for, the rapid changes to the face of global politics and democratic life, which are accompanying global capitalism.

The growing culture of individualism, together with changes in technology and the marketplace, may be seen as demanding and offering an ever-growing role to the individual's own 'agency' in determining directions, routes and pathways through many aspects of life, including the political. This constant decision-making perhaps involves, more than at any previous time, a willingness to enter unknown territory with confidence and being able to work out a pathway through it.

## Personal effectiveness, or little c creativity, as essential to thriving in tomorrow's world

Surviving and thriving in the twenty-first century, then, could be said to require a sort of 'personal effectiveness' in coping well with recognizing and making choices, above and beyond what has been needed hitherto. It could be described as a creativity of everyday life, or what might be called 'little c creativity' (to distinguish it from creativity in the arts, and/or the paradigm-shifting creativity of great figures in history). In identifying and making choices, a person is inevitably self-shaping. This is a process that Glover (1988) calls 'self-creation'. It occurs, Glover suggests, even where choices may be constrained, and includes the incremental building of identity, so is not contingent upon having an overall 'life plan'. The notion that a person may intentionally build self-identity in the exercising of choices, seems to me a quality of persons demanded by the nature of today's world. Although there may be some small logical problems with Glover's position, overall as a concept it seems coherent and useful and it is one which I plan to return to in Chapter 6.

In addition to shaping one's identity through choices (and perhaps more significantly), being able to route-find throughout the many choices to be confronted in life is important for young children, for they are now subject to a much greater range of choice. Children as young as two may become involved in consumer choices when shopping with a carer, and are targeted by advertising accordingly. The case for fostering capability in identifying and making effective choices seems just as relevant, then, to early education as it may to later stages of it. Shaping one's identify and route-finding by making choices, are what I call 'little c creativity' (Craft, 1997, 2000).

What then does personal effectiveness, or 'little c creativity', involve? The first observation to make is that the terms 'little c creativity' and 'personal effectiveness' are distinct ideas, as follows. Little c creativity is the capacity to route-find, life-wide. Personal effectiveness is the capacity to take action that is in some way evaluated as 'effective' or successful. Implied in the term personal effectiveness, is the inclusion of the 'personal' domain. It is as relevant, then, in parenting and other forms of social interaction, as it is in getting and holding down a job.

I am wanting to use the term 'little c creativity' to encompass personal effectiveness, and little c creativity will be used throughout the book to mean life-wide resourcefulness (Craft, 2001a, b) that enables the individual to successfully chart a course of action by seeing opportunities as well as overcoming obstacles. This may occur in personal and social matters, or in undertaking an activity in a curriculum area such as mathematics or the humanities. Implied in 'little c creativity' is the notion that it is essentially a practical matter akin to Ryle's (1949) 'know-how', in that it is concerned with the skills involved in manoevering and operating with concepts, ideas, and the physical and social world. This practical element I return to in Chapter 6.

The kind of personal effectiveness being proposed here is in keeping with the liberal tradition, in paying attention to the well-being of the individual. It focuses on the individual making something of his or her life, whilst being tied in to the wider social, economic, and ethical framework of society. It has something in common with the Romantic movement in the sense that it celebrates individuality and the potential for going beyond existing traditions. In Chapter 6, I shall be exploring, among other themes, the connections between the kind of personal effectiveness being proposed here and Nunn's ideas, in particular his ideas on self-expression. The more detailed exploration of connections, though, between the kind of personal effectiveness being proposed here and Nunn's ideas in particular on self-expression, J. S. Mill's on liberalism, and those of other political thinkers, is unfortunately beyond the scope of this book.

Although it is a concept which emphasizes the individual's freedom, little c creativity may also be developed in a context of constraint. Here I refer to Berlin's (1958) distinction between the notion of 'negative freedom' as being free through constraints, and 'positive freedom', that is being free to be one's own agent, being free to undertake a course of action, determined not by the collective but by the individual only. It seems to me that little c creativity could arise out of either form of freedom. A playgroup, for example, may at times provide for children to explore the play activities entirely independently, with a large degree of freedom. In such circumstances, a child may exercise personal effectiveness in the making of choices, in making something of friendships, and in exploring specific activities such as role play and construction with bricks. By contrast, at other times it may constrain the children's choices so that they must choose between specified activities, for example, cutting and sticking, quiet time in the book corner, painting, or a number activity. The constraining of choices does not necessarily mean that creativity may not be developed. These practical questions of freedom and constraint will be returned to later in the book, in Part Three.

This kind of creativity is not necessarily tied to a product-outcome, for it involves exercising imaginativeness, and this is discussed later, in Chapter 5.

The notion of little c creativity goes beyond 'doing it differently', 'finding alternatives' or 'producing novelty', for it involves having some grasp of the domain of application, and thus of the appropriateness of the ideas. It involves the use of imagination, intelligence, self-creation and self-expression. These philosophical ideas and their role in little c creativity are examined in Part Two of the book. Little c creativity also goes beyond the provision in both the Early Learning Goals and the National Curriculum 2000. Although it can be argued (Craft, 2000;

Rowe and Humphries, 2001) that creativity can be encouraged in children aged five to eight through these existing curricula, I want to suggest that this occurs in spite of, not because of, the statutory curriculum framework. Fostering young children's resourcefulness and encouraging them to consider and implement alternative possibilities, in a range of contexts, whether in play, in relationships, in a collective activity such as circle time, or in a 'formal' curriculum area such as early mathematics, is not necessarily embedded in the curriculum, and yet a case can be made for this to be a more dominant part of the curriculum. Given that the National Curriculum aims statement published in 1999 (QCA, 1999a, b) does highlight creative thinking as an aim for the school curriculum, this book forms in part a call to see that aim through squarely into the definition and implementation of the whole curriculum.

Little c creativity has something in common with the 'democratic' version of creativity proposed by the NACCCE Report (1999), discussed in Chapter 1, which was: 'Imaginative activity fashioned so as to produce outcomes that are both original and of value', in that little c creativity is held out as something which all children are capable of (as opposed to an elite notion of creativity, to which only some may aspire), and in the recognition that originality and value are necessary to creativity. But one significant distinctive feature of little c creativity is its emphasis on resourcefulness, lifewide. Later chapters will explore similarities and differences between the NACCCE definition and little c creativity, as follows. Chapter 3 will explore the outcomes dimension of little c creativity, together with the issues of originality and value. Possible links between views of intelligence and little c creativity are explored in Chapter 4. Chapter 5 will explore the imagination dimension of little c creativity.

Overall, my proposal is that there is a case for early education enabling children to develop confidence and skills in shaping themselves and their lives, both now as children and later as adults, and that the existing Early Learning Goals and National Curriculum are insufficient on their own.

### Little c creativity: a third wave?

I have been developing an argument, then, for little c creativity (encompassing personal effectiveness) as an aim in early education. This advocacy of 'ordinary' creativity is quite distinct from the two other dominant ways in which creativity has been conceived of in recent years and which were discussed in Chapter 1, the first being the wave of activity in practice and policy in the 1960s, and the second being the way it has been described since the late 1980s and particularly the late 1990s. I want to position little c creativity as a 'third wave'. Its distinguishing feature is *its focus on the width of ordinary life*, including, but not exclusively, the curriculum areas studied by school pupils. In this, it contrasts with the emphasis within the Plowden Report (and the practices which followed it), on a particularly child-centred pedagogy and an arts-based curriculum. It also contrasts with the Early Learning Goals which identify creativity as a curriculum area encompassing making in art, craft and design, and the expression of emotional responses, as well as various forms of dramatic play and creative self-expression. Its application across life means that little c creativity contrasts with the National Curriculum definition of creativity as a cross-curricular thinking skill applied across the subjects of the National Curriculum. However, it is also fundamentally similar to the National Curriculum definition, in that the discussion so far implies transferability across contexts. The question of how far this may be the case will be addressed in Chapters 8, 9 and 10. The breadth of application of little c creativity has much more in common with the NACCCE definition of creativity, although that latter definition is situated within a strong arts framework within the report, rather than being a lifewide approach to life.

As part of its lifewide focus, a second distinguishing feature of little c creativity (Craft, 2001a, b) is the attempt to explore the fostering of creativity across the school curriculum. Clearly, this stands in marked contrast with the characterization of creativity in the Early Learning Goals. It also contrasts with the National Curriculum. For here, the lack of any coherent account of how creativity may be applied within the National Curriculum areas, provides an illustration of the general discontinuity between its stated aims and detailed programmes of study highlighted by Bramall and White (2000). In their consideration of whether the 2000 curriculum lives up to its aims, Bramall and White recommend an aims-driven revision of the curriculum, where the traditional subjects may have to 'earn their keep' and other subject areas may come in as alternatives or replacements, in order to see the aims through into practice. I want to propose a significant place for little c creativity within the aims and detailed curriculum statements of the National Curriculum, for at present this is lacking.

In other ways, little c creativity contrasts with the 1960s (first wave) approach to creativity, but is closer to the second wave NACCCE and the 2000 National Curriculum formulations of it. One example of this is the relationship suggested between little c creativity and the wider economic, social and technological context (Craft, 2000), this being that the wider context both demands a personal resourcefulness for survival, but also offers the opportunity for generating ideas and practical outcomes. Obviously these may go beyond the personal, to benefit others too. Whereas Plowden appears to make no economic or wider argument for the fostering of creativity, NACCCE and the National Curriculum do. NACCCE, in common with this view of little c creativity, presents creativity as both a product of, and necessary to, its economic and cultural context. The National Curriculum describes creativity as being bound up with enterprising activity, with innovation and with leadership focused on helping to produce a better future. So both little c creativity, and the treatment of creativity by NACCCE and in the National Curriculum in 2000, are more closely related to the economy than was Plowden in the 1960s.

Another feature of little c creativity is that it is not necessarily tied to a particular pedagogy. This again contrasts with the Plowden conceptualization, and to a lesser degree the NACCCE perspective, but it is more similar to the way in which creativity is presented in the National Curriculum. Plowden's perspective on creativity was integrally connected with the pedagogy of child-centred teaching and learning, in turn derived from the very similar theoretical frameworks of several influential, child-centred, thinkers.

By contrast the NACCCE report instead suggests several tasks and foci for fostering creativity, but without any strong connection to an overarching theoretical framework. The report suggests that in teaching for creativity, teachers have the task of encouraging, identifying and fostering, but the report does not propose a detailed pedagogy. Similarly, although certain parts of the National Curriculum (i.e. numeracy and literacy) have become prescriptive in terms of their pedagogy, the rest of the curriculum, including how to foster creativity, remains flexible and is entrusted to the professional artistry of the teacher.

## CONCLUSION

This chapter has been concerned to make a case for the significance of little c creativity in the curriculum of young children. I have suggested that the existing curricula are insufficent on their own and have argued that what is being proposed may be seen as a 'third wave' of conceptualising creativity, distinct from the two most recent waves of thinking about creativity, the one linked with Plowden and the other associated with curriculum reform during the 1990s.

These first two chapters have been concerned with developing a rationale and context for the focus of this book, little c creativity. Next, I want to fill out some elements of little c creativity, starting with drawing a distinction between little c creativity and big c creativity. I will then go on to look at intelligence and imagination introduced briefly during this chapter, exploring the roles which these may play in little c creativity, before going on to explore points of connection between it and self-creation, self-expression and know-how. Chapter 3, then, focuses on the distinctions between little c and high c creativity.

## References

Apple, M. W. and Whitty, G. (1999) 'Structuring the postmodern in education policy', in D. Hill, P. McLaren, M. Cole, and G. Ribowski (eds) *Postmodernism in Educational Theory: Education and the Politics of Human Resistance*. London: The Tufnell Press.

Berlin, I. (1958) *Two Concepts of Liberty: An Inaugural Lecture* (lecture delivered before the University of Oxford, 31 October 1958): Oxford: The Clarendon Press.

Blake, N., Smeyers, P., Smith, R. and Standish, P. (1998) *Thinking Again: Education After Postmodernism* Westport, Connecticut and London: Bergin & Garvey.

Bramall, S. and White, J. (2000) *Will the New National Curriculum Live Up to Its Aims?* Philosophy of Education Society of Great Britain

Carlson, D. and Apple, M. W. (1998) 'Introduction: Critical Educational Theory in unsettling times, in D. Carlson and M. W. Apple (eds) *Power/Knowledge/Pedagogy: The Meaning of Democratic Education in Unsettling Times*. Boulder, Colorado and Oxford: Westview Press.

Craft, A. (1997) 'Identity and creativity: educating for post-modernism?' *Teacher Development: An International Journal of Teachers' Professional Development*, 1(1), 83–96.

Craft, A. (2000) *Creativity Across the Primary Curriculum*. London: Routledge.

Craft, A. (2001a) 'Little c creativity', in A. Craft, B. Jeffrey, and M. Leibling, (eds) (2001) *Creativity in Education*. London: Continuum.

Craft, A. (2001b) 'Third Wave Creativity? Lessons in the early years.' Paper presented as part of 'Creativity in Education' symposium, at British Educational Research Association (BERA) Annual Conference, Leeds University, September 2002.

Drummond, M.-J. (1999) 'Perceptions of play in a Steiner kindergarten', in L. Abbott and H. Moylett (eds) (1999) *Early Education Transformed*. London: Falmer Press.

Giddens, A. (1990) *The Consequences of Modernity*. London: Polity.

Giddens, A. (1991) *Modernism and Self-Identity: Self and Society in the Late Modern Age*. Cambridge: Polity Press (in association with Macmillan).

Giddens, A. (1998) *The Third Way: The Renewal of Social Democracy*. Oxford: Polity Press (in Association with Blackwell).

Giddens, A. and Hutton, W. (2000) 'In conversation', Introduction to A. Giddens and W. Hutton (eds), *Global Capitalism*. New York: The New Press.

Glover, J. (1988) I: *The Philosophy and Psychology of Personal Identity*. London: Allen Lane, The Penguin Press.

Gordon, P. and White, J. (1979) *Philosophers as Educational Reformers*. London: Routledge & Kegan Paul.

Kellner, D. (1992) 'Popular culture and the construction of post-modern identities', in S. Lash, and J. Friedman (eds) *Modernity and Identity*. Oxford: Basil Blackwell.

Pascal, C. and Bertram, T. (1999) 'Accounting early for lifelong learning', in L. Abbott and H. Moylett (eds) (1999) *Early Education Transformed*. London: Falmer Press.

QCA and DfEE (1999a) *The National Curriculum Handbook for Primary Teachers in England*. London: DfEE/QCA.

QCA and DfEE (1999b) *The National Curriculum Handbook for Secondary Teachers in England*. London: DfEE/QCA.

QCA and DfEE (2000) *Curriculum Guidance for the Foundation Stage*. London: DfEE/QCA.

Ritzer, G. (1993) *The McDonaldization of Society: An Investigation Into the Changing Character of Contemporary Social Life*. Newbury Park, CA: Pine Forge Press.

Rowe, S. and Humphries, S. (2001) 'Creating a climate for learning at Coombes Infant and Nursery School' in A. Craft, B. Jeffrey, and M. Leibling (eds) (2001) *Creativity in Education*. London: Continuum.

Ryle, G. (1949) *The Concept of Mind*. London: Hutchinson.

Schmidt, S. (1998) *A Guide to Early Years Practice*. London: Routledge.

Smart, B. (1993) *Postmodernity*. London: Routledge.

Smith, J. and Spurling, A. (1999) *Lifelong Learning: Riding the Tiger*. London: Cassell.

Usher, R. and Edwards, R. (1994) *Postmodernism and Education*. London: Routledge.

# CHAPTER 3

# Contrasting big and little c creativity

*In this chapter a rationale is constructed for understanding little c creativity and high creativity as distinct concepts, whilst possibly occupying different ends of a spectrum.*

## Introduction

In the last Chapter, I proposed 'personal effectivenes', or 'little c creativity' as way of conceptualizing creativity. I began to make the case for why little c creativity should be seen as an important aim in early education and gave examples of what little c creativity might involve, and which might be seen overall as 'shaping one's life'. I positioned little c creativity as representing a 'third wave' of thinking about creativity.

In this chapter I develop the concept of little c creativity further, drawing on the psychological literature where a major distinction is made between 'high' (or 'big c') creativity and ordinary, everyday creativity. To draw out the distinctions between the two conceptualizations of creativity, I will consider Gardner's work, which focuses on big c creativity, but will first set out some of the wider context to the psychological literature on high creativity.

## High creativity

Some influential descriptions of high creativity, i.e. the sort of publicly acclaimed creativity which fundamentally changes knowledge and/or our perspective on the world, include the following:

> *the achievement of something remarkable and new, something which transforms and changes a field of endeavor in a significant way ... the kinds of things that people do that change the world*
> (Feldman *et al.*, 1994, p.1)

*exceptional human capacity for thought and creation*
(Rhyammer and Brolin, 1999, p. 261)

*the ability to produce new knowledge*
(Dacey and Lennon, 2000)

It seems to me that these definitions all focus on the extraordinary, the boundary and knowledge-shifting, the major-contribution-to-history. Each one involves a recognition that something 'new' has been identified, discovered, or suggested.

Integral to definitions with an extraordinary, or 'high creativity' focus, is that this sort of creativity is seen as being manifested by a very few, extremely talented, people. It is the extraordinary creativity of the genius, in any aspect of human endeavour, which in some way offers a transformation of that field and is recognized as such within the field. High creativity has certain characteristics, such as innovation/novelty, excellence, recognition by the appropriate field, as indicated earlier, and a break with past understandings or perspectives.

Many studies of creativity have focused on this extraordinary, paradigm-shifting kind of creativity, or 'high creativity'. Feldman *et al.* (1994) have proposed a useful framework for understanding high creativity. They view high creativity as involving three perspectives – the individual, and their talents and interests, the domain in which they operate, and finally the field (of judges, of existing, culturally accepted experts). The model works dynamically. The acceptance of new creative minds into a domain by the field is the recognition of the potential of 'big c' creativity, a recognition of the kind of creativity that actually changes the domain; in other words, creativity that refashions it. People who are high creators are those who change domains of knowledge, or create new ones.

The high creativity literature focuses on a range of aspects of the concept, including persons, processes, products and, in the case of some researchers, places.

## Illustrating the contrast between little c creativity and high creativity

In considering differences between little c creativity and high creativity, I shall focus on persons, and on the work of Gardner. Thus, what follows is illustrative, rather than a comprehensive review.

Gardner (1993) has studied the personality and biographical factors which may be associated with 'high creativity', by looking at the work and lives of seven great creators (Freud, Einstein, Picasso, Stravinsky, Eliot, Graham and Gandhi), selected for their representation of the seven intelligences which he postulates. There are, of course, problems with Gardner's selection as he himself admits: the study includes only one woman, it is time-bound and to an extent geographically/culturally limited (that is to mainly early twentieth-century Europe).

Similarities between the seven creators included 'rapid growth in expertise and productivity, once they had committed themselves to a domain' (*op. cit.*, p. 364). Another common feature was a level of self-absorption and self-promotion, in the interests of the work itself. Another similarity was 'the amalgamation of the childlike and the adult like' (p. 365). Gardner noted that each experienced a feeling of being under siege during their 'greatest creative tension' (p. 367).

He also observed social-psychological similarities. For example he noted that love, within the homes in which they each grew up, 'seems to have been conditional on achievement' (p. 367). He noted, too, that each household was quite strict, so that 'ultimately, each of the creators rebelled against control' (p. 367) and that each creator had a personal sense of social marginality, which they used 'as a leverage in work' (p. 368) to the extent that 'whenever they risked becoming members of "the establishment" they would again shift course to attain at least intellectual marginality' (p. 368). He also described the ten year cycle of creativity experienced by each of these individuals, consisting of initial breakthrough followed by consolidation, succeeded ten years later by a subsequent breakthrough which was more integrative, and so on and so on. Gardner indicates that each of these creators was 'productive each day' (p. 372) – and that in the nature of their creativity; each demonstrated the capacity to identify and then explore 'asynchrony' or dissonance with others within their field of endeavour. For Gardner, asynchrony refers to 'a lack of fit, an unusual pattern' (p. 41). Breaking away from an established wisdom is in his view an essential aspect of the creative process as demonstrated by these seven individuals.

In a more recent study of the extraordinary mind (1997), Gardner developed a new taxonomy of creativity, distinguishing four types of extraordinary creator:

- Masters
- Makers
- Introspectors
- Influencers

This taxonomy comes out of the different foci that human beings have. Influencers and introspectors are people who are particularly involved in the social environment – introspectors in their own world, and influencers in trying to influence other people. Makers and masters can be interested in anything, including people. But they tend to approach their objective not through direct contact but more through ideas, and through symbolic representation in domains. They tend to be writers and scientists. From an early age, people seem to be drawn either toward people or toward objects. Makers and masters then, are oriented toward domains. Influencers and introspectors are oriented towards people.

The four individuals whom Gardner cites as representatives of each form of creator are:

- *Master*. Mozart, who did not have a desire to create new forms, but rather to master the art form better than anyone else.
- *Maker*. Freud, who sampled half a dozen fields of medicine before inventing his own.
- *Introspector*. Virginia Woolf, who was both personally and culturally introspective. As she was a writer, we have access to her patterns of thought.
- *Influencer*. Gandhi. He immersed himself in two cultures which contrasted with his own in order to first pursue his studies and then to work as a lawyer, through which he developed powerful views on positive human relations regardless of national boundaries, developing a new form of protest at the heart of which was non-violence.

Gardner discusses these individuals as representatives of these respective categories, and then offers three lessons which he has learned from these people:

- *Reflection*. All of these people made time to reflect, in a variety of ways.
- *Leveraging*. All of these people identified what they were good at and really pushed that.
- *Framing*. Creative people neither ignore nor are put off by failure but instead ask 'What can I learn from this?' This is an ability to look defeat in the eye and seek some benefit from it. Great creators have learned this lesson well.

More recently, Gardner (1999a) has suggested that the following factors are significant in fostering high c creators:

- early exposure to risk-takers who do not accept failure easily – both adults and peers;
- the chance to excel in at least one pursuit when young;
- discipline, enabling the mastering of one domain when young;
- a constantly stimulating and stretching environment;

- not being the first-born, or being in a family which tolerates rebellion;
- social marginality (for example through physical, psychic or social anomaly or obstacle).

His work is close to the findings of Worth (2001) whose investigation of 'localized' creators (those with a reputation for creative work in a localized context such as an organization) suggested early life experiences to be a significant factor. Although Worth's study is not looking at high creators, it is interesting to note this particular parallel with Gardner's proposals.

Some of the characteristics (childlike qualities, feeling under siege, being on the edge, high energy and productivity) that Gardner identifies in *Creating Minds* (1993) also appeared among ordinary educators in a recent small research project (Craft, 1996, 1997a, b, 1998). On that basis, we might expect to see some of the qualities described above in ordinary individuals: the childlike playfulness, the feeling of being under siege whilst being creative, the connection between love and achievement, the wish to be 'on the edge', high energy and productivity, and so on. And of course it could be that each kind of creativity involves different personal responses. For parents and teachers the feeling of being under siege for example is very common. ... 'The three characteristics', which Gardner identifies as belonging to each of the four extraordinary people from his 1997 book, reflection, leveraging and framing, may also be appropriate and relevant to the creativity of ordinary people.

One further position posited by Gardner is that creativity is not a single entity (Craft, 1996). He suggests it is not therefore psychometrically ascertainable, for example as 'thinking diversely, or divergently', around which empirical tests can be constructed. His argument is that such tests, although reliable (i.e. they can be replicated), are not particularly valid for creative thinking. It is not the case, for example, that people who are good at thinking up many uses for a rubber band, or a brick, are necessarily particularly creative. Conversely, it does not necessarily follow that creative people are able to come up with many uses for a rubber band or a brick. Nevertheless, many psychologists continue to use this single, and rather narrow, definition of creativity, which is also closely associated with an approach to measuring psychological phenomena through norm-distributed, product-defined, psychological tests.

Gardner suggests that creativity is the ability to solve problems or fashion products, pose questions, or raise new ones (an important issue to confront in education). He suggests that creative individuals do this regularly. It is their mode of existence. Something that is creative has to be both novel and has to be accepted (though of course the acceptance is culturally- and values-related, and thus we have to pay attention to the social context in which people are creative). He emphasizes, with his colleagues Feldman and Cziksentmihalyi (1994), the individuality of each person's creativity, and the mix of skills and domains which it may draw upon and be expressed within.

In his more recent work, Gardner has emphasized the moral context to creativity, discussing the notion of 'humane creativity' and suggesting that 'We seek individuals who not only can analyse but also will do the right thing; individuals who will be admirable not only as thinkers or creators but also as human beings' (1999b, p. 248).

## Little c creativity

Although it may be that some qualities present in high creators may also be found in ordinary people's creativity, I want to distinguish between the two kinds of creativity. For whereas high creativity is focused around the extraordinary contributions and insights of the few, little c creativity, by contrast, focuses on the resourcefulness and agency of ordinary people. A 'democratic' notion, in that I propose it can be manifested by anyone (and not just the few), it refers to an ability to route-find, successfully charting new courses through everyday challenges. It is the sort of creativity, or 'agency', which guides route-finding and choices in everyday life. It involves being imaginative, being original/innovative, stepping at times outside of convention, going beyond the obvious, being self-aware of all of this in taking active, conscious, and intentional action in the world. It is not, necessarily, linked to a product-outcome.

As noted in Chapter 2, the concept of little c creativity is not dissimilar to the notion of 'democratic' creativity coined by the NACCCE Report (1999), to mean the creativity of the ordinary person (recognizing, in the context of education, that creativity is something that all pupils can do).

Little c creativity then, is a way of coping with everyday challenges, which may involve knowledge-based intuition just as much as step-by-step thought. Elsewhere (Craft, 2001), I have postulated that lacking little c creativity may negatively affect a person's capacity to cope with basic challenges thrown at them by life, through an inability to pose questions which may lead to possible ways around blockages or problems. I have also suggested that a person's ability to operationalize little c creativity may vary at times through their life according to various factors, and that the broader cultural context may form a part of the background to this.

Little c creativity, then, describes an approach to life which is driven to find solutions and ways through all situations, an approach to life which in the vernacular may be labelled as 'can do'. It contrasts with an attitude of being stuck, or of being fatalistic, when faced with uncertainty or blockages. Elsewhere, I have proposed that little c creativity can be shaped and encouraged and thus that schools and our wider education provision have a role to play in fostering it (Craft, 2001). At its heart, I have argued elsewhere (Craft, 2000, 2001), is the notion of 'possibility thinking', or asking, in a variety of ways, 'what if?' (This latter is explored in more depth in Chapter 8.)

Little c creativity is driven by a particular 'mind-set' or attitude. Being creative means being inclined to be so, and being sensitive to opportunities in which to be so. This is a perspective adopted by David Perkins and his colleagues of Project Zero at Harvard University (Perkins *et al.* 1993). They argue that *ability* to be creative at any level, whether at the everyday ('little c') end or the paradigm shifting ('big c') end of the creativity spectrum, is a third aspect of being creative, but that the *habit* of being inclined to creative behaviour and the *quality of alertness, or sensitivity*, to opportunities for creative behaviour are just as important.

Finally, the notion of little c creativity encompasses the identification of new problems (as well as the solving of existing ones), and as discussed in Chapter 2, it assumes that creative thinking can be applied across contexts.

So far, I have been considering some of the similarities and differences between big and little c creativity. The next section seeks to draw the similarities and differences together.

## Similarities and differences between big c and little c creativity

It seems to me that there are five qualities which big c creativity as described by Feldman *et al.* (1994) and Gardner (1993) has in common with little c creativity. These are:

### Innovation
- creativity as demonstrated through acts of innovation in fashioning new products, ideas or questions, rather than through tests separate from the real life concerns of individuals
- the involvement of 'possibility' in acts of creativity
- the likelihood that creative acts will necessarily involve development or change

## Domains and Knowledge

- that creative acts come out of a depth of knowledge and understanding in any particular field
- the notion of creativity as multi-faceted (and thus as drawing on different intelligences and being expressed in different domains)

## Risk

- the need for creative acts to entail some element of risk

## Audience/context

- acts of creativity as requiring an audience, for some kind of appraisal or recognition (thus requiring some form of 'field')
- creativity as having a value-context, in which creative ideas are evaluated in terms of their wider contribution to the broader social 'good'

## Idiosyncracy

- creativity as idiosyncratic (and thus *not* measurable through abstract, norm-distributed, product-defined, psychological tests)

Some of these points are of course interconnected, which is reflected in their grouping here. For example, creative acts involve innovation and therefore the application of possibility thinking, and also development and change.

*Differences* between big and little c creativity include:

## Focus

In little c creativity, the focus is on personal agency rather than on field(ie 'large' outcomes which may shift paradigms and which are subject to the scrutiny of a field). In little c creativity, the outcomes of a creative process are likely to be small steps, working out how to find a new place, making up a rhyme, inventing a meal, developing a new game.

## Field

In acts of little c creativity there is no necessary reference to a field of experts, but rather to a spectrum of reference-points of non-expert peers, which provides the 'field' that scrutinizes the little c creative act.

It seems to me that a useful way of understanding the connection between big and little c creativity, is to see them as occupying different ends of a continuum. At one end of the continuum are acts of creativity that change the world (and which are thus both focused on larger-scale outcomes and subject to the judgements of a field of experts). At the other end of the continuum is personal agency, which is likely to involve working in small steps, and where innovation is judged at a 'local' level where the judge may range from the agent to their peers, to their wider context. Some of the issues raised by the locus of judgement in little c creativity are explored among other questions in Chapter 10. At both ends of the spectrum, though, creativity may involve problem-finding, or problem-identification, just as much as problem-solving.

## CONCLUSION

In this chapter, I have proposed that little c creativity is not only distinct from the two approaches to creativity (or 'waves') in curriculum policy affecting the early years of schooling since the mid 1960s, but that it is also conceptually quite distinct from big c creativity. I have, however, identified some qualities which little c creativity appears to share with big c creativity, and I have suggested that little c creativity may be seen as occupying the opposite end of a continuum to big c creativity.

## References

Craft, A. (1996) 'Nourishing educator creativity: a holistic approach to CPD'. *British Journal of In-service Education*, **22**(3), 309–22.

Craft, A. (1997a) 'Identity and creativity: educating teachers for post-modernism?' *Journal of Teacher Development: An International Journal of Teachers' Professional Development*, **1**(1), 83–96.

Craft, A. (1997b) 'Defenders and born again learners: teachers' reflection on practice at MA level'. *British Journal of In-service Education*, **23**(3), 375–86.

Craft, A. (1998) 'UK educator perspectives on creativity'. *Journal of Creative Behavior*, **32**(4), 244–57.

Craft, A. (2000) *Creativity Across the Primary Curriculum*. London: Routledge.

Craft, A. (2001) 'Little c creativity', in A. Craft, B. Jeffrey, and M. Leibling (2001) *Creativity in Education*. London: Continuum.

Dacey, J. and Lennon, K. (2000) *Understanding Creativity: The Interplay of Biological, Psychological and Social Factors*. Buffalo, NY: Creative Education Foundation,

Feldman, D. H. Csikszentmihalyi, M. and Gardner, H. (1994) *Changing the world: A Framework for the Study of Creativity*. Westport, Connecticut and London: Praeger Publishers.

Gardner, H. (1993) *Creating Minds: An Anatomy of Creativity Seen Through the Lives of Freud, Einstein, Picasso, Stravinsky, Eliot, Graham and Gandhi*. New York: Harper-Collins.

Gardner, H. (1999a) *Intelligence Reframed: Multiple Intelligences for the 21st Century*. New York: Basic Books.

Gardner, H. (1999b) *The Disciplined Mind: What All Students Should Understand*. New York: Simon & Schuster.

National Advisory Committee on Creative and Cultural Education (NACCCE) (1999) *All Our Futures: Creativity, Culcture and Education*. London: DfEE.

Perkins, D., Jay, E. and Tishman, S. (1993) 'Beyond abilities: a dispositional theory of thinking'. *Merrill-Palmer Quarterly*, **39**(1), 1–21. Detroit, Michigan: Wayne State University Press.

Rhyammar, L. and Brolin, C. (1999) 'Creativity research: historical considerations and main lines of development'. *Scandinavian Journal of Educational Research*, **43**(3), 259–73.

Worth, P. (2000), 'Localised, Creativity: A Lifespan Perspective'. Unpublished PhD Thesis, Milton Keynes: The Open University Institute of Educational Technology.

# PART TWO
# Exploring and Evaluating Little c Creativity

This second part of the book, entitled Exploring and Evaluating Little c Creativity, continues the conceptualization of little c creativity, exploring the roles played in it by intelligence, imagination, and self-creation, self-expression, know-how and possibility thinking – suggesting that little c creativity involves all of them.

Chapter 4 explores what kind of intelligence might be relevant to little c creativity, first with reference to the intelligence quotient approach, and then the broader approach proposed by Gardner, and arguing that a broad view of intelligence is a necessary assumption underpinning the concept of little c creativity. Chapter 5 explores imagination, its nature and its connections with little c creativity. An argument is made for one particular aspect of imaginativeness as congruent with Elliott's 'new creativity', but draws some distinctions between this 'new creativity' and little c creativity. Being imaginative and imagining are proposed as necessary to creativity. Chapter 6 explores how the concepts of self-creation, self-expression and, to a lesser extent, know-how, connect with the notion of little c creativity. Chapter 7 explores the idea of possibility thinking, making the case for its centrality in creativity in bringing together the other elements discussed in Part Two so far. In this chapter, the relationship between creativity and play is also explored. Finally, in Chapter 8, the overall coherence of the proposed concept of little c creativity is critically appraised, but the overall argument is that little c creativity has an important role in the education of young children.

Together, the chapters in this part of the book form the conceptual core for the notion of little c creativity, forming a foundation for Part 3, which explores the application of little c creativity in practice.

# CHAPTER 4

# Little c creativity and intelligence

*In this chapter I explore what kind of intelligence might be relevant to little c creativity. Having distanced the concept from the IQ approach to intelligence, I make the case for little c creativity involving a broad approach to intelligence such as the multiple intelligence (MI) theory developed by Gardner, (although there are specific problems with that theory, which are explored). However, ultimately it is proposed as a useful example of how a broader view of intelligence must underpin little c creativity.*

## Little c creativity and intelligence

How is intelligence relevant to little c creativity? As a case to draw on during this discussion I start with a brief story about Norah, a person known to the author.

Norah arrived in London from rural Kenya at the age of 22. She had come in search of work and also hoping to study computers as an undergraduate at university. Although she had prior work experience in her village of teaching the youngest children in the local school, she had no qualifications. On arrival in London she found employment and a university place difficult to attain, encountering some racism in her search but also discovering that the costs of being a university student were beyond her means. Within weeks, she had adjusted her expectations and had registered with a company providing cleaners, while also registering at her local college for evening classes in dressmaking; at that time a hobby. Within months she had gained a certificate in dressmaking, had made several successful garments and had persuaded her employers to take her on direct for a lower cost to them, instead of paying a cut to the cleaning agency for her services. She found she got a great deal of personal satisfaction from the dressmaking and set about developing her skills, persuading one employer to loan her their sewing machine and registering for a soft furnishings course at her local college. Within three years she had set up a small business, making curtains and other soft furnishings, alongside her cleaning work. She has plans to venture into fashion design, using the cleaning work as a reliable source of income in the meantime.

It seems to me that, alongside her persistence in wanting to make a success of her life in London, Norah demonstrated little c creativity. She was resourceful in finding ways around the obstacles and difficulties that her new life presented, in order successfully to create a balanced way of living her life which offered her novelty, value and use – and paid the rent. She did this by operating 'possibility thinking' and by being imaginative about what might be feasible, rather than accepting a situation of no employment and no course of study, which would have meant returning home to Kenya and abandoning the dream of living in London. In other words, in my terms she was successfully manifesting little c creativity.

In doing these things, Norah made thoughtful, insightful, resourceful choices, which it seems to me can be described as intelligent. But what do I mean by that?

In Ryle's (1949) terms, Norah manifests intelligent behaviour which does not necessarily involve expert knowledge, demonstrating that intelligence and the intellect are not the same. Ryle suggests that intelligent behaviour is not necessarily born of theory ... proposing that 'theorizing is one practice amongst others and is itself intelligently or stupidly conducted' (p. 26). For Ryle, theorizing is usually done silently and in private, in one's own head. Intelligent behaviour by contrast is 'visible'. On the other hand, Norah did have some knowledge of her domains of activity, i.e. paid domestic work, dressmaking, and running a business. Thus, although not intellectual, her behaviour was nevertheless not devoid of knowledge; indeed, I suggested in Chapters 2 and 3 that a person's creativity depends upon their knowledge of a domain.

In Ryle's terms, Norah was using a mixture of know-how (procedural knowledge) and know-that (propositional knowledge). For Ryle, procedural knowledge concerns how things are done – and is therefore applied knowledge rather than 'theoretical'. Propositional knowledge on the other hand does not necessarily involve any application but may be exclusively theoretical. Although 'knowing that' may not necessarily involve 'knowing how', 'knowing how' by contrast must logically involve some 'knowing that' even if that knowledge is implicit. Norah accumulated procedural knowledge about dressmaking, about running a small business, and juggling time and commitments to enable her to make a career shift. She also accumulated propositional knowledge about the properties, for example, of certain fabrics, and about the basic accountancy rules on book-keeping, as her business grew.

Norah could be said also to have demonstrated intelligent action in selecting what knowledge to use, and when and how to do so in order to manifest her dream – which was to find a way of living and working in London. White's (1998) recent discussion of intelligence is helpful here. He proposes that 'intelligent action has to do with the flexible adaptation of means in the pursuit of one's goals' (p. 4). Norah persistently adapted with flexibility to the opportunities and barriers facing her, without losing sight of her goal, in order to achieve it. Her resourcefulness was concerned with giving shape to her life. Of course, intelligent action is not necessarily associated exclusively with life-shaping. Indeed, views of intelligence are various and include those which count certain kinds of activity (such as logical-mathematical ability) exclusively as relevant to defining and measuring intelligence, as well as those which see the range of intelligences as being potentially limitless.

I want to suggest that to be little c creative assumes a broad approach to intelligence and not a narrow one. Certainly, it involves resourcefulness in varied situations – and this broad canvas includes much narrower specifics. For example, little c creativity could be applied in maths lessons in school; being able to work with hypotheses and possibilities in exploring aspects of number, for example. But little c creativity also requires a 'can-do' attitude and approach to life, which may also manifest itself as flexibility and resourcefulness in other aspects of activity too, and not necessarily or even exclusively ones which are part of the traditional school curriculum.

It is its potential breadth of application that requires little c creativity to draw, then, on similarly broad approaches to intelligence. It is incompatible with the narrower definition of intelligence. To demonstrate this, I look briefly at the narrow definition of intelligence proposed by Burt and others in the psychometric tradition during the 1950s, as discussed by Kleinig (1982), together with some of its criticisms.

## The IQ approach

The psychometric tradition, of which Burt was a noted exponent, viewed intelligence as 'a fixed, innate endowment which places a ceiling on what people can expect to achieve in life' (Kleinig, 1982, p. 133). Burt of course linked this notion to later life paths, the measure of intelligence being 'IQ' – intelligence quotient. Some of the criticisms of this school of thought's attempts to define and measure intelligence are pertinent to demonstrating the wider foundations of little c creativity. I look at four here.

## 1 Validity

The validity of testing intelligence in a context-free way has been challenged. Critics often focus upon the difference between the use of the term intelligence in everyday discourse compared with its use in the 'scientific' sense. Kleinig (1982) for example notes that in ordinary conversation, intelligence can mean being 'clear-headed', 'quick-witted', 'talented', 'clever', 'sharp', 'adroit', 'astute', 'discerning', 'thoughtful', 'wise', 'logical', 'creative' and 'prudent' ... among other things. Furthermore, intelligent behaviour in one of these areas may not correlate highly with intelligence in another and no attempt is made to generalize. On the other hand, in the scientific sense intelligence is taken to mean performance on a set of logical-mathematical tasks against certain standards. Here, despite the fact that the tests occur in a context-free environment, they are taken to be applicable across numerous domains of human endeavour. Thus, a person's IQ score is seen as an indicator of their ability in any aspect of life, not purely in logico-mathematical tasks. The validity of this claim is questionable.

## 2 Biologically predetermined performance ceiling

There is a logical problem with the assumption, built in to the psychometric approach to intelligence, that there is a 'performance ceiling' which is biologically predetermined. How can it ever be proved to be so? A person might continually achieve at a certain level on some sort of test or in some sort of assessment situation. This could be seen as evidence that the person's intelligence is unmodifiable. However, it could never be proven conclusively except by falsification, as Popper pointed out in the context of the sciences (Popper, 1972). In other words, a person might achieve beyond their current ceiling, thereby falsifying that presumed ceiling and suggesting another. But it could not be proven that the new presumed ceiling was fixed either. Thus, if we can never know what a person is really capable of achieving, we cannot talk meaningfully of unmodifiable intelligence either.

As to the genetic aspects of the IQ claim, there are further questions, for example the extent to which it is possible to separate and identify genetic and environmental influences on the development of skills. For if we cannot be sure that we can separate out the genetic from the environmental, we cannot either be sure that the IQ tests provide a reliable index of these influences.

### 3 Moral questions

Other problems associated with the narrow definition of intelligence are of a moral nature. Some, for example Kleinig (1982), have argued that IQ test research has been determined, as he puts it, 'more by the needs of an elitist and competitive social structure than by an interest in understanding and ameliorating the human condition' (p. 142). He argues that consequently, under the banner of 'being scientific' these tests have 'served to reinforce the values of a particular form of society, locating within individuals and groups the reason for their station in life rather than the changeable socio-economic and socio-political structures which they inhabit' (p. 142). By contrast, the concept of little c creativity is a democratic one, proposing and assuming the potential in all individuals to improve their lives.

### 4 Other kinds of intelligent behaviour

Because IQ tests emphasize cognitive/relational abilities, other aspects of assessing performance are neglected, including those involving the body and feelings. How, for example, is the 'intelligence' of the psychotherapist to be measured? Or that of the surgeon? Or the musician, actor, director, or dancer? Or for that matter Norah's 'intelligence' in finding her way through a maze of life possibilities?

Little c creativity cannot be 'measured' with tests which are context-free. It does not begin with an assumption about a biologically predetermined ceiling to intelligence. Instead, it comes out of a liberal, egalitarian, rather than an elitist, political stance. It acknowledges the potential for developing creativity in a potentially infinite range of contexts and drawing on a potentially infinite span of human abilities. It assumes a much broader idea of what it is to be intelligent. One such broader schema that has been very influential in recent years is that of Gardner, and it is this that is now considered below.

## Multiple intelligences

Gardner's pluralist theory of mind (1983 and various subsequent texts) aimed to recognize the different cognitive styles and strengths of individuals. He called it the 'theory of multiple intelligences'. Gardner claimed that his was a new definition of what it meant to be a human being, in taking the view of humans beyond Socrates' emphasis on humans as rational animals. Gardner's perspective was that human beings were animals with a range of intelligences. Initially, he proposed seven of these.

1 *Linguistic intelligence*: facility with language.

2 *Logical-mathematical intelligence*: ability in logical, mathematical, and scientific thinking. Gardner notes that Piaget, the influential developmental psychologist, whilst claiming to be studying the development of all intelligence (including moral development), was in fact studying only the logical-mathematical form – a claim which Piaget would probably not have denied himself.

Gardner also suggests that 'if you do well in language and logic, you should do well in IQ tests and SATS [Standard Assessment Tasks – i.e. national tests in England and Wales for children aged 7 and 11, and you may well get into a prestigious college' (1993, p. 8). His argument though is that what happens to you once you leave full time education depends on 'the extent to which you possess and use the other intelligences' (*ibid.*, pp. 8–9).

3 *Spatial intelligence*: facility with forming a manoeuvrable and operational mental model of the spatial world. Surgeons, painters, sailors, engineers – and, presumably, carpenters and plumbers – are all examples of professions or trades involving spatial intelligence.

4 *Musical intelligence*: facility with music and sound. Performers, composers, and conductors require this kind of intelligence.

5 *Bodily-kinaesthetic intelligence*: ability in solving problems or creating products using the whole body, or parts of it. Athletes, craftspeople and dancers for example all utilize bodily-kinaesthetic intelligence.

6 *Interpersonal intelligence*: ability to understand and relate to other people. Successful politicians, teachers and salespeople all have this kind of intelligence.

7 *Intrapersonal intelligence*: capacity to understand oneself accurately and to apply that understanding effectively in life.

Toward the end of the 1990s, he began working on a further intelligence or more, referring to the revised list of possible intelligences as 'eight and a half intelligences'. He explored various other candidates at this point (1996), including *naturalist intelligence, spiritual* and *existential* intelligences, and later *moral*, or even *philosophical*, intelligence (1999). The exact number of intelligences that could be detected is perhaps unimportant. Gardner's is a theory of plurality and individual difference. The mix of strengths is drawn from birth, values, training, motivation. We can, Gardner suggests, either ignore the individual mixes, which is what he suggests educational systems tend to do, or we can exploit them.

Gardner's work appears to relate intelligences to their domains of application. Thus, logico-mathematical intelligence may be seen as 'played out' in the sciences and in mathematics. However, Gardner is now at pains to point out that the domain is distinct from the intelligence. He suggests that 'intelligence is a biophysical potential; a domain is an organized social activity in which degrees of expertise can be distinguished' (1998). Thus, a person may have a powerful biophysical potential in a number of domains but not in others.

The idea of there being many capabilities of which we each possess different combinations, is not new. The Great Britain Board of Education Consultative Committee's 1933 report (the Hadow Report), which recommended a rationale for the provision of the nursery and infant stages of primary education and a smoother transition for children from the nursery school or class to the infant department, recommended the following for children aged under five:

- attention to careful treatment of 'eating, sleeping, excretion, and the exercise of the sensory and muscular organs' (Recommendation 26, p. 179)
- provision of an open-air environment designed for exploration so that children are 'surrounded by trees, plants, animals, places that they can explore, pools in which they can paddle, and sandpits in which they can dig' (Recommendation 27, p. 179)
- attention to sensory development, so that 'the child's constant desire to look at things and to handle them should be restricted as little as possible' (Recommendation 28, p. 179)
- encouragement of 'imagination and thought' (Recommendation 29, p. 179) and acknowledging the imaginative worlds of the child, although 'the world of fancy should not exclude the world of reality' (Recommendation 29, p. 180)

For children aged 5 to 7+, this report recommended the development of the senses: touch, hearing, sight, fine motor control, observation and perception, reproductive imagination/vistual memory, attention and reasoning powers, and emotional development (Recommendations 31–9, p. 180–2). The curricula recommended by Hadow for the five to seven year olds were correspondingly broad, and it classified these into four areas:

a)  Religious instruction
b)  Natural activities, including physical training, open-air life, rest and play

c) Expression training, including speech, dancing and singing, handwork and drawing
d) Formal instruction in the 3Rs (Recommendation 58, p. 185).

So, the Hadow Report 1933 clearly identified a number of significant areas of achievement appropriate to young children.

As far as junior-aged children were concerned, an earlier Hadow Report (1931) recommended that although the '3R's (reading, writing and arithmetic) should be seen as the fundamental grounding of the upper end of the primary school, the curriculum should be seen as broad, and as 'supply[ing] children between the ages of seven and eleven with what is essential to their healthy growth – physical, intellectual, and moral – during that particular stage of their development' (*op. cit.*, para. 74, p. 92). The Report provided an important precursor to Plowden's recommendations in its proposal that the curriculum for junior-aged children should be both made relevant and also encourage their active engagement, as shown in the following quotation: 'the curriculum is to be thought of in terms of activity and experience rather than of knowledge to be acquired and facts to be stored' (para. 75, p. 93). But to return to the breadth of the curriculum, the 1931 Hadow Report recommended children's capabilities should be developed in language, manual skill, aesthetic subjects, physical education and 'other subjects' (para. 80, p. 99), i.e. science, maths, geography and music.

Some years later, the Spens Report (1938), which considered the field of secondary education, concluded that in general children possess either a practical, technical, or academic aptitude, and that the education system should provide appropriately for these different strengths in learners. Conveniently, of course, the existing school system was a tripartite one, corresponding to these perceived needs.

In the 1960s, an example from psychology of a similar argument was produced by Thorndike (1963). In his discussion of the problems in measuring achievement, he suggested that achievement is not exactly congruent with the notion of the scholastic aptitude test, one problem being the narrowness of the criteria for scholastic performance. As he put it, 'there is no more *a priori* justification for expecting an exact correspondence of academic achievement with a scholastic aptitude measure, than there is to expect perfect correspondence between age and height' (Thorndike, 1963, p. 3).

Nor is Gardner's the only contemporary formulation of a broad approach to intelligence. A similar set of nine intelligences has been proposed by Charles Handy, the management guru: these are the factual, analytical, linguistic, spatial, musical, practical, physical, intuitive and interpersonal (1994). And, from the adult learning field, the various different approaches to 'learning style' also acknowledge different cognitive strengths in individuals (for example, Honey and Mumford, 1986). Some of what I am about to argue could be applied to any of these formulations, but for the sake of depth I shall make my points in relation to Gardner's work only.

I want to comment on two specific aspects of Gardner's concept of multiple intelligence (MI) theory.

## 1. Multiple intelligence as a contrast to intelligence as a unitary concept.

First, it represents a notion of intelligence which is at odds with the traditional IQ approach to intelligence as a 'unitary' concept, described above. The IQ position, which sees intelligence as measurable, as having a 'ceiling' for each individual and where achievement from tests which measure intelligence can be shown on a normal distribution graph, is, Gardner suggests, bounded. It is bounded by its application only in logical-mathematical activity but also by its ceiling. Gardner's MI theory suggests a perspective on intelligence that is not 'bounded' but is, rather, limitless. He rejects the notion that intelligence is purely an unfolding of what is within, offering culture a role in its expression, through his suggestion that intelligence is a bio-physical potential. The potential may or may not get crystallized, he suggests, depending on what is available within a culture.

## 2. Application in many domains

Gardner's approach emphasizes the many domains in which intelligent behaviour may occur, widening these beyond the logical/mathematical.

Gardner's concept of multiple intelligences has been widely debated, and the theory has its critics, notably and most recently, the philosopher John White (1998). White's critique focuses on the foundations of the theory; in other words, the criteria which Gardner uses to select and define his intelligences. Since Gardner's discussion of possible forms of intelligence candidates has grown over the years but his criteria remain unaltered, White's critique seems to me to be important.

In this next section I look at four major areas of White's critique. I explore first each of the three criteria: 'importance within a culture', 'distinctive developmental history', and 'susceptibility to being encoded in a symbol system'. I go on to consider the application of these criteria, and finally the breadth of intelligences that Gardner proposes.

## 1. Importance within a culture

White suggests that there is a lack of logic in the way that Gardner applies his criterion that an intelligence must be important within a culture. For, he asks, 'Why is linguistic intelligence in, but the ability to recognize faces out?' (p. 6). White's point is that it is hard to imagine how any form of communal living would be possible if we were unable to recognize the faces of those close to us as well as those of community figures such as politicians and other leaders.

I would challenge this. For 'culture' in Gardner's terms seems to me to be at a different level from that of 'survival'. Culture, for Gardner, is a refinement of human interaction, i.e. at the level of 'the made environment' – so his choice of what counts is directly related to the human capacity to construct artefacts and tailor the natural world. On this basis, linguistic intelligence could reasonably be selected as an intelligence more significant than recognizing faces.

## 2. Distinctive developmental history

Gardner posits that each intelligence must have a distinct developmental history, together with a clearly definable set of 'end-state performances'. Essentially the developmental model is one where biological 'unfoldment' of the genetic code is reflected in the mental. White critiques the notion of developmentalism in two ways.

First, he suggests that 'the assumption that the unfolding with which we are familiar in the biological realm is also found in the mental' is flawed. He notes that although it is widely recognized that a seed, for example, holds within it the power to unfold into more complex forms of the same organism, the same cannot be said of mental capacities and desires. White suggests that whilst mental capacities and desires change and become differentiated, they do not 'unfold' in the same way that a seed does. For socialization plays an important role in how these capacities and desires become differentiated (indeed, in his account Gardner gives a role to culture). White contends that the cultural environment cannot be equated with the physical environment of the seed (i.e. water, light, air, etc.). This seems to me to be a reasonable argument. Through the social and cultural context, unique mixes of capacities and desires are differentiated and refined. What is needed to nourish these, and the predicted outcome, is not fixed in advance for human beings in the same way as it is for a seed.

Second, White challenges Gardner on the notion of the end-state, which implies that there is a 'ceiling' on development in the mature state. White's position is that Gardner appears here to be espousing the view that 'all human beings have mental ceilings – e.g. in each of Gardner's intelligences – beyond which they cannot progress' (White,

1998, p. 9). White notes that although this position has been and is held by some psychologists, that position has been deeply criticized and still is. Indeed, I would add to this that Gardner himself has challenged the ceiling-on-intelligence notion. So, it would seem that Gardner is open to the criticism that this aspect of his theory is inconsistent with his wider position.

I would counter that although (as White points out) it is unclear what counts as 'maturity' in Gardner's account, this lack of amplification does not necessarily undermine the account. He could, in theory, identify 'end states' in each intelligence, and offer hand-picked examples of these. Of course, these might reflect Gardner's own values rather than being 'objectifiable end states'. It seems to me however that the challenge to refine what is meant by maturity does not invalidate the theory, but rather identifies an aspect which needs tightening. Although such elaboration could help make clearer the consistency of Gardner's position, equally, it may by the same token highlight an inconsistency between this aspect of his theory and his wider position.

### 3. Susceptibility to being encoded in a symbol system
One of Gardner's criteria is that there is a special symbol system, distinct for each intelligence, through which it is expressed and communicated. The symbol system for logico-mathematical intelligence, then, is the language of number, algorithms and the encoding of logic through these and words, too. White challenges Gardner's argument that symbol systems across domains are equivalent (White, 1998, pp. 12–14), and following Scruton (1974) suggests that Gardner relies over-heavily on Goodman's thinking. White thus proposes that symbol systems in, for example, art, are not equivalent to symbol systems in mathematics, as the encoding of an idea in art cannot be applied in a new context, in the same way that a mathematical symbol can be. Further, White suggests that not all intelligences involve a symbol system. He gives the example of interpersonal intelligence and also the problem of athletics. This seems to be a fair argument, for there are recognized musical symbols and linguistic ones – but the symbols in art, or sport, or interpersonal interaction, are not as clear.

### 4. Application of criteria
White challenges the way in which Gardner has applied the criteria, noting Gardner's own acknowledgement that the selection is not necessarily systematic, but rather, as he puts it, 'an artistic judgment' (Gardner, 1983, p. 63). White's point is that Gardner's application of these criteria appears to be subjective rather than scientific.

Overall, White's critique of these criteria is persuasive, as it does suggest firstly a potential arbitrariness in the choice of criteria under-pinning Gardner's intelligences (indeed, he gives no explanation for having chosen these particular criteria). Second, White's critique highlights that it is not clear whether all the criteria must be met, or only a majority of them. If the latter, it is not clear how many would need to be met. All of this somewhat undermines the notion of the criteria being in some way fundamental. Both of these points seem to seriously weaken Gardner's theory, since it is presented as if it were scientific. On the other hand, perhaps what is significant about Gardner's account is that it has opened up discussion about what counts as being intelligent action.

White proposes a much simpler framework for multiple intelligence. He suggests that, 'Since there are an indefinite number of human goals, intelligence can be displayed in countless different ways' (1998, p. 21). He emphasizes the 'embeddedness' of intelligent action and thus dismisses IQ tests as both narrow and invalid. White suggests that intelligent action *does not* involve transcending what would normally be expected, and that everyday actions such as putting a key in a door, could in fact be called intelligent. This is significant if we are to take the broad definition of intelligence to be synonymous with little c creativity, for in this sense the latter would be at odds with the wide definition. For, here, White's notion of intelligent action does not necessarily involve innovation in thought and action, although it may be about performing as expected within a domain. Little c creativity then may draw upon a wide definition of intelligence but is not equal to it, in that little c creativity does involve innovation.

Returning to Gardner's MI theory, as an attempt to acknowledge the breadth of human capability in a very practical way many teachers have found Gardner's framework useful because it has implications for teaching and learning in schools. Clearly, the emphasis through stat-utory curriculum and assessment arrangements is on linguistic and logical-mathematical intelligences. But the implication of Gardner's theory is that, in order to develop each child's capabilities approp-riately, we need to broaden our own awareness of the intelligences in which individual children may be strong, and in which individual children may be weak. The implication of Gardner's theory and also its applications by schools and teachers, is that individuals' capacities may be affected by 'nurture' and socialization. If, as I have argued, a broad view of intelligence underpins the idea of little c creativity, then in fostering it in schools, teachers need to be geared toward individuals, their passions and their capabilities.

Although Gardner's theory, then, has been criticized, and perhaps weakened, in the above discussion, and is at this stage in need of some amplification and clarification, it seems nevertheless to form a useful challenge to the narrower approaches to intelligence such as the IQ school of thought. It also provides a useful challenge to other narrow definitions, posed by philosophers, for example that proposed by Barrow (1993). He couches intelligence as residing within a 'rationalist' framework: as he puts it, 'an intelligent person is one who has broad understanding of certain fundamental ways of thinking that structure our way of looking at the world' (p. 57). He proposes that understanding enables both insight and imagination.

Barrow does recognize the breadth of human achievement, indeed he notes that how to assess understanding in any quantitative way is difficult, particularly in some domains, such as art. He also acknowledges the normative nature of the term 'intelligence', so that different kinds of understanding hold different social 'worth'. He notes too that the kinds of intelligence overlap, so that for example, 'it is ... very likely the case that getting on with people is enhanced by a reasonable degree of rational understanding' (p. 55). Yet ultimately the framework that he espouses is one of rational understanding, for he suggests that 'the intelligent person is one who is able to engage in rational argument in a way that observes the rules of sound reasoning' (p. 56). Barrow appears to place philosophers at the pinnacle of his spire of intelligence.

Barrow gives a role to knowledge, proposing that understanding enables insight and imagination, which appears comparable to the role given to knowledge in little c creativity. Nevertheless, little c creativity transcends Barrow's range of intelligent phenomena. Little c creativity holds the potential for non-rational impulses to creativity (such as may come through dreams and daydreams, and such as are written about by, for example, Bohm and Peat, 1989).

## Little c creativity and its place in the context of theories of intelligence

Overall, I am suggesting that little c creativity has a great deal in common with some wider definitions of intelligence, and little in common with narrower views.

Gardner's MI notion of intelligence seems particularly relevant to little c creativity because it highlights the importance of the domain in which activity takes place. The forms of activity are distinct from one another in MI. Similarly for little c creativity, the domain of application is integrally significant; although since little c creativity is about one's own life, the domains of application will both include and be broader than the formalized domains of knowledge taught, for example, in the school curriculum. Two aspects of this are, firstly, that little c creativity is not about the arts alone; and secondly, that in order to behave creatively, a person must have some knowledge of the domain.

There are at least two fundamental differences, however, between the view of creativity I am proposing here and MI theory as noted during the foregoing discussion. First, as argued by White (1998), the multiple notion of intelligence appears to presume a ceiling on performance or ability. The little c creativity notion makes no such presumption about performance ceilings, and in this sense is distinct. Having said this it must be acknowledged that the inclusion of the notion of ceilings on performance in MI is inconsistent with Gardner's wider position as discussed earlier.

There is another and more fundamental sense in which MI and little c creativity are distinct. Little c creativity is necessarily concerned with behaviour which involves or produces innovation, whereas MI is concerned with performance. In other words, while multiple intelligence theory is focused on the encouragement of excellent performance in a range of domains, little c creativity is concerned with activity that produces change, difference, novelty. Thus, a skilful piano recital might be seen as having elements of high musical intelligence, but not necessarily any little c creativity. For it to involve little c creativity, it would have to involve novelty or innovation, in the interpretation of the piece in some way.

In common with White's position (1998) that 'Intelligent action has to do with the flexible adaptation of means in the pursuit of one's own goals and there are as many types of intelligence as there are types of human goals', little c creativity is concerned to foster creativity across any aspect of human activity. It is also about effectiveness, i.e. the successful pursuit of goals. In common with White's perspective, it does not assume any end-state or ceiling on performance. However, it involves more than the effective achievement of goals across many possible aspects of life. As discussed in the paragraph above, it necessarily involves innovation in the process of realizing goals.

In contrast to Barrow's perspective on intelligence, little c creativity is couched in a framework which includes but is not exclusively concerned with, rational thinking. In other words, it is conceived of as involving a broader range of processes than those that Barrow suggests are involved in his version of intelligence. On the other hand, Barrow's concern to understand the role of knowledge in intelligence, in different domains, places little c creativity closer to Barrow's concept of intelligence than it is to other conceptions of intelligence, such as the IQ approach.

As already indicated, little c creativity has little in common with the IQ approach to intelligence. It does not assume a ceiling on performance. It does not see intelligence as reducable to context-free tests or tasks. It does not assume that as a consequence of measuring it, we can produce an elitist data curve representing human potential. It is a much looser, more liberal and egalitarian approach to human capability and potential.

## CONCLUSION

In this chapter, I began by with a case study of little c creativity to build the foundation for arguing that a wide view of intelligence is necessary to little c creativity. I compared little c creativity with a narrow view of intelligence, arguing that not only were there logical problems with that approach but that it was inconsistent with little c creativity.

As an example of a particular formulation of a wide definition of intelligence, I examined Gardner's (1984) MI theory (the theory of multiple intelligences), going on to discuss White's (1998) critique of this. At the end of the discussion I argued that, although Gardner's theory had perhaps been weakened by the criticisms of it, it was not invalidated by them, but was merely at this stage in need of some clarification on certain points.

Finally, I returned to a narrower view of intelligence, that of Barrow (1993), and explored briefly some contrasts between little c creativity and this perspective.

In pursuing the idea of little c creativity then, I have suggested that intelligent behaviour, in a broad sense, is necessary to personal effectiveness. But is it enough to behave intelligently? If we return to the case study of Norah which opened this chapter, the imagination, as well as intelligence, seems to play a role in her story. She conceived of new possibilities; she imagined how else her life could be shaped.

In Chapter 5, the focus therefore turns to what role imagination may play in little c creativity.

## References

Barrow, R. (1993) *Language, Intelligence and Thought*. Aldershot: Edward Elgar Publishing Ltd.

Bohm, D. and Peat, P. D. (1989) *Science, Order and Creativity*. London: Routledge.

Gardner, H. (1983) *Frames of Mind: The Theory of Multiple Intelligences*. London: William Heinemann Ltd.

Gardner, H. (1993) *Multiple Intelligences: The Theory in Practice*. New York: Harper-Collins Inc.

Gardner, H. (1996) 'Are there additional intelligences? The case for naturalist, spiritual, and existential intelligences', in J. Kane (ed.), *Education, Information and Transformation*. Engelwood Cliffs, NJ: Prentice-Hall.

Gardner, H. (1998) Unpublished correspondence with John White on multiple intelligences.

Gardner, H. (1999a) *Multiple Intelligences for the New Millennium*. Unpublished talk given at University College, University of London, for The Harvard Club.

Gardner, H. (1999b) *Intelligence Reframed: Multiple Intelligences for the 21st Century*. New York: BasicBooks.

Great Britain Board of Education Consultative Committee (1931) *Infant and Nursery Schools* (also known as the Hadow Report). London: HMSO.

Great Britain Board of Education Consultative Committee (1933) *Infant and Nursery Schools* (also known as the Hadow Report). London: HMSO.

Great Britain Board of Education Consultative Committee, (1938) *Report to the Consultative Committee on Secondary Education with Special Reference to Grammar Schools and Technical High Schools* (also known as the Spens Report). London: HMSO.

Handy, C. (1994) *The Empty Raincoat: Making Sense of the Future*. London: Hutchinson.

Honey, P. and Mumford, A. (1986) *A Manual of Learning Styles*. Maidenhead: Peter Honey and Alan Mumford.

Kleinig, J. (1982) *Philosophical Issues in Education*. London: Routledge.

Popper, K. R. (1972) *Conjectures and Refutations: The Growth of Scientific Knowledge*. London: Routledge & Kegan Paul.

Ryle, G. (1949) *The Concept of Mind*. London: Hutchinson & Co (Publishers) Ltd.

Scruton, R. (1974) *Art and Imagination*. London: Methuen.

Thorndike, R. L. (1963) *The Concepts of Over- and Under-Achievement*. New York: Bureau of Publications, Teachers College, Columbia University.

White, J. P. (1974) 'Intelligence and the logic of the nature–nurture issue'. *Proceedings of the Philosophy of Education Society of Great Britain, Annual Conference, Vol. 8 No. 1*, pp. 30–51. Oxford: Basil Blackwell.

White, J. (1998) *Do Howard Gardner's Multiple Intelligences Add Up?* London: University of London Institute of Education (*Perspectives in Education Policy* Series).

# CHAPTER 5

# Imagination and creativity

*The main questions explored in this chapter include the nature of imagination and its connections with creativity; and the extent to which small children can exhibit each.*

*An argument is made for one particular aspect of creativity, imaginativeness, being congruent with Elliott's notion of a 'new creativity', but some distinctions are then drawn between little c creativity and the 'new creativity'. The creativity and imagination manifested by young children is explored, and finally, the case is made for both being imaginative and imagining as essential to little c creativity.*

In Chapter 4, I argued that intelligence (in a wide sense) is necessary to little c creativity. In this chapter, I explore the role of imagination in little c creativity. In doing so I draw on the philosophical literature on imagination, illustrated by both the real-life case of Norah, given in Chapter 4, and also examples from the lives of other young children known to me.

Norah's persistence and success in making a successful life for herself in London having travelled there from rural Kenya, was offered as an example of little c creativity. She made what I described as intelligent choices, demonstrating resourcefulness in conceiving of possibilities for her life in London, as well as finding practical ways of making these come to pass, overcoming obstacles which life placed in her path. Norah's case also demonstrates the ways in which imagination is also necessary to little c creativity. Norah envisaged alternative futures, conceiving of possibilities beyond the 'given' ones. She shaped a new future for herself, rather than accepting her life as it was. She imagined new possibilities. Without having imagined these, she could not have manifested little c creativity, in making significant changes occur.

But what is meant by imagination in this context? For imagination as a term is used in the philosophical literature to incorporate a range of meanings, including imaging, imagining, and being imaginative (this tripartite distinction was made by Passmore, 1980). These are, as discussed elsewhere (Craft, 1988), distinct concepts but with logical connections between them. It seems to me that little c creativity involves both imagining and being imaginative, but not necessarily imaging. To explore why this is, I want to sketch out these three aspects of imagination found in the literature.

*Imaging*, of which visual images are one sort, and where olfactory, auditory, gustatory, etc. are others, involves a kind of private process. Thus, we say, 'in the mind's eye', or 'having a song on the brain' or 'I could smell the scent of my university hall of residence', while being at the time nowhere near genuine originals of the images produced. A child may recall their first school dinner, or the sound of their newborn sibling.

In his account, Kenny (1989) uses the term 'fancy' to separate out imaging from being imaginative. For Kenny, the imagination, in contrast to the fancy, is creative, involving 'the ability to imagine the world different in significant ways; the ability to conjecture, hypothesize, invent ... possessed *par excellence* by persons such as poets, story-tellers and scientists of genius' (p. 113). He suggests that imagination is superior to the intellect, as it enables the thinker 'to form new thoughts and disover new truths and build up new worlds' (p. 114). As he puts it, 'the objects of imagination are created, not discovered' (p. 117). The creative imagination is, according to Kenny, an aspect of the intellectual faculty. It is both more disciplined and more original than the fancy, which generally comprises unintentional meanderings into alternatives, and which includes fantasy. I have no difficulty with Kenny's distinction between fancy and imagination, nor with his account of either. What is useful about Kenny's account is its attempt to flesh out the intellectual element of what we might call being imaginative, in contrast with the whimsical, 'supposition' based fancy.

*Imagining*, by contrast, refers to supposing or entertaining a hypothesis, or hypothesizing. It is again a private process which may be shared and indeed developed by doing so. Imagining involves intention and may also include memory. I can intentionally imagine many aspects of my first day in a new school, aged six, when a wasp stung me in the face during morning playtime – thus drawing on memory, with intention. Sometimes, however, the intention may be less conscious than in the first-day-at-school example. A child at play can imagine what it might be like to be a pirate, or a doctor, or a princess. The process of becoming a princess or a pirate seems to be seamless with the child's real life. Take the real-life case of Natasha. One minute she is Natasha, aged four, living in Kentish Town in London with her family, and the next she is Princess Natasha, who wears sparkly long dresses, high-heeled shoes, lives in a palace and is going to marry a Prince. Moments later she may be a ballerina, on a stage, and her living room is transformed into a theatre. Any adults or children in the room then become her captive audience while she dances for them. Moments later again Natasha may re-emerge in her real-life self to go swimming, or to get ready for dinner. Returning to the adult case of Norah, it seems to me that she in some way *imagined*, or supposed, what her life could be like in the future and then found ways of bringing that to life.

Imagining, may in certain contexts, involve 'pretending' – indeed Ryle (1949) suggests that imagining is a species of pretending. This is so for children at play, and on some levels, for actors at work. Considering other domains though, creativity must, it seems to me, necessarily involve some element of 'acting as if', or a suspension of belief. Thus, a chemist may think 'as if' in hypothesizing about a relationship between two elements. Or an artist may suspend belief about an object in order to explore it in a new light. A writer may enter into the characterization and plot of a story, 'as if' they were real. It may be that 'acting as if' is a natural part of being new to any activity, including, for example, work. So, as Norah made her shift from cleaning work into dressmaking, and gained her first commissions, she acted 'as if' she were an experienced dressmaker toward her clients, and in this way 'grew' this new aspect of her identity.

Within education, it seems to me that there are at least two levels of acting as if: that of the teacher and that of the learner. I have a powerful recollection of beginning teaching, and 'acting as if' I were a teacher before beginning to assume my own personal professional mantle including all its mannerisms and beliefs. All children beginning school have a similar process to go through – they start by 'acting as if' they are familiar with the routines and life of the big school, before assuming their own mantle in it. Both children and teachers, then, learn to play the roles of pupil and teacher. Similarly, as discussed already, children at play in the classroom or in playtimes, often act as if they were something other than what they are, through their play. Through such playing out of 'as if', imagining may also involve fantasy to some extent, although fantasy is not necessary to imagining.

*Being imaginative*, a third element of imagination, is surrounded by much discussion in the literature and again seems to me to be necessary to little c creativity. 'Going beyond the obvious' or 'seeing more than is initially apparent' or interpreting something in a way which is unusual, seem broadly to encompass what many writers mean by being imaginative. Hence, Norah's realization that the local college could in fact offer her a means, through vocational qualifications, to a new way of life, was an example of her being imaginative. The important point here is that Norah was able to envisage a new horizon – beyond her previous expectations.

Being imaginative, I have argued elsewhere (1988), must involve the agent being aware of the unconventionality of what they are doing/ thinking. Norah chose, with intention and self-consciousness, a path distinct from the one that would have forced her into a downward spiral of disadvantage. This I would say was being imaginative. By contrast, a child drawing a lion in a swimming pool may be unaware of the unconventionality of the representation and thus in that activity could not be described as being imaginative.

The example of the lion in the swimming pool does bring in another element of being imaginative, however, which is originality. Young children's language development is rich with examples of originality. Another child, five-year-old Naomi, for example, declared on one occasion that she had a 'brown hungry' (for example, a hunger for chocolate) and a 'white hungry' (which might be satisfied with milk). She was making associations between descriptors which for her were original. She may, perhaps, also have been original in wider terms.

To be imaginative, does something have to be original in both ways? It seems to me that it must be original in the first sense, for the creator, for it follows that if being imaginative involves departing from some rule or convention, the outcome must have some originality in it for the creator. Thus in a way, finding an original idea or way through something may be a form of learning itself (as Beetlestone, 1998, has argued) in that it involves making new connections for oneself. It seems to me that being imaginative must also involve a wider original- ity, because it involves a departure from what is the norm, as discussed above. The spectrum of originality however is vast: a child may request spaghetti with apple sauce for a special tea, an original idea for her or him and a break with convention, thus original in both senses, but not of ground-breaking significance. Toward the other end of the spec- trum, a child may write a poem for a competition which is selected for a prize and publication. This again would demonstrate both kinds of originality, but is of a wider significance than the spaghetti and apple sauce example. At the extreme of this end of the spectrum are the massive leaps of imagination which change paradigms, which it is rare to find in young children.

Being imaginative must, I propose, also involve some kind of out- come. To be able to say that someone has been/is being imaginative, there must be a potentially public indication of some sort to show for it

– a decision, a book, a behaviour, a poem, etc. As Scruton (1974) notes, imaging and imagining are mental acts, whereas being imaginative need not be. The outcome of creativity could be described along a scale, at one end of which might be outcomes which are within the agent's head – for example, an idea – but not yet shared with others. Somewhere in the middle of the scale might be an outcome which is external but not yet disseminated in a wide field – e.g. an idea which has been expressed to others, but not scrutinized by the field in which it is generated. At the other end of the scale might be an idea which has been turned into some sort of public product which can be scrutinized by the field in which it has been produced. Thus, the outcome may not necessarily be one which has been publicly debated, but must be in a form where this could happen.

There are, of course, limits to being imaginative. The person who hears voices in their head may be not imaginative, but rather disturbed. But the line is a thin one. Jana, a composer of piano music and lyrics, hears sounds in her head which she believes to be sent to her, and not of her own making; but these eventuate in written form as musical lyrics. Some of her work offers social commentary on moral issues. Her work is ultimately performed and enjoyed by others, and is thus in the public arena. It is scrutinized within her field and considered to be original, in that she goes beyond what was there previously, creating both musical and moral dilemmas in what she writes. Jana, it seems to me, is being imaginative. Her experience is not dissimilar to the accounts of other composers. Mozart (in Holmes, 1878, pp. 211–13) described hearing his compositions, in 'a pleasing lively dream' which he could then take 'out of the bag of my memory'. Tchaikovsky (in Newmarch, 1906) described inspiration coming to him through periods of very deep and intense concentration. In contrast, the man who listened to the voice in his head which told him to climb the fence around the lion enclosure in the zoo, and who was consequently mauled to death, was clearly disturbed. The Jana example illustrates another aspect of being imaginative: it does not necessarily involve conscious intention, in that the sounds appear, to Jana, to be 'sent' to her, a phenomenon often quoted by individuals concerning their own creativity.

But to return to the man in the zoo. What he may have been experiencing was some sort of fantasy world. To what extent are being imaginative and fantasy the same? Several writers have pointed out that the fantasy can only recombine what is already known; in other words, that it involves non-imaginative imaging. If fantasy involves recombinations of the known, it is close to 'fancy' as discussed by Kenny (referred to above) and to 'imaging'. As Coleridge wrote: fantasy 'has no other counters to play with, but fixities and definites' (cited by Jackson, 1969). In fact the interpretation of dreams relies upon this, taking into account that some of what is known is represented symbolically and therefore may be disguised, in dreams. Being imaginative, by contrast, not only goes beyond the known as suggested earlier, but many writers, including Dewey (1933), Montessori (1989), Kant (Churchton, 1899), de Bono (1967) and Barrow (1988), have claimed that being imaginative has an objective. As de Bono puts it: 'chaos by direction, not chaos through absence of direction' (p. 18). It is this sort of idea, that 'free-floatingness' is not (and will not produce) imagination, which seems to underlie Mary Warnock's call for rigidly time-tabled study, set up so that through boredom the child becomes purposively imaginative. It is also what seems to underly Murray's (1964) claim that being imaginative requires motivation. Kant's discussion of imagination having an objective is framed in relation to other mental attributes, as follows: 'no mental faculty is to be cultivated by itself, but always in relation to others; for example, the imagination to the objective of the understanding' (Churchton, 1899, pp. 70–71).

Earlier in the chapter I discussed fancy, and its relationship to being imaginative. A fear of the free-floatingness and the lack of objective in fancy seems as Passmore (1980) notes, to underlie the hostility of Dewey (1933), Montessori (1989), and Kant (Churchton, 1899) to the notion of imagination as the undisciplined exercise of 'fancy', and yet all were in favour of 'the exercise of the imagination within a form of work' (Passmore, 1980, p. 151). Interesting questions are raised here as to whether play is fantasy, and whether it can be considered imaginative,if purposive, going beyond the given, or a form of work. I argued in the section on being imaginative, that children's make-believe play could be imaginative. Similarly I would suggest that role play fostered in, say a drama or humanities lesson, could involve being imaginative. In the case of young children, it seems to me that play can be seen as a combination of both fantasy and being imaginative. A child role-playing a parent in the home corner of the reception classroom may fantasize that she is faced with a conflict of interests in her family. On one level then she may be modelling known adult behaviours. Her response to the conflict however *may* illustrate imaginativeness; she may be directed in her response, that is she might be aware of how her response may depart from what might be expected; she may be breaking with convention.

The lack of objective or direction in fantasy, the sense in which fantasy can involve ideas being 'blown' like a feather in the wind, is one of the reasons why I would distinguish it from being imaginative.

Another is that dreams, hypnotic states, nightmares, and so on do not necessarily involve unconventionality or going beyond the given. Likewise, they do not necessarily involve intention to depart in some way from convention.

Elsewhere (Craft, 1988) I have noted and discussed a number of difficulties with the concepts of imaging, imagining, and being imaginative, and have explored logical relationships between these three different aspects of imagination. In that work, I made the following connections between being imaginative and both imaging and imagining:

## 1. Imaging and imagining
### Visual images and imagining
Visual images may involve imagining and vice versa. Thus, I can visualize a medieval street scene and imagine I am in it; but by the same token they may *not* involve each other, as in Ryle's (1949) example of a man conjuring up an impression of his nursery.

### Olfactory images and imagining
Imagining may involve olfactory images (my father says he can conjure up the smell from his primary school days of cabbage cooking – and he still retches at the thought of it). I cannot produce olfactory images myself, although particular smells can trigger memories of places and events.

### Auditory images and imagining
Auditory images may involve imagining and vice versa; I may have an auditory image of my son crying, and imagine I am there in the room with him. On the other hand, they may also neither of them involve each other. I may imagine my son's first night in the world without the sounds of the hospital ward and his newborn cry; and I may hear a hymn from a school assembly over and over again in my head during the day without imagining I am actually *at* assembly.

## 2. Imaging and being imaginative
### Visual images and being imaginative
I can visually image without being imaginative (picturing myself on the motorway, driving home, for example). Conversely, one can be imaginative without visually imaging. (For example, when one baked potato popped just as guests arrived for dinner, my mother was able to think of a way of solving the problem of having not enough for the meal – by roasting the surviving potato remnants, and cutting all the remaining potatoes into pieces so that no one noticed.) Alternatively, one can be imaginative and also visually image. (I can picture a

television programme I am planning with a colleague, in order to map out the next step; or I can picture what I think might be added to our developing scheme.)

*Auditory images and being imaginative*
I can have auditory images without being imaginative, (I can find the theme tune from a radio series in my head after the programme, as a sort of background noise, undemanded, unwanted). Conversely I can be imaginative without having auditory images (I can find a back route in a strange town to avoid a traffic jam without any accompanying auditory images). And I can also experience auditory images and imagination together (I can alter the words to a song I know and listen to it in my head).

### 3. Imagining and being imaginative
I can imagine without being imaginative (I can, during role play, act out a part in a stereotyped way). I can also be imaginative without imagining (I can make up a joke without mental pictures). I can be imaginative and imagine at the same time (I can envisage an unusual way of decorating a room in my house).

## Imagination and mental acts
It may be, as the philosopher Roger Scruton (1974) suggests, that imaging and imagining are essentially mental acts, and that being imaginative may not necessarily be a purely mental act. He suggests that doing something imaginative means 'doing it thoughtfully, where one's thought is not guided by the normal processes of theoretical reasoning, but goes instead beyond the obvious in some more or less creative way ... by doing X imaginatively one does more than X, and this additional element is one's own invention, added because it seems appropriate to X' (p. 100). His emphasis seems to me to be on the kind of thinking that accompanies some sort of 'doing', thereby suggesting that some kind of action other than mental is undertaken.

He suggests that imaging and imagining can be conjured up at will. 'It means that the request to imagine or form an image of something makes sense. Someone can assent to it directly' (p. 95). But Scruton also says that, 'This does not mean that "picturing" or imagining are always or nearly always voluntary.' (pp. 94–5). However, for example, someone can be 'ordered' or instructed to see the other picture in Wittgenstein's duck–rabbit (Wittgenstein, 1958). This is, of course, an important point in terms of education. A teacher may invite children to conjure up an image of a place they have recently visited as a class, or to image aspects of the story which she is reading to them. Or she may invite children to imagine what it would be like to live in Tudor times, or to take someone else's point of view in a dispute.

Being imaginative, by contrast, may not necessarily be conjured at will. Imaginative responses or ideas often come through the twilight of consciousness rather than being intended. Thus, according to Adams (1986), Coleridge claimed to have composed 'Kubla Khan' in a dream. I have taught children who said that stories they were writing, or paintings they were doing, 'created themselves'. Again, there are important educational implications of imaginative behaviour not being conjured up at will: it may be that teachers cannot 'make' children be imaginative, although they may guide them in ways which support their imaginativeness and do not suppress it.

The notion of not being able to conjure being imaginative at will seems to be embedded in the view of Warnock (1977), who suggests that being imaginative relies on *not* forcing it. Her claim, rather, is that the curriculum should provide so much structure that children become imaginative as a direct result of not being required to be so. As she puts it, 'The familiarity and the safety of accustomed rituals can allow great freedom to the thoughts and feelings and act as a source of refreshment' (p. 163). It may be the case, in empirical terms, that 'willing' oneself to be imaginative by surrounding oneself with an apparently 'conducive' creativity environment, may either suppress or destroy it.

Warnock's view of structure and predictability forming a safe context in which children may be imaginative, is perhaps a rather 'formal' response to not being able to conjure imaginativeness at will. In some respects I would agree with Warnock's analysis (e.g. in the fostering of children's creative writing, or problem finding and solving, I consider silence and space to be important so that they can 'hear' their own thoughts (Craft, 1988)). Other strategies, appropriate to different parts of the curriculum, might include mentoring imaginativeness in, say, maths investigations, offering opportunities in which children can depart from the obvious in, say, design and technology, and in general creating a classroom climate where children's ideas about anything from behaviour to scientific hypotheses, are valued and 'heard'. I would argue that an important ingredient in fostering creativity in the classroom is balancing curriculum content against being open to possibility across the curriculum, thus making space both conceptually and physically for being imaginative. And whilst being imaginative may not necessarily be 'willed', this is not to say that it is without intention. In other words, being imaginative is not accidental, and indeed may involve a great deal of intention and concentrated activity toward the goal as documented by the poet Spender (1952) and the mathematician Poincaré (1924).

Having then sketched out some distinctions between imaging, imagining, and being imaginative, I want to concentrate now on how these connect with creativity in the philosophical literature, before going on to little c creativity in particular.

## Imagination as the 'new creativity'?

A landmark in the way creativity is understood in the philosophical literature was Elliott's (1971) definition of what he called 'the new creativity'. It is distinct from other conceptions of creativity in that it is not necessarily tied to a tangible product-outcome; nor is it necessarily tied to the notion that creativity can be measured, has a 'ceiling' or may be illustrated on a normal distribution curve.

Elliott places creativity very close to imagination, suggesting that 'Creativity is imaginativeness or ingenuity manifested in any valued pursuit' (p. 139). He does not, importantly, tie the concept to an object, but only to a 'pursuit'. As he puts it, under his new concept of creativity, 'it is not necessary to make or create anything in order to be creative' (p.139). This means that *the process* by which someone proceeds can be considered to be creative. For Elliott, the processes involved are 'problem-solving' and 'making something of an idea' (these he describes as related but distinct versions of the 'new creativity'). He claims that 'under the new concept, to proceed imaginatively is *ipso facto* to be creative. All creativity is creative (i.e. imaginative thinking') (p. 147). This contrasts with the traditional concept where 'to be creative a person had to produce some object of a sufficiently impressive kind' (p. 147).

On Elliott's analysis, it is clear that creativity necessarily involves imagination. For example, it could be argued that problem-solving involves imagination, in order to envisage possibilities. Making something of an idea, finding something valuable in some way in an idea, or having a novel idea, likewise must all require having imagination to frame possibilities.

## Being imaginative and 'the new creativity': the same or distinct?

I have been considering the concept of being imaginative as distinct from imaging and imagining, and as distinct from fancy and fantasy, and have now introduced Elliott's notion of 'the new creativity' which seems to involve the concept of being imaginative as discussed so far. Are they, in fact, the same concept?

Certainly, there are similarities in what is meant by these terms. What follows is a sketch of similarities as I see them, after which I shall address what differences there may be between the two terms, and as I do so, I shall introduce some discussion of little c creativity. It seems to me that there are six similarities between being imaginative and Elliott's 'new creativity'.

## 1. Intention

'The new creativity' and imaginativeness, it seems to me, each involve intention. When Aneurin Bevan envisaged a national health service, he knew from what traditions he was departing; it was no accident that he thought creatively/imaginatively about health care in Britain. His plans for the beginnings of the NHS, it could be argued, involved both problem-solving and making something of an idea. The idea/solution was not hit upon unwittingly, unknowingly or unintentionally. The 3-year-old who negotiates with a friend to use a blanket as a 'ceiling' for a pretend rocket, intends to do so; the plan is not 'accidental'. Norah, in choosing to be a dressmaker and not a cleaner, intended to do so.

## 2. Departure from rules

The departure from rules is shared by both processes, being imaginative and 'the new creativity'. As White (1972) notes, ' "creative", like "free", is not a term that has any application on its own, unqualified' (p. 135). We need to know from what it is to be free; from what it departs.

As Olford (1971) puts it, ' "Creativity" seems to imply a departure from rules; a liability to stray from, rather than competence enshrined in, the observance of rules' (p. 78). As I have already suggested, so does being imaginative. Olford continues, however, 'divergence may not ... be creative; it may result in chaos rather than cosmos' (1971, p. 78) – in other words, the boundaries of being imaginative or being creative are still governed by the normative values of what is appropriate, even where there is a departure from rules. Bevan's plan for the NHS, for example, might not have been considered imaginative/ creative if he had advocated that it should embody a different medical model to the traditional Western one, since it would not have been appropriate to have proposed such a radical change all at once. By contrast, the gradual inclusion of complementary therapies such as osteopathy, acupuncture and the Alexander Technique into the NHS, seems to display imagination on the part of therapists/physicians and administrators responsible for their introduction, and perhaps illustrating a departure from familiar rules and conventions in a culturally acceptable way. The three-year-old who uses a blanket for the ceiling of the rocket, is departing from the usual convention in blanket use, but within certain norms. If the child were to decide to cut up, set fire to, or paint all over, the blanket in question without license to do so, we might describe their activity as destructive rather than being either imaginative or creative. Norah chose to depart from the norm in her peer group from rural Kenya in making more of her life than she might otherwise have done.

### 3. Disposition

Logically, it seems that 'the new creativity' and being imaginative must involve the *disposition* to create or imagine. They both involve, in other words, having an intellectual 'can-do' approach, as it were, one which is open to the possibility of ideas 'popping into one's head' and being taken seriously, and this approach being brought to a range of situations, repeatedly. Disposition can be seen as conceptually distinct from intention, for the purposes of this discussion, since it really refers to a basic orientation, rather than going after a specific goal in the way that intention might be seen to imply. Testing the presumption that disposition is necessary to 'the new creativity' and being imaginative, one might ask whether it would be possible for a person to see their way around a problem, or to depart from convention, while *not* having such a 'can-do' approach. The answer to this must surely be no, although we could imagine a situation where a person's usual can-do approach is undermined by unusual circumstances, such as illness.

Having the disposition to create, though, may not always have a creative outcome, as the following discussion explores.

First, having a disposition to create does not automatically mean being able to do it consistently across all domains. Like imagination, creativity can at times be 'willed' but it is also vulnerable to being stifled by attempts to consciously be creative. This inconsistency across domains may be more obvious in a high creator. Thus, a ground-breaking surgeon may be a poor creative writer. There is no logical reason why this inconsistency should not hold true for little c creativity also. So, a person may be creative in finding paid employment but not in the invention of new food combinations. One nursery child may be creative in the sand tray but less so in relationships, but another may be creative with small bricks and other construction equipment, whilst less so in role-play.

Second, being disposed to create does not necessarily mean being able to do so consistently across time. This again may be more obvious in the case of high creators, where a writer or artist, for example, becomes 'blocked' in their creative endeavour. Again the logic seems to apply to little c creativity. For a person may be creative in successfully seeking paid employment during some periods of their life, but may find it much more onerous and feel blocked in doing so, during other periods, whilst nevertheless maintaining a disposition to be creative. To an extent this may reflect personal maturity, but it may also be to do with external circumstances and mental or physical health. An eight-year-old child may be creative with written language in a way that they could not be at the age of three, simply because they knew and could do less in that domain when they were younger.

What I have suggested so far, then, is that disposition is common to both the 'new creativity' and being imaginative; but the disposition to be creative may be domain-related, and there may be times when the disposition to be creative is inhibited. One of the questions raised by the above discussion is the question of whether creativity could be considered to be something like a personality trait – in other words, do creative acts belong to creative persons? If we take on board the domain and temporal limitations to actually being creative which were discussed above, it may be that some individuals exhibit creative behaviour across many domains and others far fewer; while some people can be creative more continuously than others. Studies of the creative personality have, as noted in the Introduction, formed an important line of creativity research since the 1950s, and in terms of high creativity, these studies suggest that persistently successful high creators do share certain characteristics (summarized by Brolin, 1992).

## 4. Possibility thinking

From the above discussion, we might conclude that both imagination and creativity involve an approach to life which begins with: 'perhaps if' or 'what if?', that is to say, a questioning way of operating which could be described as 'possibility thinking'.

At first glance, the term 'thinking' implies orderly, intentional thought. But I would want to include in my notion of possibility thinking a wide gamut, from the sort of possibility thinking of which we are not necessarily conscious and which flows from an apparently 'other' source, to the kind which we intentionally conjure up. For example, I am not necessarily conscious that I take a new route back from a friend's house in the heavy rain which has flooded some roads. Similarly, a teacher trying to motivate a child to read may not necessarily be conscious of all the strategies she is using to model the process and entice the child into reading. And a child exploring a new role in the home corner may not consciously think, 'I want to try out being a daddy', but may be motivated to do so in a much less conscious way. For a composer of music, the sounds may flow in to their awareness from a wellspring of orginality, but they may not be 'working' at the composition with a problem-solving approach to it.

On the other hand, a more conscious manifestation of possibility thinking might be the kind of 'puzzling' which may occur to a researcher looking at a phenomenon which they are studying (as described by Minkin, 1997), or which may be invoked in a small child as they notice the patterns made by a multiplication table. An even more conscious manifestation of possibility thinking would include the intentional problem-solving involved in, say, a commercial marketing campaign, or in the creative department of an advertising agency. For further discussion on self-consciousness (the overall intention to be creative), see Chapter 6.

It seems, then, that both imagination and Elliott's 'new creativity', involve 'possibility'.

## 5. Problems posed for the teacher
The question of 'the new creativity' and imagination each seem to me to raise a number of problems for the teacher. One of these is how to make children aware, in the classroom, of novel possibilities which the teacher may not be aware of him or herself. Another is how to foster divergence, difference, individuality while at the same time managing a group of perhaps thirty individuals, within a curriculum which may be to some or even a large extent, laid down.

## 6. Different domains
It seems to me that for both imagination and creativity it is possible to find commonalities and distinctions across different domains of human endeavour. Fostering imaginative and creative approaches to mathematics and art, for example, may involve quite different outcomes to one another, as White (1972) notes. Yet, what is common to both domains, I have suggested, is 'possibility thinking' – or the asking of 'what if?', and any differences lie in the various structures and values of the domain, for in each respective domain the agent requires knowledge in order to operate creatively. The question of how far there is commonality or difference is a major theoretical one, for the suggestion that creativity in different domains has the same root, begs the question of what precisely can therefore be transferred from one domain to another. The question of transfer is considered in more depth in Chapter 8.

Thus far then, logically, the two concepts of Elliott's 'new creativity' and being imaginative, appear to be identical. The above discussion has suggested that creativity and imagination are each associated with intention, departure from rules, disposition, and involve possibility thinking. Both raise similar problems of making children aware in the classroom of what may also be novel to the teacher, and in the tension between managing and fostering individuality. And for both the 'new creativity' and 'being imaginative', different fields of endeavour, or domains, demand different kinds of creativity/imagination but are equally underpinned by possibility thinking.

Are there, then, any fundamental differences between imagination and Elliott's 'new creativity'? It seems to me that there may be. I suggested at the start of the chapter that imagination was necessary to creativity. If this is the case, then rather than being the same concept, one may be a pre-condition of the other. But, on the other hand, if we accept Elliott's definition of the 'new creativity', then we *must* see being imaginative as *the same* as being creative. As he puts it, 'to proceed imaginatively is *ipso facto* to be creative. All creativity is creative (i.e. imaginative) thinking' (Elliott, 1971, p. 147). Being imaginative must logically involve the generation of an idea or ideas. Being creative must logically involve an outcome of some sort, too, an idea or some other product. The notion of an outcome is built into each concept. It does, indeed, seem as though these are one and the same concept. So, although the suggestion that being imaginative is a necessary pre-condition to being creative is seductive, it is difficult to see how the terms are distinct when we are discussing Elliott's 'new creativity'. How similar then, is Elliott's 'new creativity' to little c creativity?

## Comparing little c creativity with Elliott's 'new creativity'

Little c creativity is similar, it seems to me, to 'the new creativity' proposed by Elliott, for both involve proceeding with imagination. So, how, if at all, is little c creativity *distinct* from Elliott's 'new creativity'?

One clear distinction between the two is the ordinariness of little c creativity. The latter refers exclusively to the actions of ordinary people and not to those of high creators. Thus, LCC would include the sort of eccentricity and idiosyncracy which is illustrated by the so-called 'Ya-Ya Sisterhood' in Rebecca Wells' novel, *Divine Secrets of the Ya-Ya Sisterhood* (1996). A complex tale of female friendship and the mother-daughter relationship, in this novel Wells celebrates the ways in which an ordinary group of Louisiana housewives stamped their own special set of interpretations on their local world in the 1950s.

By contrast, Elliott's concept of the 'new creativity' embraces both high and low creativity (the nature of this distinction was explored in Chapter 3). Thus, although Elliott's concept would include the ideas and ways of the Ya-Ya Sisterhood, it is also broader than this, incorporating, for example, the genius of Einstein's theory of relativity, too.

Another distinction between the two concepts is that Elliott's 'new creativity' does not involve having what I have termed any physical 'product-outcome'. He suggests that the 'new creativity' contrasts with the 'old creativity' in that, rather than being tied to a product outcome, such as an artefact of some sort, the 'new creativity' is concerned with making something of *ideas*, and with *solving problems*. Thus, Elliott draws a distinction between these two kinds of creativity by contrasting the kinds of outcome they may have. Indeed, he suggests that, 'Since the new concept allows that a person is creative simply by having and making use of novel ideas, it is nothing but a part of our existing concept of imaginativeness' (Elliott, 1971).

Since both concepts, little c creativity and Elliott's 'new creativity' each involve the generation of ideas, they clearly overlap. Where it seems to me they are *distinct*, however, is that little c creativity incorporates both product *and* ideas outcomes. Little c creativity encompasses things which are made as well as also ideas.

A further distinction is the inclusion of problem-finding as an inbuilt assumption in the concept of little c creativity (discussed briefly in Chapter 3 and explored more fully in Chapter 7), which is a dimension not present in Elliott's 'new creativity'.

Finally, then, we may examine imagination and creativity in young children. I start with a general discussion of definitions used so far but move quickly to examine little c creativity.

### Imagination and creativity in young children

In the earlier discussion of imagination above where distinctions were drawn between imaging, imagining, and being imaginative, I referred in passing to children's play. It seems to me that play must, necessarily, involve *imagining*, i.e. supposing. Thus, Natasha's Barbie doll can be 'getting married', and 3-year-old Isaac's Postman Pat slippers can 'run away' and refuse to go to bed. Even players in a Monopoly game or, possibly, in a game of chess, are 'supposing' to an extent; they are players in a world where, like the theatre, disbelief is suspended temporarily and new, special rules organize behaviour.

Play may also involve *being imaginative* (say, inventing a new food combination), as discussed already. It may also involve *imaging*. A child who is being a fairy princess may have visual images of her ball gown and her palace. A child who is 'cooking beans on toast' in the home corner may have clear images of the meal.

Some play, as discussed earlier, involves fantasy; it seems to me that imaging and imagining are necessary to fantasy play, but that being imaginative may not necessarily be. Thus, whereas Natasha must suppose that Barbie is 'getting married' and she must image various aspects of this play (including the groom, the building in which the ceremony takes place, the ballroom for the reception, etc.), she does not necessarily need to depart from convention in any way in playing out the wedding and the associated celebrations. Similarly, whereas the child 'cooking beans on toast' in the home corner must suppose that this is indeed what they are doing, and may have both visual and gustatory images of these, they are not likely to be being imaginative in this particular sequence of what is effectively imitative play.

If children's play involves the three aspects of imagination (i.e. imaging, imagining, and being imaginative), it seems probable that their thinking in other contexts in the school curriculum does too. As part of a humanities project, for example, children may imagine (or suppose) that they are living in a different set of circumstances from the ones they in fact live in. In mathematics, a child may visualize the continuation of a geometric pattern. In a science investigation, a child may demonstrate imaginativeness, first postulating the reasons for a phenomenon (i.e. hypothesizing), and then proposing methods for testing their hypotheses. Thus far, then, I would suggest that it is possible for young children to demonstrate all three kinds of imagination in their thinking.

Turning now to creativity, to what extent can young children be said to be creative? Clearly, the creativity of most young children is unlikely to be of the same order as that of a person with a rare talent or gift in a particular domain: it is unlikely to be high creativity. But nevertheless, I am suggesting that little c creativity is both possible and common in young children. The child who persuades an adult carer to permit the wearing of an unusual combination of clothes in a public place, or who invents a way of attaching their home-made mobile to their bedroom ceiling, or who finds ever-more reasons for putting off bedtime, could, it seems to me, be described as creative. In Chapter 7, I explore further ways in which young children are creative.

## Distinctions between aspects of imagination, and little c creativity

I have already suggested that little c creativity and Elliott's 'new creativity' are similar concepts. As regards imagination, it seems to me that all three kinds of imagination (imaging, imagining, and being imaginative) may at times be involved in little c creativity.

At the core of little c creativity, it seems to me, is possibility thinking: postulating, interpreting, considering options, being open to possibility. Thus it would seem that being imaginative is centrally involved in little c creativity. Imaging, by contrast, is perhaps not necessary to little c creativity. Thus, if I am setting up a spreadsheet to deal with income and expenditure on a proposed Open University course, I will need to hypothesize about audience and usage, and to 'go beyond what is given' in inventing course content, but I will not really need to visualize or image anything. I would need to imagine and to be imaginative, but not to image. An eight-year-old considering the options for a creative writing task, will need to consider audience, style, plot line, characters, how much time and energy they have for the task itself; but they will not necessarily need to visualize.

Sometimes however, little c creativity may involve all three kinds of imagination. A teacher of young children planning a learning environment may well image what it is going to look like, as well as hypothesizing about how her pupils will respond to it. She may also go beyond what is given by 'interpreting' a corner of the room so that it now becomes a post office, or a bakery, or a hospital, for example. In this example, the teacher uses all three kinds of imagination as part of little c creativity.

Similarly, to pathfind my way to a new set of working practices when I became a mother for the first time, I created visual images in my mind of working as an academic part-time and parenting part-time. I did this as well as hypothesizing about what might be possible – (i.e. 'supposing'), and as well as thinking up a variety of ways of being an academic and a mother – (i.e. being (hopefully) imaginative). In this example then, all three kinds of imagination were necessary. Again, a 3-year-old playing with a stick which becomes, respectively, a bunch of flowers, an umbrella and a rocket, may 'suppose' (i.e. imagine), and visualize (i.e. image) what the stick has become, as well as being imaginative in conceiving of the unexpected in the first place.

The extent to which imaging is necessary to little c creativity may also be related to the individual and their style of thinking. So, I would like to suggest that little c creativity may require, depending on the context, imaging, imagining and being imaginative. But in these examples, the notion of imaging has been more dispensable. Essential however to all little c creativity, must be imagining and being imaginative.

## CONCLUSION

Having explored the interconnections between different meanings of 'imagination', I have identified 'being imaginative' as an essential element of being creative. I have proposed that fantasy and fancy are distinct from being imaginative, although these are closely related to other forms of imagination. I have discussed Elliott's views on the 'new creativity', viewing his definition as a useful one, in that, first, it separates being creative from making fashioned products; second, it does not propose creativity as measurable on a normal distribution scale; and lastly, it links creativity with being imaginative. I have discussed the extent to which being imaginative and 'the new creativity' can be said to be the same concept, and have argued that Elliott's 'new creativity' and 'little c creativity' are distinct concepts.

Having sought to define the terms, I then looked at whether young childen can be said to be both imaginative and creative, and have proposed that they are able to be both. Finally, I have looked briefly at some distinctions between imagination, Elliott's 'new creativity' and LCC, suggesting that imagining and being imaginative are necessary to little c creativity.

Having, in Chapters 4 and 5 explored the ways in which intelligence and imagination are integral to the idea of little c creativity, in the next chapter I explore the role of self-creation, self-expression and know-how in little c creativity.

## References

Adams, J. L. (1986) *The Care and Feeding of Ideas: A Guide to Encouraging Flexibility*. Reading, MA: Addison-Wesley Publishing Company Ltd.

Barrow, R. (1988) 'Some observations on the concept of imagination', in K. Egan, and D. Nadaner, *Imagination and Education*. Buckingham: Open University Press.

Beetlestone, F. (1998) *Creative Children, Imaginative Teaching*. Buckingham: Open University Press.

Brolin, C. (1992) 'Kreativitet och kritiskt tandande. Redsckap for framtidsberedskap' [Creativity and critical thinking. Tools for preparedness for the future], *Krut*, **53**, 64–71.

Churchton, A. (1899) *Kant on Education*, trans. A. Churchton: London: Kegan Paul, Trench, Trubner & Co.

Craft, A. (1988) *A Study of Imagination*. Unpublished MA thesis, University of London Institute of Education.

de Bono, E. (1967) *The Use of Lateral Thinking*. Harmondsworth: Penguin.

Dewey, J. ([1909] 1933) *How We Think*. London: D. C. Heath.

Elliott, R. K. (1971) 'Versions of Creativity' *Proceedings of the Philosophy of Education Society of Great Britain*, **5**(2), 139–52.

Holmes, E. (1878) *The Life of Mozart Including his Correspondence*, London: Chapman & Hall.

Jackson, J. R. de J. (1969) *Method and Imagination in Coleridge's Criticism*. London: Routledge & Kegan Paul.

Kenny, A. (1989) *The Metaphysics of Mind*. Oxford and New York: Oxford University Press.

Minkin, L. (1997) *Exits and Entrances: Political Research as a Creative Art*. Sheffield: Sheffield Hallam University Press.

Montessori, M. ([1948] 1989) *To Educate the Human Potential*. Oxford: Clio Press

Murray, E. J. (1964) *Motivation and Emotion*. New York: Prentice-Hall Inc.

Newmarch, R. (1906) *Life and Letters of Peter Illich Tchaikovsky*. London: John Lane.

Olford, J. (1971) 'The concept of creativity'. *Proceedings of the Philosophy of Education Society of Great Britain*, **5**(1).

Passmore, J. (1980) *The Philosophy of Teaching*. London: Duckworth.
Pepler, D. J. (1982) 'Play and divergent thinking', in D. J. Pepler and K. H. Rubin (eds), *The Play of Children: Current Theory and Research*. London: S. Karger.
Poincare, H. ([1908] 1924) *The Foundations of Science*, trans. by G. B. Halstead. London: Science Press.
Ryle, G. (1949) *The Concept of Mind*. London: Hutchinson.
Scruton, R. (1974) *Art and Imagination: A Study in the Philosophy of Mind*. London: Methuen & Co Ltd.
Spender, S. ([1946] 1952) 'The making of a poem', reprinted in B. Ghiselin (ed.), *The Creative Process: A Symposium*. Berkeley: University of California Press.
Warnock, M. (1977) *Schools of Thought*. London: Faber & Faber.
Wells, R. (1996) *Divine Secrets of the Ya-Ya Sisterhood*. London: Macmillan.
White, J. (1972) 'Creativity and imagination: a philosophical analysis', in R. F. Dearden, P. H. Hirst and R. S. Peters (eds), *Education and the Development of Reason*. London and Boston: Routledge & Kegan Paul.
Wittgenstein, L. (1958) *Philosophical Investigations*. Oxford: Basil Blackwell.

# CHAPTER 6

# Self-creation, self-expression and know-how

*In this chapter, I explore how the concepts of self-creation, self-expression and, to a lesser extent, know-how, connect with the notion of little c creativity.*

In the previous chapters, I have been building up the concept of little c creativity as agency, or personal effectiveness. I have suggested that it is essentially about individual and collective agency, that it involves both intelligent behaviour (drawing on a broad definition of intelligence) and being imaginative. It also seems to me to be related to the notion of *self-creation*, written about by Glover (1988), *self-expression*, written about, amongst others, by Nunn (1920) and *know-how*, written about by Ryle (1949).

## Self-creation
Focused on the notion of shaping oneself, self-creation is a human ability which Glover suggests has implications for society and its political organization. He suggests that even where our choices are constrained, we may shape ourselves according to our own values, and that this is central to human existence, even where the choices are partial – or where we are only partially aware of the values underpinning our choices. For Glover 'unaware' self-change is also an aspect of self-creation, which involves a spectrum of being conscious.

He includes a number of processes as contributing to self-creation. These include:

- work (or the lack of it)
- personal style – as he puts it, 'style combines chosen forms of self-expression with what we are given naturally. The way people do things is partly chosen.' (p. 135).

- 'the real me' – self-creation can be a process of discovery as we find that parts of ourselves are not able to find expression in certain activities; he gives the example of a job which stifles aspects of oneself, or a relationship

Glover argues that we become aware of the need to self-create quite naturally: 'When a way of life does not fit with what you think you are really like, you can feel like a plant away from the light, distorted by having to twist and grope towards the sun. ... These strong affinities we have for some kinds of life and the sense of drowning which others give us, are likely to have been created by the interaction of our genetic make-up with things we have come across and responded to.' (p. 137).

However, he also stresses that 'self-creation need not be the most important thing in someone's life ... to have a project of self-creation need not involve a 'life plan': a unitary blueprint of how your life is supposed to turn out ... for most of us, self creation is a matter of a fairly disorganized cluster of smaller aims: more like building a medieval town than a planned garden city' (p. 135). He also points out that 'it is absurd to suppose that all our psychological characteristics can be altered substantially and at will ...' but makes the analogy of gradually encouraging 'tendencies which are already natural to us ... Self-creation is not like the instantaneous transformations of magic, but more like sculpting a piece of wood, respecting the constraints of natural shape and grain' (p. 136).

There are a number of themes in Glover's concept of self-creation which could be challenged.

First, a question could be raised about how meaningful the maintenance of the status quo is under the umbrella phrase 'self-creation', a term which would suggest the development of aspects of oneself, rather than the maintenance of how things are. To what extent, in other words, is self-creation actually about 'development' as opposed to re-creating what one already is, or is doing.

Second, Glover speculates on the source of individuality and individuation, suggesting that perhaps individuality is developed as a matter of biological survival. He suggests our pattern of reproducing the species involves leaving the family group in which we grew up. Perhaps, he suggests, individuation is a preparation for leaving the family. But this is a culturally specific model, as he himself recognizes; for the cult of individualism is a peculiarly Western one which may well be related to other notions and values, such as the free market. Glover's speculation may also be less applicable today, i.e. at the end of the twentieth century, as his model relies heavily on leaving the family home in order to make a new shared family life with a specific other. As family, employment, and wealth patterns shift in post-industrial societies, this is a less common dominant model. For example, young people leave their parents and then return, parental partnerships do not necessarily last, and individuals have relationships, some of which may include children (and with more than one partner over the course of adult life). It must be acknowledged that the tone of this part of Glover's account is speculative rather than explanatory, and that his point applies to other animals than humans. It appears, too, that Glover may be concerned with interpreting the self-creation concept in its origins in the human species over aeons. Glover does also locate the origins of self-creation as fairly specifically in the 1500–1700 period, in Western culture. Nevertheless, the cultural saturation of his explanation of individuality and individuation could be challenged.

Third, Glover suggests that that 'the inner story' drives self-creation, i.e. our beliefs about what we are now like, or the stories which we tell ourselves. As he puts it:

> Many projects of self-creation can only be understood in the light of the inner story of which they are part. My attitudes towards my past influence, and are influenced by, what I want to become. Both the content and emotional tone of the story so far make intentions about the next part more intelligible (p. 140).

Clearly, Glover suggests, one's inner story relies upon a story of memory, and 'the process of involuntary comparison' (p. 141). He discusses the notion of 'charged memories' – i.e. the most emotionally charged, which are often unconscious. Such charged memories can affect our inner story.

The inner story can be seen as non-fiction, or we tinker with it so that we accept what is an apparently more continuous story than in fact is the case; when it is convenient to do so we ignore some of the conflicts and inconsistencies. As Glover puts it, 'we have only simplified sketches of each other, which leave out the fuzzy edges' (p. 147) and 'The inner story involves a good deal of selection' (p. 149). He discusses the notion of 'abridgement' – that over time, we tell ourselves shorter and more schematic versions of our own story. He talks about there being two forms of abridgement, or editing, of our stories:

a) to allow 'wishful thinking, fantasy and self-deception' to take a role: 'bits of the film we do not like are lost in the cutting room' (p. 149).

b) to not leave out or add any incidents, but 'colours what happened by taking an attitude towards it' – like a voice-over or commentary might do in a film (p. 150)

He discusses desires which conflict with our inner story, such as reacting politely to a racist joke and then feeling very guilty about 'not being true to oneself'. He describes this as 'doubling' – there are two different stories, the one in the moment (in this case not to give offence), and the inner story (in this case to eschew racist behaviour).

For Glover, then, the inner story about 'the real me' is essential to self-creation. He implies that we are conscious, or aware, of our inner stories, although we may not be aware of the level of reality of these; thus, if we are prey to for example, wishful thinking, fantasy etc., as in (a), we are not necessarily aware that we are.

However, I would argue that much self-creation is not necessarily fully conscious. We tell ourselves inner stories, so must be aware of them, but we may not be aware of *why* we have the stories we do. Thus, I would want to challenge the extent to which, in reality, the 'real me' story is as conscious as this.

Although these three aspects of Glover's concept may be challenged, the concept has an overall coherence and, it seems to me, is close to, but distinct from, the notion of little c creativity.

## Self-creation and little c creativity

There are several distinctions which I want to draw between little c creativity and self-creation.

### Development and change

One of the problems with self-creation as argued above, is that it does not necessarily involve change. The notion of little c creativity, on the other hand, does necessarily involve development and change, in order to take the self beyond what is to what might be – even if this means no action but thoughts alone. Acting on possibilities, and seeking change, is, I would argue, by contrast with self-creation, fundamental to little c creativity, which is about taking opportunities, and exploiting possibility. Just as imagination involves seeing beyond what initially seems possible, so this is integral to little c creativity as argued in Chapter 5. There is implied 'movement', or 'development' in the term. Whereas in Glover's account, self-creation is also about self-definition, what I am proposing as embedded in little c creativity is the capacity to route-find through life at the start of the twenty-first century. This implies, as discussed in Chapter 3, a capacity both to innovate and to cope with change arising from others.

## Choice

In a similar way to Glover's concept of self-creation, the concept of little c creativity which I am advancing draws upon non-conscious mental life in a way which is mediated by an 'I' which struggles to balance first and second-order desires. Frankfurt's (1971) account of these concepts, to which Glover also relates self-creation, is, I think, helpful here. He suggests that human beings who are not 'wantons' have the ability not only to have certain desires, but to 'want to want to have' certain desires. This ability to choose enables humans to make longer term plans. He calls those people who do not exercise second-order desires, and live by first-order desires only, 'wantons'. For Frankfurt, first-order desires which are expressed through choice, are the same as 'will'. And as humans are able to mediate their first-order desires through their second-order ones, in other words to choose what to value, they have what he calls 'freedom of will'. Choice over possible alternatives at different levels in the psyche is central to my concept of little c creativity.

A psychoanalytic writer, not referred to by Glover, is Assagioli (1974), an Italian medical doctor and psychiatrist who practised and wrote in the early and mid-twentieth century. His theory is drawn from clinical observation over many years. He suggests we can think of ourselves as having two selves. Our conscious self, which is rational and aware, and the one we are not conscious of, which is more intuitive, impulsive, emotional and subject to sensation. Our conscious self, has *choice*, and can 'transcend' or rise above the deeper self, selecting out elements to emphasize. I find Assagioli's notion of transcendent choice helpful in the formulation of little c creativity, which is about personal change and path-finding.

Although Frankfurt and Assagioli seem to be referring to similar concepts, one obvious difference between them, it seems to me, is in the importance placed by Assagioli on intuition and the emotions in the non-conscious self. These are implied in Frankfurt's notion of first-order desires; but whereas Frankfurt's first-order desires may be interpreted as specific habits, by contrast it seems to me that Assagioli is really highlighting the creative function of intuition and feelings.

Thus, an early years practitioner faced with a child exhibiting challenging behaviour, may stand back from an impulsive, first-order response of, say, frustration, to draw on second-order desires to inspire rather than to force, learning. The notion (as Assagioli would have it) of the transcendent self helps to explain the course of action which might follow from standing back, and which might involve acknowledging the disaffection but working with rather than against it. This it seems to me is an example of little c creativity. It may also be an example of self-creation, in that the 'I' mediates between the first and second order desires.

When applied to small children, though, it seems to me that this element of intuition in choice plays a highly significant role. So, a three year old who is playing with a paddling pool, exploring what happens to water when it comes out of a hose may find they have flooded their play area temporarily and may move to working out how to stop the flood, rather than how to water everything in sight. Their focus will move, but not necessarily with all that much conscious intent. They may persist with the activity, to explore what happens and how. Their activity may be creative in their own terms (although what they are discovering may not be new to others).

### Self-consciousness, or 'realization'

Self-consciousness is necessary for little c creativity in a way in which Glover does not suggest it is for self-creation. Consider the following example:

When a practitioner plans a learning environment such as a class-rom, they bring to bear on the layout of furniture including the availability and scope of resources, a wealth of insight about the way they consider learners will be best supported. In making decisions about the environment, their intentions will be explicit in their thinking about how the space may be used. If asked to explain why they have chosen this particular form of organization, they will probably be able to explain it in terms which demonstrate awareness of many of their own insights into learners and learning.

On the other hand, there may be aspects of the way the space is organized which the teacher cannot explain, or is not aware of, until questioned about the specifics. For example, in the case of planning an environment for very young children, the teacher may not have considered what the space will look like from the height of the child; they may have *unconsciously* imported their own adult height-perspective into their organization of the space. Similarly, a teacher may have a particular unconscious view of learning which they only become conscious of when they are asked to do an exercise of this kind. It is only when the teacher becomes aware of what they have done – i.e. gains some insight into it, *realizes* what they are doing, perhaps through being questioned, that I would describe their action as little c creativity. Little c creativity involves, in other words, some level of insight into one's actions, an awareness of one's own intentions, or 'self-consciousness'.

Glover is, of course, writing about the adult. What does it mean for a child to have insight into their own creativity? Let us take an example from an inner London nursery class. Four-year-old Jacob at play in the sand tray may create a miniature landscape within which small plastic toys talk to each other, engage in battle or in some adventure. It is not uncommon for children to act out a process going on elsewhere in their lives in their play: for example, the birth of a sibling, the discovery of snow or of a new place, the loss of someone close to them. It is also not uncommon for children to explore new possibilities through their play, although there is some evidence that such play can be gendered. The point, however, is that at some level there is an intention to play, to experiment, to act out, and an inner story which supports, or even 'drives' this. How far is the child aware of this? I would suggest the intention and inner story are not well-developed in terms of the child's consciousness, but that they must be there at some level, in order for the playing to happen at all. The child may not be aware of anything more than the story itself – i.e. not necessarily the explanation for it in terms of the sibling, the loss of someone, etc.

There are, of course, many levels of awareness or self-consciousness, as Wittgenstein argued in the case of levels of fluency in reading (1953). In other words, although we may suddenly become aware of our intentions, or have a moment of realization, this is only one point in a spectrum of awareness.

Glover writes of self-consciousness developing in part through the things that we do. He suggests that there is 'a hierarchy of control which contributes to our idea of the self' (p. 58), in that our awareness of specifics may be overridden by a complex of ideas about something. He gives examples which include one of a young child whose frenzy of distress or anger may be overridden by becoming absorbed in an interesting exchange on a different topic. He suggests that self-consciousness (a 'prime feature', p. 60, of being a person) involves having 'I-thoughts' or 'single-stream thoughts' (p. 61); and that self-consciousness thus involves a range of degrees of being so. As he says, 'being a person does not require any moment of illumination ... it does not matter whether their acquisition [i.e. the I-thoughts] was in a sudden conscious moment or through slow, unconscious conceptual growth' (p. 61). In so far as Glover is suggesting that self-consciousness can be gradually developed, his notion of self-consciousness differs from the one I would advance for little c creativity, where I would suggest that there is, necessarily, a moment of illumination, or realization.

In suggesting 'awareness of insight into one's actions', I am drawing the line more tightly around what counts as self-consciousness. I am proposing that, in an act of little c creativity, self-consciousness involves not simply having 'I-thoughts', but also having a meta-awareness of these, in which the moment of awareness sets apart non-self-consciousness from self-consciousness. For example, the practitioner who is explaining why they have arranged their classroom in a particular way, would be self-conscious in my account only at the point at which they realize that they have chosen the layout of resources for specific reasons.

It seems to me then, that if little c creativity is to enable individuals to route-find and thus to make a practical difference to their lives, it must necessarily encompass insight at a range of levels as indicated.

## Additional concepts forming part of little c creativity

Two aspects of little c creativity which do not form part of Glover's conception of self-creation, are willingness to work positively with adversity, and 'possibility thinking'.

### Willingness to work positively with adversity

Although not included in Glover's account of self-creation, this notion is used by Gardner in recent work on 'high creativity' (1997), where he suggests that highly creative individuals use 'leverage' successfully; in other words, even 'failures' are perceived as having potential for positive success. I would also hypothesize that 'leverage', or willingness to work positively with adversity, is an aspect of little c creativity as well as of high creativity, as the following example may indicate.

Eliza, a seven-year-old child whom I know, was taking a piano exam recently. Full of nerves, she set off early that morning with her mother, and having decided to avoid the traffic by going on the train, they clambered aboard what they thought was the correct one. To their horror they found themselves on the wrong line and by the time they got to the exam, it was too late. Although bitterly disappointed, as well as embarrassed, Eliza's reaction to this disaster was to suggest they enquire, then and there, about when she could next try for it. She worked with determination for the new exam date and passed with flying colours. Her attitude throughout was 'can-do'.

Litte c creativity, then, involves a willingness to work with adversity. The omission of this feature from self-creation seems to me quite appropriate. For self-creation is less about change and path-finding, although Glover does accept that self-change may happen, and that this may involve a spectrum of being conscious.

### Possibility thinking

As suggested earlier in the book, 'possibility thinking' is a fundamental aspect of little c creativity, located at its core. Possibility thinking manifests itself through being imaginative, being open to possibilities and having an explorative attitude to life and all that it involves, i.e.

lifewide, as well as lifelong. It involves, I suggested in Chapter 5, a spectrum of consciousness, from non-conscious to conscious.

*Examples of children manifesting possibility thinking include the following*:

- Five-year-old Kate is on her way to the zoo with her class but their bus gets stuck in a traffic jam. Kate decides to spend her time in the traffic jam making a verbal list with her friend Gregory of all the different ways they could get to the zoo (e.g. running, biking, going by scooter, by rocket, by jet-propelled feet, etc.).

- Two-year-old Rebecca pretends that she has something in her hand and places the imaginary item into the hand of an adult with whom she is playing. She enters into a dialogue with her mother about the qualities of the item (it can do magic, it heals bumps and bruises, it can turn into a bunch of flowers).

- Four-year-old Bina negotiates with her mother about what she is prepared to eat from her packed lunch, and since the chocolate biscuit has more appeal than the white bread cheese sandwich she says she only has the right-sized space in her tummy for the biscuit.

- Eight-year-old Natasha is making a friendship bracelet for a friend. She has no cotton left so she uses some thin leather laces instead.

- Six-year-old Jack loses his PE bag in the cloakroom. He does not panic, but asks his teacher if he can search for it in the lost property box.

In Chapter 7, I explore possibility thinking in some depth, considering how it relates to the other aspects of little c creativity and examining what it involves for teachers and learners in the early years in particular.

### SUMMARY

So far, then, I have explored the notion of 'self-creation' as proposed by Glover, discussing some problems with the concept and then making a comparison between little c creativity and self-creation. I have suggested that the two concepts have a lot in common, although little c creativity necessarily involves additional concepts. These are development and change, as well as self-awareness. It also involves willingness to work positively with adversity, and has at its core, possibility thinking.

The next sections of this chapter will go on to consider, more briefly, self-expression and know-how.

## Self-expression

The kind of personal effectiveness being proposed in little c creativity may also have something in common with Nunn's notion of 'self-expression' (1920), a manifestion of biological individuality, which was referred to briefly during the discussion of Plowden in Chapter 1. For Nunn, the ultimate aim of education is the realization of individuality and self-expression. Each of these seem to me to be fundamentally necessary to enacting personal, individual effectiveness, in the social and physical environment.

Nunn aligned his thinking with the elitist Burtian IQ approach, suggesting that full expressiveness and creativity would only be fully developed among a few, a position which is currently unfashionable, as demonstrated in the 'democratic creativity' approach taken by the NACCCE Report discussed in Chapter 1. He also proposed a child-centred pedagogy, which enabled the growth of the child without interference. For Nunn, the growth of the child is driven by the bio-logical unfolding of an inner 'blueprint', and the teacher, as Gordon and White (1979) put it, is therefore 'a servant of nature, an adjutant of evolution' (p. 212). As discussed in Chapter 1, the Plowden Report focused some of these ideas and they have been criticized in a number range of ways. Nevertheless, although the elitism and 'growth' assumptions in Nunn's thinking may be unpalatable and problematic respectively, I would argue that a fundamental aim of education must be to promote individual self-expression. In this sense, a version of Nunn's ideas have some currency in early years education.

I would argue, however, that *all* children (rather than the few) are capable of individual self-expression, and would propose that fostering collective self-expression is equally desirable and important as an aim (not *the* fundamental aim, but one of several) for education. The embracing term I would use would be 'little c creativity', encompassing both individual agency discussed in earlier chapters, and also collective agency. The puzzle is that some people seem to find it easier to access their self-expression and little c creativity than others.

### Individual and collective agency

Agency refers to the capability to self-direct across life. It may be put into action both by individuals and collectively, as these two real-life examples should illustrate:

### Individual agency

Seven-year-old Cai was hoping to find his friend, Jake, in the play-ground before school, to invite him to tea that night. When Jake's mum and big sister explained to Cai that Jake was not well and therefore off school, Cai was disappointed. Rather than leaving the question of tea unresolved, Cai asked Jake's mum and big sister how soon Jake would be back at school and therefore how soon he might be able to come to tea.

### Collective agency

A group of six children in a Year 2 class, encouraged by a session on 'social inventions', came up with the idea of getting the school playground cleaned up (i.e. free of litter). They put this into action with the head teacher and school keeper, and within a few weeks had not only produced a litter-free environment but had also created an incentive scheme for those using the playground not to drop litter.

## Know-how

As discussed briefly in Chapter 4, know-how is a distinct form of knowledge identified originally by the philosopher, Ryle (1949), but since taken up by cognitive psychologists and others. Ryle drew a distinction between 'knowing how' and 'knowing that'. Knowing how is the procedural knowledge which you need in order to operate a personal computer, ride a bike, or swim. In other words, it is 'doing' knowledge. I suggested in Chapter 4 that although skill-based, it seemed that understanding was also necessary to it. For example, how could a person ride a bike without some knowledge of brakes, steering, roads, balance, etc., even if known implicitly?

'Knowing that', by contrast, implies conceptual understanding of a part of a knowledge system. For example, contextual information that helps us to understand an archaeological fragment, or the knowledge that a surgeon needs in order to decide whether and how to operate on a patient, or the understanding that, at present, it is impossible to shop at a supermarket outside of certain hours. 'Knowing that' may exist separately from 'knowing-how'. For example, I may know how to make a certain recipe without ever having done it before, or indeed being able to do so. In the practical world, we often need to use both knowing how and knowing that, in other words, both procedural and conceptual knowledge. A musical conductor, for example, needs a thorough understanding of music and musical notation, as well as the skills to lead musicians working from a score. And a child learning to draw, needs both the conceptual knowledge about representation, and about drawing materials, as well as the procedural knowledge of how to hold a pencil/use the materials to hand. In fact, any system of knowledge will include both procedural and conceptual knowledge, to differing degrees.

Little c creativity must logically involve a large degree of know-how since it is ultimately about making a difference, by having an idea or taking an action. Since 'knowing that' is also necessary to some know-how, there will be times when little c creativity involves both kinds of knowledge.

## CONCLUSION

In this chapter, I have explored Glover's notion of self-creation, comparing it with little c creativity. I found that the two concepts had a lot in common, although they are ultimately distinct in that there are some fundamental concepts (including development and change and also possibility thinking), which are central to little c creativity. I went on more briefly to explore the relationship between little c creativity and self-expression and then know-how, suggesting that little c creativity involves both individual and collective agency and that it necessarily involves know-how, and at times, may involve conceptual knowledge.

## References

Assagioli, R. (1974) *The Act of Will*. London: Wildwood House.

Frankfurt, H. (1971) 'Freedom of the will and the concept of a person'. *Journal of Philosophy* **63**(1).

Glover, J. (1988) I: *The Philosophy and Psychology of Personal Identity*. London: Allen Lane, The Penguin Press.

Gordon, P. and White, J. (1979) *Philosophers as Educational Reformers*. London: Routledge & Kegan Paul.

Nunn, T. P. (1920) *Education: Its Data and First Principles*. London: Arnold.

Ryle, G. (1949) *The Concept of Mind*. London: Hutchinson.

Wittgenstein, L. (1953) *Philosophical Investigations*, trans. by G. E. M. Anscombe. Oxford: Basil Blackwell.

# CHAPTER 7

# Possibility Thinking

*This chapter examines further the idea of possibility thinking, and makes the case for its underpinning role in little c creativity with young children. The relationship between possibility thinking and play is explored, and the final part of the chapter discusses some practical implications of possibility thinking for pedagogy.*

Over the course of the book so far, I have introduced and developed to an extent the notion of possibility thinking as core to little c creativity. Possibility, I have argued elsewhere (Craft, 2000), is fundamental to creativity, and may be manifest in any aspect of life. In the preceding chapters, I have explored imagination, intelligence, self creation, self-expression, and know-how, and suggested that they are all necessary to little c creativity. I now want to suggest that possibility thinking is the means by which these different sets of attributes are brought together and expressed, bringing about creative acts and ideas. Towards the end of Chapter 6, I gave some examples of children manifesting possibility thinking, and in this chapter I want to explore in greater depth what it is.

Possibility thinking encompasses an attitude which refuses to be stumped by circumstances, but uses imagination, with intention, to find a way around a problem. It involves the posing of questions, whether or not these are actually conscious, formulated or voiced. The posing of questions may range from wondering about the world which surrounds us, which may lead to both finding and solving problems; and from formulated questions at one end of the spectrum, through to nagging puzzles, to a general sensitivity at the other. Possibility thinking, also involves problem finding. Being able to identify a question, a topic for investigation, a puzzle to explore, a possible new option, all involve 'finding' or 'identifying' a problem (using the word problem in a loose way, to mean 'other possibilities').

It involves, then, the exploration of any knowledge domain and the perception of alternative possibilities. Before focusing on what this means for children in the early years of education, I want to explore how possibility thinking may be seen as underpinning apparently contrasting types of thinking in domains of knowledge.

## Possibility thinking as a foundation to knowledge in any domain?

It has long been argued that some domains of knowledge involve convergent thinking (where there is one 'right answer') and that others require divergent thinking (finding multiple possiblities). Hudson (1973) in his work on intelligence, suggested that children who excel in science, maths and technology, are also children who do well on traditional IQ tests, where there is one right answer. In other words, they are good at convergent thinking, where there is just one solution to the problem. On the other hand, those children who are divergent thinkers, finding several possibilities for each question, tend to excel in the arts (and, we presume, may not, necessarily, excel in IQ tests). These children are good at thinking of many possible solutions to a problem. Hudson's thesis was that the arts and the sciences demand different kinds of thinking.

One implication of this view is that science, maths and technology are fundamentally uncreative, in that they involve a very focused perspective on possibility thinking. Yet, this is clearly refuted at the level of high creativity, by the very existence of scientific and technological invention. What was Einstein's work if not creative? What of the invention of the internet? Of plastics? Of new medicines? All of these innovations occurred within a scientific or technological context and yet none could be called uncreative. At times, divergent thinking will surely occur within any domain, certainly at the level of the expert.

I want, then, to challenge the idea that the domains of science, maths and technology are uncreative – although they clearly require more convergent thinking than other domains. What the two kinds of thinking, convergent and divergent, have in common, it seems to me, is the foundation of possibility thinking. This does not mean that different domains of knowledge operate in identical ways.

This last point has led other writers to a very different position, however, to the one I am proposing. For example, White (1972) suggests there is no logical connection between creativity in different domains. In his critique of Read's (1943) theory of education as flowing from and through the arts, White notes that creativity in art is not the same as creativity in other subjects; or as he puts it: 'the thesis ... ignores differences in what counts as being creative in different areas' (p. 145). He notes that Plato, too, puts education in the arts as the foundation of his education curriculum, 'with mathematics and dialectic emerging from it' (p. 145) – and underpins this with a psychological theory. This, too, White nevertheless rejects, as 'There is no such logical connexion between free activity in art and creativity in mathematics, etc.' (p. 146). White suggests that 'what counts' as creativity differs between domains. What counts as creativity in art, differs from what counts as creativity in mathematics. Likewise, we might add that what counts as creativity in role-play differs from what counts as creativity in design and technology. This cannot be denied.

But, what underpins the ability to be creative in any domain, it seems to me, *is* driven by the same attitude toward the activity. To be creative in any domain, the agent needs to be able to operate possibility, to be able to ask 'what if?' or to wonder, 'perhaps if . . .?' Not only, suggests White, does what counts as being creative differ from one domain to the next, but consequently, there is no logical connection between creativity in different domains.

However, if both are driven by postulation, by 'what if?', by possibility thinking, as I have proposed, then we can see how they *are* necessarily logically connected, a position I want to maintain.

Possibility thinking is what drives the capacity of individuals to find their way through the life experiences which they meet with a creative attitude and approach, enabling them to make the most of situations, even those which appear to pose difficulties. It provides, I propose, the underpinning conceptual process for all creative activity, whatever the domain of application. Just as little c creativity is conceived of as lifewide, so, it follows, is the possibility thinking which underpins it.

I would suggest, though, that possibility thinking involves a continuum of thinking strategies, from 'what does this do?' (i.e. essentially coming to grips with the procedural and conceptual knowledge of a domain), to 'what can I *do* with this?' (i.e. generative thought, engaging the agent in the manipulation of the domain in some way), at the other end of the continuum. It is this generative sense of possibility thinking that seems to me to be the driver of little c creativity.

## Possibility thinking in the early years

In the early years, creativity is often perceived to be closely linked with certain activities, for example painting, play dough, drawing, modelling, performance, imaginative play, etc. As acknowledged in Part One, this is in part encouraged by the way in which creativity is put forward in curriculum policy guidelines such as the Early Learning Goals. But it is also a legacy from the culture and practices of early years education and care, where the creative expression of children is closely linked with areas of activity such as these, rather than being seen, additionally, as a lifewide skill.

Little c creativity is conceptualized as wider than this and I have argued that it forms a 'third way' or 'third wave' of conceptualizing creativity in the early years. Nevertheless, I will include in this chapter analysis of activities traditionally associated with creativity, exploring in particular children's play. I start with a brief observation of a child, Shakil, based on my field notes from a recent visit to his reception class.

> Shakil has made the water tray into an ocean in which his plasticine animal can swim and have adventures. A few minutes later on his return from the toilet, Shakil notices that the lunch-boxes are always stacked outside the classroom, and asks the teaching assistant why that is so – suggesting that if they were inside the classroom they would be less vulnerable to 'accidents' (being knocked over, food 'disappearing' from them, etc.).

In both cases, Shakil seems to me to have been asking himself, 'What can I do with this?' He does this in the context of play but also in the 'lifewide' context too.

I want to use these two brief observations of Shakil, to explore how possibility thinking could bring together imagination, intelligence, self-creation, self-expression, and know-how. For it seems to me that the activity in the water tray and the suggestion about the lunch boxes each involve Shakil in being imaginative. In the water tray, he conceives of possibilities beyond the literal, in a stream-of-consciousness of playing. In the lunch box example, Shakil reasons logically, thinks consciously and goes beyond what is given in the structure of the classroom rules and physical layout, to suggest something original to himself – and quite possibly, those around him. In the second example particularly, he proposes an intelligent intervention. Both examples involve self-expression in different forms and the second in particular, self-creation; Shakil is shaping himself and his identity by voicing the question at all. Both involve procedural knowledge, or know-how.

What may be clear however, from the brief discussion of Shakil, is that the water play example did not necessarily involve the use of intelligence. This could be seen as one manifestation of the complex relationship between play and possibility thinking and it is this I want to examine next.

## Play and possibilities

Many early years practitioners and commentators contend that, for children in the early years, play is a core learning mode and vehicle for learning and expression. The word 'play' is used in combination with creativity in many contexts and by commentators and policy makers alike. As noted already in this book, it forms a part of Creative Development as an Early Learning Goal. It formed a core part of the Plowden perspective on creativity. However, the meaning of 'play' is extremely wide and it is often used very loosely. In Chapter 10, I explore some other claims made by researchers for the role that play occupies in creativity, as well as exploring further the notion that although some kinds of play are creative, others are not necessarily. In this part of the chapter, however, I will be concentrating on the connections between possibility thinking and imaginative play.

I would suggest that possibility thinking underpins much imaginative play just as it does innovation in other domains. However, the components of possibility thinking in imaginative play may not always be equally present; in particular, in some instances (such as the example of Shakil and the water tray, above), intelligence may not necessarily be involved.

On the other hand, it is difficult to see how imagination and self-expression could not be present in all imaginative play. Similarly, all imaginative play is a form of self-creation, or expression of agency, although often in role rather than as oneself. Imaginative play, then, provides practice arenas for trying out individual and collective agency, or self-creation.

Know-how, though, poses more of a challenge, as although much imaginative play is practical, and relies on practical knowledge (know-how), it is not always actually enacted – sometimes imaginative play can remain, at least partly, in the realm of ideas. Take, for example, the actual case of three-and-a-half-year-old Joshua, returning home in the car with a bag of popcorn in the dark. He announced to his father, 'It's very dark in here. I am in a cinema. I have my popcorn and I am watching the film.' Looking out of the window, he gave a commentary describing what he was watching in the 'film' – houses and trees going by. When they arrived home, he announced, 'Now we are in the film, daddy.' In this example, Joshua used both procedural and conceptual knowledge – in other words, not just what he knew how to do but also what he knew about, cinemas and films. He was demonstrating know-how but did not enact it fully, remaining in the 'storytelling' mode.

The story, then, of which elements that go to make up possibility thinking and how they relate to the play of young children, is complex, in that they may not all be present in all imaginative play.

This noted, what of the role of the environment and teaching and learning opportunities surrounding the child at play? In the next part of this chapter, I look at some pedagogical implications of valuing children's possibility thinking.

## Some pedagogical implications of valuing possibility thinking

Part of the challenge in early years education is to find a balance between managing large numbers of learners and a pre-determined curriculum on the one hand, and encouraging, rather than inhibiting, the curiosity and possibility thinking of individual children, on the other. It seems to me that a creative practitioner will stimulate and support possibility thinking across the curriculum and across the setting, in a variety of ways. These will include encouraging the exploration of possibilities through, for example:

- storytelling
- simulations
- dramatic play
- open-ended scenarios
- empathy work
- role play
- fantasy modelling
- puppetry
- improvisation

Some of these activities will involve a deliberate structuring of activities, and others will involve much less. For example, drama improvisation in pairs, or a simulation, may be set up quite deliberately in a way that free play in the home corner, or playing with ready-made puppets, may not be.

Actively fostering young children's possibility thinking involves moving their thinking on from 'What does this do?' to 'What can I do with this?' and, in the case of difficulties, 'How can I get around this problem?' It involves a move from the concrete into the more abstract, but is present even in the concrete experience of very small children.

So, even when a child of three or less engages in literal play, acting out a scene which mirrors life in a fairly faithful way (e.g. playing homes), they may nonetheless be operating with possibility thinking. As their play becomes more abstract, complex, and symbolic between the ages of four and seven (for example, Shakil's ocean in the water play), so possibility thinking continues to be a powerful driver of their actions and ideas.

For the practitioner in the learning and teaching environment, this means encouraging and celebrating the expression of possibilities across contexts. Modelling 'I wonder if' thinking strategies and celebrating diversity in children's ideas, encouraging the individual and collective generation and evaluation of ideas and actions, are all practical implications of valuing possibility thinking. It would follow that the resourcing and management of the learning environment need to reflect this principle of valuing and nurturing possibility thinking. In the final part of the book, Chapters 9 and 10 explore these broad pedagogical and resource issues further.

## CONCLUSION

I have advanced the argument in this chapter that possibility thinking underpins all domains of knowledge (those traditionally associated with convergent, as well as those associated with divergent, thinking), although to differing degrees. I have also developed the case that it provides a vehicle for bringing together a number of different attributes of little c creativity: imagination, intelligence, self-creation, self-expression and know-how. In the case of young children, possibility thinking is expressed in part through play, and some aspects of possibility thinking may be expressed more strongly through play than others.

Although I have looked at some school-based examples, and have explored children's imaginative play, clearly there is no limit to the possible life contexts or domains of knowledge in which possibility thinking could be exercised. It is, I would suggest, like the little c creativity that it drives, lifewide in its potential.

In the next chapter I widen the overall focus to discuss the overarching concept of little c creativity, exploring its conceptual and practical limits, developing the rationale for fostering it in the early years and exploring some practical aspects of this.

## References

Craft, A. (2000) *Creativity Across the Primary Curriculum*. London: Routledge.

Hudson, L. (1973) *Originality*. London: Oxford University Press.

Read, H. (1943) *Education Through Art*. London: Faber.

White, J. P. (1972) 'Creativity and education: a philosophical analysis', in R. Dearden, P. Hirst, and R. S. Peters, *Education Development and Reason*. London and Boston: Routledge & Kegan Paul.

# CHAPTER 8

# Evaluating the coherence of little c creativity

*Chapter 8 lays the ground for the later chapters, which will explore some practical implications of little c creativity for curriculum, pedagogy, assessment, and practitioner and system development. It explores the coherence of the concept, and takes further the argument for the place of little creativity in the education of young children.*

## Introduction

What kinds of conceptual issues arise from the notion of little c creativity? Some of the questions which can be asked about it, have been considered earlier in the book, for example the distinction between it and 'big c' or 'high' creativity. Other issues will be examined later: for example, the problem of who judges whether something is creative will be discussed in Chapter 10 on teaching and assessing. But it seems to me that there are five further conceptual issues which are fundamental to its coherence as a concept and which need some discussion in this chapter. They are,

- its possible cultural specificity
- the extent to which it can be said to be context-free, or 'transferable'
- the extent to which little c creativity may be said to be the same in adults and in children
- the issue raised only very briefly in Chapter 3, of the extent to which a person can be said to be little c creative across the domains of their life and over time
- the extent to which little c creativity is a 'political' concept

## Cultural specificity of a 'universal' concept?

It could be said that little c creativity has been presented so far as a universally applicable concept. But, it may, by contrast, be culturally specific, in that it places high value on individuality, and being able to think independently of social norms. In other words, what is being described may reflect peculiarly Western values, for in a culture where the individual and the marketplace are held in high esteem, little c creativity is a prized virtue. In a more conformist or repressive culture, little c creativity might be perceived as an inappropriate process, not to be encouraged. Clearly, the cultural context is likely to affect a person's experiences of little c creativity and their ability to operationalize it. Of course, this may not be a predictable relationship. For example, in a social context where choice and personal autonomy are severely restricted, the drive to find alternatives may be quite strong; but on the other hand, it may be that avoidance of social or political sanctions and socialization into submission would, in such conditions, militate against creativity. The point, though, is that the relationship between the cultural context and creativity is unpredictable.

It is also possible that what is being described is imbued with what might be described as *social class based* assumptions such as resilience, self-reliance, persistence, and control over one's environment. The American social anthropologists, Kluckhohn and Strodtbeck (1961) argued that basic value-orientations in society vary in a number of ways, and that these could be divided into values on several fundamental aspects of life, 'activity' being one of them. Their contention was that that there was a modality of value orientations as regards 'activity' in one's life, from 'being', to 'being-in-becoming', to 'doing' (pp. 15–16). In the 'being' orientation, the preference is for spontaneous activity, or 'a spontaneous expression in *activity* of impulses and desires' (p. 16). 'Being-in-becoming', by contrast, emphasizes activity that is focused on the development of all aspects of the self. Finally, 'doing' is about taking actions with the aim of achieving goals which 'are measurable by standards conceived to be external to the acting individual'. They suggested, in their analysis, that the 'doing' mode was dominant at that particular time in American culture. It could be that little c creativity, too, reflects a good measure of the 'doing' value-orientation.

There may be further biases within the models presented in this book, which reflect the cultural context, for example, the basic attitude towards time, or the relational orientation (two further categories used by Kluckhohn and Strodtbeck). In the case of time, Kluckhohn and Strodtbeck identified three distinct value-orientations, i.e. past orientation, present orientation, and future orientation. Little c creativity is quite strongly focused on the future (as are other formulations of general creativity, too – such as Bruner's where he discusses the 'deferral' of creativity, i.e. that creative activity often involves time, to hone the outcome (Bruner, 1962)). In the case of the relational orientation, Klukhohn and Strodtbeck propose three modalities here: the 'lineal', the 'collateral', and the 'individualistic' (p. 17). The lineal mode refers to the fact that there is always a biological and cultural link through time, from one generation to the next. So, in the lineal mode, a careful and ordered system for succession over time, has primacy. By contrast, the collateral mode emphasizes a more laterally extended group, and its goals. And by contrast again, in the individualistic mode, as one might expect, the individual's goals have primacy over either lineal or collateral ones. Thus, using the framework of Klukhohn and Strodtbeck, it could be said that that the concept of little c creativity is very much drawing on the individualistic mode.

Although Klukhohn and Strodtbeck did not propose their categories as indicators of social class-based attitudes, but rather used the categories for the analysis of five distinct cultural groups in North America, it has been argued that some of the modalities reflect differences in social class-based attitudes (Craft, 1970, 1974). And little c creativity could be said to reflect some class-based value-orientations, in being focused on 'doing', being future-orientated, and operating in the individualistic mode.

However, the concept of little c creativity also reflects the globalization of significant aspects of Western culture. My contention has been that the development of possibility thinking is of growing importance for basic survival in a world of decreasing certainties, increasing fragmentation, but also increasing commonality in this phenomenon, globally and across diverse cultural contexts. Thus, although the concept may reflect culturally-specific values, I would argue that it may have an accelarating 'universal' currency across diverse cultural and class contexts. The notion of the individual's flexible approach being significant in societal development is not new, although the emphasis is. Indeed, as long ago as 1961, McClelland argued that flexibility in the ways in which people relate to their various contexts, would be essential for the successful development of 'modern society' (1961, p. 194). Although McClelland was referring in this instance to relationships, his overall concern was to identify psychological factors which would support a society's economic development. The flexibility then that McClelland referred to was less about individual 'survival' and more about 'society's development'.

To animate the argument for little c creativity, I introduce next an adult counter-example, discussed elsewhere (Craft, 2001), i.e. to look at what might *not* count as little c creativity. The example which follows is contextualized both within British (i.e. Western) cultural values, and also social class values that perhaps are less supportive of little c creativity. The person described is known to the author, although not by this name.

### Jimmy

Jimmy is an upholsterer by training. In his early thirties now, he worked from his late teens until his late twenties as an upholsterer for a local small business. When the owner retired, however, Jimmy lost his job and since then has worked only sporadically. Initially, with strong encouragement from his partner, Jimmy worked as a painter and decorator for one of his friends. However, that came to an end when Jimmy took a short-notice holiday for three weeks at a busy time of the year, leaving his friend with jobs to fill and nobody to do them. By the time he returned, his spot had been filled by someone else. Since that time, he has not worked in paid employment. He has found it difficult to seek out any other paid job and has sunk progressively into a despondent pattern of television watching, beer drinking, late nights and late mornings. He now takes on some child care responsibilities in that he collects his two primary-aged children from school, but does this unwillingly, as he does not see this as his role. He feels this despite the fact that the reason his partner is not available to collect the children from school is that she has now taken the initiative and gone back to work as a nanny, to earn the family some income.

Jimmy believes that the world is unfair, that he has been punished in some way and that he is unfit for employment. Although he exhibits macho behaviour when with his male friends, he does not feel at all confident as far as employment is concerned. His attitude and behaviour is a source of conflict between him and his partner and he feels there is no way out.

It seems to me that Jimmy does not exhibit little c creativity, for faced with equivalent challenges in his life to those which faced Norah in Chapter 4, he is unable to initiate any response to these. He seems to find it impossible to generate possible alternatives and to follow these through to gain a better life for himself. This much seems undisputable.

As a counter example then, Jimmy's behaviour perhaps demonstrates that lacking an ability to operationalize little c creativity may affect a person's ability to cope with basic challenges which life throws at them, through an inability to pose questions which may lead to possible ways around blockages or problems. Thus, although culturally-embedded, something like little c creativity might have enabled him to make something of his life. Lacking that capacity will do Jimmy no favours in surviving and thriving in the twenty-first century; it seems reasonable to assume that tomorrow's world will be even less tolerant of the Jimmy approach, than today's is.

## Little c creativity as a general phenomenon or as domain-specific

This is a major theoretical issue. The question is, is little c creativity a generalizable phenomenon which can be 'transferred' by the agent from context to context? Or is it domain-specific, in that it may be developed by an agent in one domain but not necessarily in another? I have argued that little c creativity, although driven by possibility thinking which underpins all domains of knowledge, is manifest uniquely in different domains. I have made the case for its importance in early education, because of its lifewide application.

But if little c creativity is manifest differently in each domain, how can it be said to be transferable? It seems to me that the answer to this question rests on the conceptual structure of little c creativity. I have argued so far that underpinning it, and driving it, is possibility thinking. In Chapter 7, where possibility thinking was explored, I suggested that it is this notion that underpins all little c creativity, and which is so-called 'transferable', i.e. which can be nurtured in any knowledge context. This is not, I would argue, inconsistent with the different manifestation of creativity in different domains. So, a child may be encouraged to apply little c creativity in imaginative play and this may appear quite different to the way they manifest their little c creativity when painting, when negotiating a friendship, when working on the computer, or when exploring an aspect of number. This is not, of course, to say that each person is equally capable of applying little c creativity in any domain, as I discuss later in this chapter.

In Chapter 10, I explore how little c creativity can be stimulated across the curriculum, discussing pedagogical strategies for helping children to 'transfer' it from context to context.

## Adults and children

From the above discussions, we might conclude that little c creativity is a concept which has its place in the adult world. Young children might thus be initiated into it, rather than exhibiting it. So, at six months, Jacob, a child known to me, was introduced by his nanny, Kay, to the idea that almost anything can be made into a play object and/or can be made fun. For example, she improvised the tray of his high chair as a water tray, and using bottle tops and lids of containers filled each with water to pour from different heights into each other and into the tray itself. Later, at twenty-one months, Jacob was keen to experiment with all kinds of uses of household objects, realizing that each has its usual purpose, but also experimenting with unusual ones. Thus, on a cold day he suggested that a tea-towel could be used as a hat (since this was nearer the garden door than his actual hat). On another occasion, he mixed this with humour, suggesting in fits of hysterics that a multicoloured jumper which he had inherited from a cousin, was a 'rug' when his father tried to get him to put it on. He was encouraged by Kay to explore possible solutions to situations which he found himself in, as well, which means that already at nearly two he could argue and suggest other possible courses of action. For example, when hoping for more small change to put in his musical money box, Jacob was told that his mother had no more change in her purse. His response was that there was some upstairs in the coppers jar kept by his father, and thus although his mother had none, there was a source of what he wanted elsewhere in the house.

What I want to suggest from these examples from Jacob's early life, is that little c creativity may be encouraged in small children and, indeed, manifested by them. This is not to say that it is an all-or-nothing attribute.

To return to the example of Jimmy given earlier in the chapter, we might ask ourselves if it is it conceivable that Jimmy might have manifested little c creativity at another stage in his life, for example when leaving school and deciding to become an upholsterer's apprentice, and that indeed he might at a later stage in his life again manifest more little c creativity? It seems undisputable that people are not necessarily consistent across the span of their lives, in their responses to similar instances. Nevertheless, it might be reasonable to expect individuals over time and with experience, to get more accomplished at little c creativity rather than less so. It seems a likely empirical expectation that the more successful experience of little c creativity an individual has, the more likely they are to continue to operate in this way in other contexts.

This point forms a critical foundation for the proposal that what happens in schools is in any way relevant to little c creativity. For my thesis is that little c creativity can be shaped and encouraged, and that clearly schools and early years settings therefore have a role to play in doing so.

## Little c creativity as lifewide?

In the discussion of Jimmy above, I suggested that individuals may be better at little c creativity at certain points in their lives, than at other points. But what about contexts for little c creativity? For example, if a person is able to use little c creativity easily in cooking does this necessarily mean that they are also able to do it in finding a job?

Empirically, individuals may, indeed, have varying strengths in different domains. Thus, one person may have poor little c creativity in cooking, but excellent little c creativity in finding forms of employment. Another may have very good little c creativity when dealing with people, but very poor little c creativity when coping with directions or finding the way from one place to another. This is a matter of common observation.

It would follow logically from this that some individuals may have strong little c creativity in more domains than others. One question which arises is, are they all equal in importance or are some domains more important than others? For example, is it more important to be able to manifest little c creativity in finding a job than it is in cooking? I have argued that the driving force behind little c creativity is possibility thinking; and that little c creativity is a skill which enables individuals to route-find in their lives in a way which enables them to feel meaning and the outcomes of personal agency. Thus, what is deemed significant or important must be related to usefulness in that context. So it seems to follow that a person who is successfully able to change their job given the flux of the employment market, and yet is uncreative with regard to food, may well have a more useful balance of skills in the sense of route-finding than the person who cannot shift their mind-set to re-focusing upon possible new work contexts, and thus cannot get access to paid employment – but yet can rustle up a range of imaginative dishes to eat. Although the case could be made that the person whose little c creativity is manifest more readily in food preparation is also route-finding in that domain, it is arguably less significant than being able to earn an income. This could of course be challenged, but even if it were, the principle of certain activities holding value in certain circles over other activities, would still remain.

If this is so, then some individuals may be 'better' at little c creativity than others, for they may have a more useful mix of contexts in which to apply little c creativity than others do. Taking it a stage further we might ask, how far to the other end of the scale can we go before a person ceases to have any little c creativity at all?

Although it may be true that some people exhibit more little c creativity than others, and that this may be so across a wide range of domains, nevertheless I want to suggest that little c creativity is not a generalized term which might be applied to a person. Rather, it is a description of specific acts of behaviour. (As indicated in Chapter 2 and Chapter 3, although some outcomes of creativity may be visible, others, such as, for example, an idea, may not yet have been played out through behaviour. An act of behaviour, then, could encompass a 'non-visible' outcome such as an idea, as well as one which is more tangible, such as an actual behaviour.) Not only may a person have certain strengths and weaknesses, but they may manifest these differently at different points in their lives. Thus it seems to me that a person's *acts of behaviour* may be judged rather than judging the person as a whole. If this is so, then a person may be judged to have no little c creativity only if they exhibit no behaviour at all which demonstrates it. It follows then that as we may never know if someone is about to demonstrate any little c creativity behaviour, we can never say that an individual is not capable of it.

## The political significance of little c creativity

What of the broader political significance of little c creativity? It might be argued that it may appear to offer a response to a political context of technical rationality in that it posits an individualist stance of 'resistance'. In the early years (and elsewhere) in English education, the political context can be seen as one in which the artistry of teaching is being undermined by a technicist view of pedagogy (Jeffrey and Craft, 2001, Woods *et al.*, 1997). One example of the latter, was the introduction, for primary schools, in the late 1990s, of a range of centrally drawn-up, compulsory programmes of curriculum content to be taught within literacy and numeracy in particular. These were accompanied by detailed, recommended strategies to achieve the successful 'delivery' of the progammes. For some schools, the implementation of the literacy strategy is compulsory; for others it is not, although other factors have contributed to a majority of primary schools taking up both. The major pegagogical assumptions which underpin the national strategies for literacy and numeracy, appear to be:

- that successful teaching is a quantifiable, 'technical' activity which can be prescribed by policy makers
- that if teachers are 'told' what to do they will be able to carry out instructions in a way which produces high results in learner achievement

In this context, a teacher who applies a little c creative response to the literacy and numeracy hours (by, for example, working holistically with the curriculum whilst meeting both pedagogical and curriculum demands of the strategies) may be regarded as offering a form of resistance to such a technicist approach. For she/he is adopting an approach which assumes that it is both desirable and feasible as a professional to keep open the possibility that even tightly drawn up instructions may be carried out in a variety of ways. Such a response may be considered to be 'resistance' in that it seems to assume that teaching is at least partly artistry rather than being a purely technicist activity.

Certainly, little c creativity is a concept that emphasizes individual agency. On the other hand, little c creativity is not framed with reference to 'resistance' within a political context. Although little c creativity may appear to offer a counter position to what some might call a currently dominant form of political climate, this is not an intention embedded within the concept itself. Rather, it is proposed as necessary for individual survival in a rapidly changing and chaotic world.

On the other hand, it could be argued that almost any theory of human behaviour, by virtue of its subject, will have political aspects, even if it is not posited as such.

## CONCLUSION

In conclusion, then, I have explored and tried to clarify a number of potentially challenging aspects of little c creativity, as follows:

- Although the concept may be culturally situated, it is rapidly becoming universalized in a globalized world, as an important tool for surviving and thriving.
- Although little c creativity may be manifest uniquely in each knowledge domain, the concept itself, being driven by possibility thinking, is effectively 'domain free' and thus in principle a transferable phenomenon.
- Little c creativity can be shaped and encouraged in children; clearly schools and early years settings therefore have a role to play in doing so.
- A person may be judged to be exhibiting little c creativity only by virtue of specific acts of behaviour, rather than in some generalized way, and this may vary over contexts and time. Broader cultural context may have an interaction with this.
- Although little c creativity may appear to offer a counter position to a technical-rationalist approach to life, it is not a 'political' concept in intention. I have acknowledged, however, that it could be argued that any theory of human behaviour is by dint of its subject, political, even if it is not posited as such.

Despite the several contentious points addressed so far, the coherence of the concept seems reasonably intact. This may also be borne out by the various ways in which practitioners, schools and Local Education Authorities are taking up the idea in practice. This uptake may perhaps be partly gauged from the increasing number of requests to the author for presentations, mentorships, studentships, and projects, all of which are driven by the desire to explore the concept both conceptually and in its application to practice.

In the course of seeking to clarify the concept itself, the argument for little c creativity in early education – that it is 'a good thing' – has been implicit in the discussion. Being more explicit, then, what is it that I am proposing children might be able to do as a result of developing little c creativity? The benefits of little c creativity could, I would suggest, be grouped together into three areas. The first of these, is *resilience* It seems likely that encouraging children to apply little c creativity across the various contexts of their lives, would stimulate their resilience to the situations with which life may confront them. The second is *resourcefulness*. It seems reasonable that encouraging children to generate possibilities seems likely to contribute to their capacity to act resourcefully, both now as children and later as adults. Finally, it seems likely that encouraging children to exercise little c creativity in any context will support their *confidence* in finding a way through the situations which they meet in life, now as children and later as adults.

In the next two chapters in particular, I explore some ways in which children's little c creativity may be encouraged and developed.

## References

Bruner, J. (1962) 'The conditions of creativity', in H. Gruber (ed.), *Contemporary Approaches to Creative Thinking*. New York: Atherton Press.

Craft, M. (ed.) (1970) *Family, Class and Education: A Reader*. London: Longman.

Craft, M. (1974) 'Talent, family values and education in Ireland', in S. J. Eggleston (ed.), *Contemporary Research in the Sociology of Education*, pp. 47–67. London: Methuen.

Craft, A. (2001) 'Little c creativity', in A. Craft, B. Jeffrey and M. Leibling, *Creativity in Education*. pp. 45–61. London: Continuum.

Jeffrey, B. and Craft, A. (2001) 'The universalization of creativity', in A. Craft, B. Jeffrey and M. Leibling (eds), *Creativity in Education*. London: Continuum.

Kluckhohn, F. R. and Strodtbeck, F. L. (1961) *Variations in Value Orientation*. Westport, Connecticut: Greenwood Publishers.

McClelland, D. C. (1961) *The Achieving Society*. Toronto: D. Van Nostrand Company.

Woods, P., Jeffrey, B., Troman, G. and Boyle, M. (1997) *Restructuring Schools, Reconstructing Teachers: Responding to Change in the Primary School*. Buckingham: Open University Press.

# PART THREE
# Applying Little c Creativity in Early Years Education

So far, I have positioned little c creativity as a possible third way, or wave, in conceptualizing creativity in the early years. In the first part of the book, I characterized the sociological background to little c creativity as one of intensified change and uncertainty in a range of contexts in complex societies. These include the changing character of social institutions such as the family, and the social structures of local communities and the wider society where the formerly perhaps more predictable roles and relationships are now much looser, less fixed, and more varied; where changes in the local and global economy include an increased emphasis on innovation, and a weakening of the formerly greater certainties in terms of employment; where developments in technology, particularly in information and communication technology, mean that these now pervade all aspects of life. I have suggested that one of the effects of the intensification of change in each of these directions is that individuals need to be increasingly self-directed and able to make their own choices about lifestyle.

I proposed little c creativity, then, as a means of self-direction which enables people to live in and with such intensified changes, lifewide. Little c creativity has to do with a 'can-do' attitude to life. I positioned little c creativity as distinct from both the Plowden approach, and the later 1990s approach (characterized by the NACCCE Report, the National Curriculum, and the Early Learning Goals) to creativity in education.

Part Two involved an exploration of various constituents of little c creativity: imagination, intelligence, self-creation, self-expression, and know-how. I proposed that these are brought together in possibility thinking, which 'drives' little c creativity.

The final part of the book, Part Three, Applying Little c Creativity in Early Years Education, now turns to the practicalities of implementing the notion of little c creativity. It does this first in respect of the curriculum (Chapter 9), then with reference to terms of teaching and assessment (Chapter 10), and then in terms of the educator's engagement with their own creativity and that of others (Chapter 11). Finally, Chapter 12 touches on some wide-ranging aspects of fostering this kind of creativity in education.

# CHAPTER 9

# Creativity and the curriculum

*In this chapter, I explore approaches to curriculum in the early years, considering recent initiatives in the light of underpinning philosophy and values. I go on to consider creativity policy and practice in the early years, analysing some issues arising from the Early Learning Goals, the National Curriculum, and the NACCCE Report in particular. Finally, I consider the possible place of little c creativity in the early years curriculum.*

## Approaches to curriculum in the early years

I begin with a broad discussion of the whole curriculum in the early years in England, as a context for the discussion of little c creativity.

There has, over recent years, been some tension in the early years educator community over the curriculum. The source of this tension is essentially curriculum definition and scope, particularly as the curriculum for school-age children becomes codified, creating a division between pre-school and school-age educators. As David has noted (1990), the term 'curriculum' was seen by many as meaning provision that 'smacked of subjects, set lessons, and a syllabus, rather than their own view of what was important in the lives of young children – holistic development through free and spontaneous play' (David, 1990, p. 72). Yet this open-ended and apparently unstructured form of provision referred to by David has been challenged by some early years practitioners and writers as inappropriate for children who are pre-school age. There are two interrelated sets of issues here. One is the meaning of 'curriculum' and the other is how it is codified for the early years age range, which in this book means from age three to eight.

On the meaning of curriculum, as David (1996) notes, there is general agreement now among curriculum theorists that an educational curriculum is made up of myriad aspects of provision; as she puts it, 'the whole curriculum is made up of the aims and objectives;

teaching and learning styles, including assessment and evaluation; content; resources available (people, space, equipment); use of resources; relationships; and rules' (David, 1996, p. 87). To this, I would add the hidden curriculum, i.e. the values encoded in the physical, emotional, and spiritual terrain of the specific provision. Curtis argued as early as the 1980s, that a non-codified and non-statutory whole curriculum certainly existed in the early years, prior to the introduction of various curriculum policies. She described this as a 'recognizable curriculum ... based on skills and competencies to be developed in a flexible and child-centred environment' (Curtis, 1986, p. 2). The term 'curriculum', then, can carry both broad and narrower meanings.

In analysing the breadth of curriculum, the following framework from primary education (Craft and Claire, 1993) may be useful. Craft and Claire drew a distinction between the formal and informal curriculum. The formal was defined as taking place in official learning time, drawing where appropriate on policy statements or requirements and often planned in a ritualized way, involving specific people. The informal curriculum took place outside official learning time, during playtimes, on entry to and departure from school, etc. Craft and Claire also discussed the overt (surface, or face-value) communication contained within both formal and informal curricula, as well as hidden messages which are implied beneath the surface. Over the last hundred years, the changes in the overt and hidden messages in the early years curriculum have been enormous. In developing her own arguments for resisting an overly outcomes-based model of curriculum, Hurst (1997) records the polarity between the traditional early years curriculum and the more recent one.

The former, i.e. the traditional early years curriculum, described by many including Kelly (1990), acknowledged since at least the 1920s and codified in the Hadow Committee's report on pre-school and infant provision (1933), has, as Hurst writes, 'influenced generation after generation of practitioners' (Hurst, 1997, pp. 50–1). It arose from a number of key theorists/commentators such as Isaacs (1929) and others, as well as from a shared value-base among the early years practitioner community, prioritizing developmentally appropriate practice in supporting children's own strategies for learning. Its emphasis was less on demonstrating learning gains according to performance criteria, and more about the individual child learning at their own pace, and informally. Identification with, and adherence to, this traditional early years curriculum, is a major source of resistance to the recent more structured curriculum policy and practice. As Hurst puts it, the individual, personal, spontaneous, and creative nature of [young children's] learning requires a curriculum which is not seen simply in terms of particular knowledge or skills to be acquired but in terms of the negotiation between the child and the adult of meaning about the world, about how people work and about the child's self-knowledge (Hurst, 1997, p. 60).

In significant contrast is the more recent curriculum policy with its focus on learning outcomes and what some call 'performativity' (Ball, 1997, 1998, 2000; Jeffrey, 2000), for as I noted in Chapter 1, massive changes were made in the last decade of the twentieth century for children aged three to eight. The introduction in 2000 of the Early Learning Goals and of the foundation stage, covering all provision up until the end of the Reception year in school (QCA, 2000), was a milestone in introducing expectations regarding learning outcomes for all children, and thus separating itself in many ways from the traditional early years curriculum approach. At the same time, it was also quite distinct from the arrangements for children in Year 1 upwards. Whilst distinct from the traditional early learning curriculum, the foundation stage can be seen as having grown out of the much earlier HMI notion of areas of experience (DES, 1985), which was originally intended for children up to the age of 11. The Early Learning Goals identified a specific set of learning objectives for children in the Foundation Stage, around six areas of learning:

- personal, social, and emotional development
- communication, language, and literacy
- mathematical development
- knowledge and understanding of the world
- physical development
- creative development

The introduction of the National Curriculum meant that, initially children from age 5 and over, and later from Year 1 and up, were to be educated around a subject content-specific curriculum and assessed at regular stages (i.e. the baseline – on entry to school, and at Year 2 – i.e. at age 7). The subjects were:

- English
- Mathematics
- Science
- Design and technology
- Information technology
- History
- Geography

- Art
- Music
- PE

In the late 1990s, the Numeracy and Literacy Strategies were introduced; these were formalized, compulsory, highly structured teaching outlines for Key Stages 1 and 2. In 2001, Citizenship was also introduced as a compulsory area of study. In addition, various forms of curriculum guidance were issued, including, in 1999, the report of the National Advisory Committee on Creative and Cultural Education (NACCCE), as briefly explored in Chapter 1. Overall, then, the emphasis in curriculum policy has been on outcomes of learning rather than the processes involved, a significant shift for the conceptualization of early years provision.

Embedded in the (international) shift towards outcomes and performance is a powerful discontinuity between the two dominant curricula (i.e. National Curriculum and Foundation Stage Curriculum) in both content and approach, and in both the overt and hidden messages carried within them. The very introduction of two curricula, replacing the traditional early years curriculum approach used by practitioners from birth to eight, represents a severing of the former developmental approach. In addition, it can be seen as cementing the distinction between 'formal' and 'informal' curricula, and carrying various overt and hidden messages within it. One of the *overt* messages carried by the very existence of the dual curricula is that children in the Foundation Stage learn differently to those following the National Curriculum (although the emphasis on outcomes and performance remain a continuous feature of both). One of the *hidden* messages, perhaps, is the implication that the formal curriculum has a higher status and importance in the education of young children, than the informal. A further hidden message, associated with the National Literacy and Numeracy Strategies in particular, was that teachers' artistry was no longer held to be of value, an enormous shift away from the conception of the early (and later primary) years teacher as a professional artist.

Although the early learning goals for the Foundation Stage have had their supporters, there has nevertheless continued to be consternation among many early years educators. Curtis (1998) offered early commentary on this (although at this stage she was commenting on the Desirable Outcomes for Children's Learning, the precursor of the Early Learning Goals). She noted that the introduction of the Desirable Learning Outcomes, the National Curriculum and of Baseline Assessment for children shortly after entering primary school, had all pressured early years practitioners into feeling they must provide a more formalized curriculum and also assess children in pre-school provision. She also argued that 'Early childhood educators should not feel pressurized into taking a subject approach to the early years curriculum even though the government guidelines for children below statutory age are subject-based' (Curtis, 1998, p. viii). Her stance was that there was plenty of scope in both curricula for a competence-based, child-focused, informal approach to provision. The adaptive line taken by Curtis is countered by a far more resistant one, presented by others, for example Hurst (1997). Others taking a resistant approach have questioned the marginalization of play in the Foundation Stage curriculum (for example, Bruce, 1999), and the fundamental need to maintain a broader curriculum perspective incorporating play, resisting a 'funnel-based' curriculum policy, narrowing what is big into something small (Drummond, 1996).

## SUMMARY

So far, then, I have briefly explored the nature of the early years curriculum in England, developing a rationale for a broad view, and suggesting that the codification of the curriculum has been problematic. I want to go on next to look at some of the practicalities of curriculum policy on creativity, in particular.

## Creativity policy and practice in the early years

As noted in earlier parts of the book, creativity has been codified in a number of different ways in curriculum policy. To recapitulate:

* creative development is codified as an early learning goal for children in the Foundation Stage
* creativity is described as a cross-curricular thinking skill in the National Curriculum
* creativity is characterized in the NACCCE report as a democratic notion which can be both fostered in learners and demonstrated by teachers (teaching for creativity and creative teaching respectively)

However, as also noted in Chapter 1, and as argued in earlier work (Craft, 1999), there are a number of conceptual problems with the curriculum area 'creative development', as well as a lack of coherence between the various policy statements. These are summarized below.

First, within creative development:

- The formulation of creative development in the policy documents implies that it is relevant only in certain approaches to learning and parts of the curriculum (and thus not completely cross-curricular).
- The developmental aspect of creative development is problematic, for it implies a static end-state or ceiling.
- It is implied that play and creativity are the same when they are not, since play may be but is not necessarily, creative.

Second, within the National Curriculum, identifying creativity as a skill:

- could be seen as an over-simplification, for to operate creatively must necessarily presuppose an understanding of the domain and thus creativity cannot be seen as knowledge-free
- raises the question of whether creativity manifested in different domains is a transferable skill or a domain-specific one

Third, regarding the NACCCE Report:

- while conceptually coherent, it has connections with Plowden in that it values pupils' self-expression as part of their creativity and also in that it is a universalist or democratic approach, assuming that *all* have the potential for self-expression rather than simply the elite few
- it is nevertheless quite distinct from the earlier statements from Plowden, in that it states that the acquisition of knowledge and skills are the necessary foundation to creativity, and since its focus was exlusively creativity, it had a great deal more to say on it than Plowden did. Also, it distinguished between teaching creatively and teaching for creativity, suggesting that teaching creatively was necessary to teaching for creativity.

Finally, regarding all three initiatives:

- the initiatives lack coherence as a set of measures, both in focus, status (statutory or non-statutory) and the way that creativity is defined – suggesting that the placing of creativity more centrally in the curriculum has not yet occurred, despite a growing recognition of the need to ensure creativity is fostered in learners and teachers.

Perhaps the most significant aspect of curriculum policy development is the new role being carved out for creativity, in both the curriculum and pedagogy as applied to children across the early years. In the next part of this chapter, I focus further on the contribution to thinking about creativity made by the NACCCE Report in particular, because it is significant in being the only curriculum policy statement to focus on creativity in the late twentieth century, and bears closer scrutiny.

## The NACCCE Report and Creativity

As noted in Chapter 1 and in Chapter 2, the NACCCE report addressed a wide range of issues, including the school curriculum, assessment, pedagogy, and teacher training. It also discussed the need for and nature of creativity in education. The definition of creativity used in the report and developed by Professor Lewis Minkin with the aid of a wide-ranging specialist advisory group and the Committee itself, was 'Imaginative activity fashioned so as to produce outcomes that are both original and of value' (p. 29). Each of these terms was carefully defined, as follows:

*Imagination* was focused around being imaginative and supposing, and not necessarily with imaging. As Joubert (2001) writes, 'Imagination, as defined and used by NACCCE, is principally to do with seeing new or other possibilities. It is this power that enables creative people to come up with novel perspectives to ordinary situations.' (Joubert, p. 18) As NACCCE put it, 'it is essentially *generative*; in which we attempt to expand the possibilities of a given situation' (NACCCE, 1999, p. 29)

A *fashioning process* was defined by NACCCE as an active process of fashioning, shaping, moulding, refining, and managing the creative idea or activity (NACCCE, 1999, p. 31).

*Pursuing purposes* is what takes ideas into tangible outcomes. NACCCE describes creativity as 'applied imagination' (p. 29). As Joubert writes in her interpretation of the report: 'outcomes can range from a creative thought, to a new theory, a scientific formula or a new work of art. The purpose may change during the pursuit of it, but the creative activity is still directed towards a goal' (Joubert, 2001, p. 19).

### Being original

NACCCE drew a distinction between three kinds of originality: historic, relative and individual. Historic originality is unique creativity in relation to other creators in the same field. Relative originality is creativity in relation to a specific peer group (thus, a child's approach to a task may be original in comparison to other children's approaches in the group). Individual originality is where a person's work is original in comparison to their own previous work. The report emphasized that all three forms of originality were both valid and to be encouraged in school, in particular individual originality, so that children are encouraged to improve on their performance by producing new ideas.

The report suggested that exceptional, historic talent will flourish when individual and relative originality is nurtured (NACCCE 1999, p. 31).

### Judging value

The report argues that creative ideas or outcomes must be evaluated, to determine their value (NACCCE, p. 31). This can be done both throughout and at the end of the creative activity, depending on the activity; the context and the judging process can provide formative feedback.

Furthermore, as noted in Chapter 1, the NACCCE report drew a distinction between *teaching creatively* and *teaching for creativity*.

**Teaching creatively** was seen as 'teachers using imaginative approaches to make learning more interesting, exciting and effective', and teaching for creativity as 'forms of teaching that are intended to develop young people's own creative thinking or behaviour' (NACCCE, 1999, p. 89). The report asserts that teaching for creativity cannot be achieved without creative teaching, suggesting that creative teachers take risks, are prepared to learn from their pupils, and are not afraid of not knowing everything already. Creative teachers, the NACCCE committee suggest, have 'strong motivation, high expectations, the ability to communicate and listen and the ability to interest and inspire' (p. 95).

**Teaching for creativity** was seen as involving three main tasks or principles, the first of which was encouraging certain attributes and beliefs such as risk taking, commitment, openness to new experiences, persistence, resilience, independent judgement, identifying, and fostering. The second main principle was seen as identifying the individual learner's creative strengths with reference to the whole curriculum, taking as an assumption that multiple intelligences are fundamental to identifying a person's strengths or weaknesses. The final principle was that teachers should foster the creative potential of all children and not just some; and to do this through innovative, questioning, and experimental activity, where children are encouraged to challenge fundamental assumptions of established thinking, and by actual and mental play, in a relaxed environment, which is full of experiences, ideas, and interesting resources and activities. A creative environment, the report suggested, takes fear of failure into consideration, accepting mistakes as part of the creative process and encouraging resilience and persistence in learning from mistakes and trying again.

The definition of creativity given by NACCCE seems reasonable and comparable to those offered by others (see Chapter 3). It is also carefully pitched to include both 'high' and 'little c' interpretations of creative activity, and is not tied specifically to the arts, or to a product-outcome. I will return to the distinction between creative teaching and teaching for creativity in Chapter 10, which explores pedagogy and assessment. But in this chapter, I want to take up critically the linking in the NACCCE report of creativity to multiple intelligences.

## Creativity as linked to a broad view of intelligence

The NACCCE Report situates creativity in what it calls a 'variety of intelligences' (NACCCE, 1999, p. 34), emphasizing the wide range of ways in which human beings can be both intelligent and creative. It explicitly discusses Gardner's theory of multiple intelligences, noting it as a useful categorization of a multiple view of human capacity. Although the report also acknowledges White's (1998) critique of Gardner's work, both of which are discussed in this book in Chapter 4, it ultimately dismisses any critique. The position the report takes is that 'The numbers of intelligences and the exact ways in which they are classified are less important than the fact that intelligence is multifaceted.' (NACCCE, 1999, p. 35). Whilst accepting that broad position, it nevertheless seems to me that White's critique of Gardner's theory is important in that it highlights the need to clarify the theory. In particular, as discussed in Chapter 4,

- Gardner's contention that each intelligence has a distinctive developmental history, with clearly definable 'end-state performances' raises questions about the appropriateness of an 'unfoldment' model in the mental realm and also about the incompatibility of the implication of a developmental 'ceiling' with Gardner's more general position which challenges that limited perspective on intelligence;
- the criterion of whether a 'symbol system' is necessary in the case of each intelligence is questionable; and
- the way in which Gardner applies the criteria in identifying intelligences, could be said to be unsystematic.

These are important questions to be resolved, if policy and other recommendations for education are to use Gardner's multiple intelligences as a part of their set of foundation assumptions.

## SUMMARY

So far, then, in this chapter, the introduction of Creative Development and creative thinking skills in the statutory curriculum, and curriculum advice on democratic creativity, have been interpreted against the backdrop of curriculum change and resistance to this, in the early years. Contemporary curriculum codification demonstrates a range from recommendations only (NACCCE), through general statement, not picked out in any detail (National Curriculum), to highly specific and explicit proposals (Early Learning Goals). There are a number of discontinuities and inconsistencies between the different curricula. The NACCCE advice in particular is subject to criticism in its use of multiple intelligence theory as a foundation.

Although there is scope in the curriculum for the fostering of creativity, it could be placed more centrally in curriculum policy. Technicist policy initiatives such as the National Literacy and Numeracy Strategies discussed in Chapter 8, introduced in the late 1990s, have the potential to undermine teachers' artistry and, potentially, block both teacher and pupil creativity.

On the other hand, although as suggested in Chapter 8 such strategies appear to be at odds with the curricula described in this book that codify creativity, both because of their emphasis on the basic skills and also because of their highly specific and didactic pedagogy, they need not necessarily be so. For pupils, possibility thinking can be developed within any content area. For adults, teacher creativity can occur within even a restrictive framework, as staff at, for example, Coombes First School and Nursery in Berkshire have demonstrated (Rowe and Humphries, 2001).

## Little c creativity in the curriculum

As argued so far, ordinary creativity involves intelligence, imagination, self-creation, self-expression, and know-how. It is not tied to a pro-duct-outcome, but enables a person to be in charge of their life. It is neither outcomes nor process focused, but both, and it seems to me that it is a desirable aim in early education. It has much in common with what Page (2000) has described and documented in her international work as a 'futures' approach to early childhood education, by which she means focusing on what children are and may be in the future. Futures-based curriculum foci, she suggests, include provision

- for children to develop an awareness and tolerance of other individuals and cultures
- for children to identify common needs and shared interests with different individuals and cultures

- for children to develop a respect for diversity
- for children to develop an understanding of human rights (Page, 2000)

Page emphasizes the importance of framing futures-issues in developmentally-appropriate ways. The same is true of little c creativity. Whilst ultimately little c creativity may enable a person to find ways of living a satisfying and responsible life as an adult, its foci will be child-centred in the early years.

Elsewhere (Craft, 2000, 2001), I have written at some length about what creativity could look like in the arts, humanities, maths, science, technology, and information and communication technology for children aged three to thirteen. Others have written about children's creativity in specific subject areas, for example in art (Barnes, 1987). Much of fostering little c creativity is about pedagogical approaches to encourage children's natural curiosity, and will be discussed in Chapter 10.

What follow here are some brief real-life examples, which cover the slightly lower age-span of this particular book, and which cover the range of the curriculum. What is present in each one, I believe, is possibility thinking and pedagogy focused on the nurturing of little c creativity.

> Two-and-a-half-year-old Emily was exploring the tray of orange jelly provided in her nursery class. The nursery worker co-ordinating her group asked, 'I wonder what it would feel like, if we put our hands in there?'

> Three-year-olds Ricky and Connor were making collages out of dried pulses at their playgroup. Their keyworker encouraged them first to explore in turn what they liked about each other's work, suggesting possible ways of adding to it – and then to respond to the feedback, choosing a course of action, either incorporating the suggestions, adapting them, or leaving them aside.

> Three-and-a-half-year-old Jason was drawing a picture of Buzz Lightyear (a children's video/film character). His keyworker watched carefully and then suggested that Jason draw Buzz flying.

> A small group of reception-aged children were exploring what happens to ice at room temperature, with their teacher. The teacher encouraged the children to advance predictions about what might possibly happen to the ice.

> Individual children in a Year 1 class were encouraged to make five-word poems, conveying their feelings about Bonfire Night.

A whole-class storytelling activity with children in Year 2 involved the children discussing a book which the teacher had read to them, and thinking of alternative endings to it.

Elyse and Wale, aged seven, were making up number sentences which gave the answer 'twenty'. They worked independently to begin with, then compared notes.

Six-year-olds in a Year 1 class were invited to invent some characters, as a class, which children then drew pictures of and wrote individual stories about.

Eight-year-olds Alasdair and Gregory chose to take on the characters of two schoolboy survivors in a desert shipwreck, in a drama lesson. They explored the relationship between the characters as a subsequent writing task.

Seven-year-olds in a Year 2 class researched their grandparents' generation. Part of this research involved visits from older people to the classroom, as well as interviewing a grandparent about their childhood. The children were invited to construct a diary entry describing a day in the life of a child growing up in their grandparents' generation.

As the culmination of their work on the proposed local road bypass, a class of eight-year-olds in a two-form entry Junior Mixed and Infants school were involved in a morning of off-timetable work. The class role-played different constituencies in the debate as to whether the by-pass should be approved. These included the local council planning department and councillors, local residents, local shopkeepers and service providers, and the press. Their parallel class then voted for or against the construction of the bypass.

Four-year-old Ola was exploring shapes in his nursery class. He noticed that straight edges fitted together better than curved ones. The teaching assistant working with him encouraged him to explore tesellating patterns using some coloured sticky-backed paper, cut into straight-edged regular shapes.

A three-year-old boy sat at the edge of a group of nursery children working on lego house construction, at the centre of which was a nursery worker, making her own building. The boy repeatedly asked for the house. The worker's response was that she would let him have her house if he could show her that he was able to start making his own one. After numerous interactions along these lines, the boy began, slowly, to make his own house.

Five-year-olds in a reception class were encouraged to predict what would happen to the dough they had made when it was put into the oven, and to think of reasons why.

Eight-year-olds in an English primary school were each linked to a fellow-pupil of the same age in an Australian class, by e-mail. Each pair developed and wrote-up a joint investigation using the Web amongst other sources, to gather their information.

Two three-year-olds were playing in the nursery sand pit with a long wooden plank, when it began to rain. As their teachers started to pack away the toys which belonged in the shed, one child ran indoors whilst the other began to drag the plank toward the shed, and after a few unsuccessful heaves at it, commissioned the observing researcher a few feet away, to take one end of it.

Just before lunch, four-year-old Jamie arrived at the carpeted area of the nursery classroom clutching a small Lego construction which he had been making painstakingly for the past twenty minutes in another part of the room. His teacher, frustrated at his late arrival and at his disregard for the rules that constructions are taken apart at the end of each session, scolded him, to which he responded 'I made that . . .' Despite having the toy removed from him, he continued to negotiate to have it put in a safe place until the following day when he could continue to build it. Ultimately he succeeded in persuading his teacher.

What should be apparent from each of these examples from across the early years curriculum, is that:

- little c creativity involves knowledge of the given domain but not necessarily expert knowledge
- any domain of human activity is open to little c creativity, not just the creative and expressive arts
- persistence and finding ways around obstacles are significant aspects of little c creativity
- careful observation by adults about children's engagement with any given learning situation, is fundamental to appropriate learning intervention to stimulate children's creativity

The formal curriculum, then, does not cast little c creativity as a specific, desirable aim for early years education. However, it is surely an essential foundation to enable children to cope with the challenges that an unpredictable world may bring into their lives; as well as helping them generate new possibilities which may make the world a better place for all who live in it.

## Creativity in specific domains

In Chapter 8, I argued that little c creativity should be conceived of as having a generic foundation, i.e. possibility thinking. I also argued that this was not incompatible with an approach which saw the domain of application as highly significant.

Within the applied, general creativity literature, there has been a shift toward recognizing the importance of the domain over the last ten years. The role of the domain in creativity was highlighted in the conceptual framework proposed by Feldman *et al.* (1994) where, drawing on Csikszentmihalyi (1994), they suggested that creativity could be seen as involving three analytical dimensions: the *field*, by which they mean 'the social and cultural aspects of a profession, job or craft' (Feldman *et al.* 1994, p. 16); the *domain*, by which they mean 'the structure and organization of a body of knowledge evolved to contain and express certain distinct forms of information' (p. 16); and the *individual*, which they describe as 'the site of the acquisition, organization and transformation of knowledge that has the possibility of changing domains and fields'. Although Feldman *et al.* were concerned with extraordinary creativity rather than the creativity of ordinary people, they were in tune with a general movement to take account of knowledge in the domain, in making sense of thinking skills. Evidence of the move toward a domain-situated approach to understanding creativity, is also found in recent research into 'ordinary' creativity in some subject areas, specifically music, drama, art, information and communication technology, design and technology, and mathematics.

An issue is the balance between 'programmes' that teach thinking, approaches which 'embed' thinking in the subjects of the curriculum, and finally approaches which emphasize transferability.

One area of domain-specific creativity which requires much greater exploration and development, is information and communication technology (ICT), its potential and role. A baseline for evaluating the possibilities it may offer is the Stevenson Report (1997), produced for the then Labour opposition, and focusing on ICT more generally (rather than ICT and creativity). This report pointed to the speed and extent to which ICT was likely to become a core part of the education and wider life experiences of all young people and their teachers in the early part of the twenty-first century. It painted a vision of 'a society within ten years where ICT has permeated the entirety of education (as it will the rest of society) so that it is no longer a talking point but taken for granted – rather as electricity has come to be'. This forecast is turning out to have been well-founded.

Given the core role that ICT is already assuming in the lives of learners and teachers, developing our understanding of ways in which creativity may be enhanced by ICT is going to be important. It is widely recognized that the pioneering work in the UK on ICT emphasized the ways in which computers could be used creatively, i.e. to make or to create images, music, software, text, ideas, and that it provided the foundations for our successful computer software industry (Heppell, 1999). Heppell suggests that computers offer the possibilities for children to develop a diversity and uncertainty of outcomes, and to exceed our ambitions and expectations for their progress.

Some of the ways in which computers have the capacity to enhance children's creativity are:

- by virtue of being multi-layered, multi-media, non-linear tools
- through use of specially designed programmes that encourage problem identification and solving, as well as creative expression of various kinds
- through the use of e-mail, web-based and other digital connections between teachers, learners and wider society
- through the internet (and intranet facilities), including the making and visiting of websites
- by offering an environment in which children can exercise agency with ease, in a highly visually attractive and sophisticated virtual environment
- by offering both a-synchronous and synchronous interaction

As the technology grows, its potential for young children is already expanding to include ways of interacting which are more in-the-moment and which do not rely, necessarily, on literacy.

## CONCLUSION

In this chapter, I have critically reviewed the various curriculum statements regarding creativity, in the context of a general discussion about the early years curriculum. I went on to explore what little c creativity could mean in the education of young children, giving fieldwork examples from across the curriculum and suggesting its necessity for both providing for children in the future and enabling them to generate new possibilities for themselves and others. In doing this, I discussed, briefly, some aspects of creativity in specific domains.

In the next chapter, the focus turns to teaching and assessing creativity.

## References

Ball, S. (1997) 'Good School/Bad School: paradox and fabrication'. *British Journal of Sociology in Education*, **18** (3), 317–37.

Ball, S. J. (1998) 'Performativity and fragmentation in "Postmodern Schooling"', in S. J. Ball (ed.), *Postmodernity and Fragmentation of Welfare*. London: Routledge.

Ball, S. J. (2000) 'Performativities and fabrications in the education economy: towards the performative society?' *Australian Educational Researcher* **27** (2), 1–23.

Barnes, R. (1987) *Teaching Art to Young Children 4–9*. London: Routledge.

Bruce, T. (1999) 'In praise of inspired and inspiring teachers', in L. Abbott and L. Moylett (eds) *Early Education Transformed*. London: Falmer Press.

Craft, A. (1999) 'Creative development in the early years: implications of policy for practice'. *Curriculum Journal*, **10** (1), 135–50

Craft, A. (2000) *Creativity Across the Primary Curriculum*. London: Routledge.

Craft, A. (2001) 'Creativity across the primary curriculum'. *Teaching Thinking*, **Autumn** (5), 42–5.

Craft, A. and Claire, H. (1993) *E624: Planning Learning in the Primary Curriculum*. Milton Keynes: Open University.

Curtis, A. (1986) *A Curriculum for the Pre-School Child: Learning to Learn*. Windsor: NFER-Nelson.

Curtis, A. (1998) *A Curriculum for the Pre-School Child: Learning to Learn* 2nd edn. London and New York: Routledge.

Csikszentmihalyi, M. (1994) 'The domain of creativity', in D. H. Feldman, M. Csikszentmihalyi and H. Gardner, *Changing the World: A Framework for the Study of Creativity*. Westport, CT: Praeger Publishers.

David, T. (1990) *Under Five – Under-educated?* Milton Keynes: Open University Press.

David, T. (1996) 'Curriculum in the early years', in G. Pugh (ed.) *Contemporary Issues in the Early Years*, 2nd edn. London: Paul Chapman Publishing (in association with the National Children's Bureau Early Childhood Unit).

Department of Education and Science (DES) (1985) *The Curriculum from 5 to 16: Curriculum Matters no. 2*. (HMI Discussion Document). London: HMSO.

Drummond, M. J. (1996) 'Whatever next? future trends in early education', in D. Whitebread, (ed). *Teaching and Learning in the Early Years*. London and New York: Routledge.

Feldman, D. Csikszentmihalyi, M. and Gardner, H. (1994) *Changing the World: A Framework for the Study of Creativity*. Westport, Connecticut: Praeger Publishers.

Great Britain, Board of Education Consultative Committee (1933) *Infant and Nursery Schools*. London: HMSO (The Hadow Report).

Heppell, S. (1999) *Computers, Creativity, Curriculum and Children*. Cambridge: Anglia Polytechnic University Ultralab Website.

Hurst, V. (1997) *Planning for Early Learning: Educating Young Children* 2nd edn. London: Paul Chapman Publishing Ltd.

Independent ICT in Schools Commission (1997) *Information and Communications Technology in UK Schools: An Independent Enquiry*. London: Independent ICT in Schools Commission (The Stevenson Report).

Isaacs, S. ([1929]) 1971) *The Nursery Years*. London: Routledge & Kegan Paul.

Jeffrey, B. (2000) 'Performativity and primary teacher relations'. Conference paper presented at 'Ethnography Conference' held at Oxford University, 2000.

Joubert, M. (2001) 'The art of creative teaching: NACCCE and beyond', in A. Craft, B. Jeffrey and M. Leibling (eds), *Creativity in Education*, London: Continuum.

Kelly, A. V. (1990) *The National Curriculum: A Critical Review*. London: Paul Chapman.

National Advisory Committee on Creative and Cultural Education (NACCCE) (1999), *All Our Futures: Creativity, Culture and Education*. London: Department for Education and Employment.

Page, J. M. (2000) *Reframing the Early Years Curriculum*. London and New York: RoutledgeFalmer.

Qualifications and Curriculum Authority (QCA) (2000) *Curriculum Guidance for the Foundation Stage*. London: Qualifications and Curriculum Authority.

Rowe, S. and Humphries, S. (2001) 'Creating a climate for learning at Coombes Infant and Nursery School', in A. Craft, B. Jeffrey and M. Leibling, (eds) *Creativity in Education*, London: Continuum.

White, J. (1998) *Do Howard Gardner's Multiple Intelligences Add Up?* London: University of London Institute of Education (*Perspectives in Education Policy Series*).

# CHAPTER 10

# Teaching and assessing creativity

*This chapter explores aspects of teaching and assessing creativity in the early years, starting with the distinction between teaching creatively and teaching for creativity. It goes on to consider a range of pedagogical strategies and their underpinning theoretical foundations; and finally looks at issues in the assessment of creativity in the early years. I draw on a general creativity literature to make suggestions for teaching and assessing little c creativity in particular.*

## Teaching creatively and teaching for creativity

The NACCCE Report, discussed in Chapter 9, distinguished between teaching creatively and teaching for creativity. Teaching creatively they defined as 'teachers using imaginative approaches to make learning more interesting, exciting and effective' (NACCCE, 1999, p. 89). Teaching for creativity, by contrast, they defined as 'forms of teaching that are intended to develop young people's own creative thinking or behaviour' (p. 89). The report suggested that teaching for creativity involved teaching creatively, as follows: 'young people's creative abilities are most likely to be developed in an atmosphere in which the teacher's creative abilities are properly engaged' (p. 90).

I want to consider this claim for a moment. It certainly seems plausible that if a teacher is passionately-inspired in their own creative artistry as a teacher, the childen working with them will be, too. But is it necessarily so? Take this example, concerning the potential for display work to stimulate creativity. An early years practitioner may be extremely fulfilled in their ability to put up stunning displays in the classroom, incorporating children's work in them. But there is a difference between a work of art, and a display which is carefully designed for children's interaction with it, and which may further stimulate children's little c creativity.

I recently visited an infant school in the south-east of England where a Year I teacher and her class had created a vibrant, interactive, three-dimensional pictorial representation of Eric Carle's story, *The Very Hungry Caterpillar*. The story explains how the caterpillar ate an increasing number of food items on each day of the week, until he was ready to go into his cocoon. Told in bright colours, it introduces children to counting the numbers one to seven, the days of the week, vocabulary relating to food, as well as the idea of where butterflies come from. In this particular display of the book, all of these were integrated across each week as part of the registration time each day, when children were able to move various items around. The children were also encouraged to explore the display throughout the day and to show visitors how it worked. Several children volunteered to show me the display. They were clearly getting to grips with reading the labels for the foods, days of the week and the steps of the story, and understanding the concept and order of the days of the week, as well as reinforcing the notion of storying and learning about the caterpillar/ butterfly life cycle. They displayed possibility thinking in their curiosity about the diet of the caterpillar, the fact that it made a cocoon and about what would happen to it once it was a butterfly. In addition, they talked about the parts of the display which they had been involved in making, discussing the materials they had used and showing me individual work they had gone on to create, using some of the techniques in the large display (e.g. rolled-up tissue paper ball pictures, finger and sponge paintings, experimenting with washes).

The teacher had, it seemed to me, really maximized the possibilities for stimulating the children's own creativity in a range of domains (language, art, science), whilst also operating in a highly creative manner herself. A powerful example, then, of teacher creativity. But, with less thought and skill, the display could have been done in such a way as to exclude rather than encourage, the children's creativity.

In addition, it is questionable as to whether modelling creativity and collaborating in its manifestation, in the ways described in this example, are the only ways in which children's creativity is fostered. It has been suggested that a very boring environment could be equally stimulating in that children become creative to avoid boredom (Warnock, 1994). Eight-year-old Clare regularly 'went to the moon' in her head during the weekly spelling list and spelling test at her school in the south-west of England, for example. The lesson was both boring to her and also offered her sufficient time and space to disengage, as to enable her to be imaginative in her head.

So, I want to qualify what the NACCCE report claimed, by suggesting that teaching for creativity may occur through creative teaching, but not necessarily – and that it may arise through other means too.

The NACCCE report proposed that when teaching for creativity, teachers aim for:

- both broadly and narrowly focused experimental activity, carefully pitched at an appropriate developmental level
- encouraging imaginative activity and wonder at its potential
- making adequate space for generative thought, free of immediate critique although subject ultimately to critical scrutiny
- encouraging self-expression
- appreciating the phases involved in creative activity and the necessity of time for each
- stimulating learners during play periods with possibility thinking, and combining this with rigorous testing of these possibilities
- overtly encouraging and valuing imaginativeness, originality, questioning, and curiosity.

There is some evidence from pre-school research that certain characteristics of the teacher are correlated with the extent to which creativity is effectively fostered with pupils (Angeloska-Galevska, 1996). These include teacher attitude toward creativity, social relations between teacher and pupil, the provision of optimal materials and perhaps most significantly, the educational level of the teacher (university-educated teachers were found, in this study, most likely to foster creativity). Clearly this evidence begs questions about the possible relationships between values and attitudes, educational level, intelligence, and pedagogic repertoires. It has also been suggested that the ideal learner is often characterized as one who conforms; a model which does not appear to embrace pupil creativity. As Sternberg and Lubart say, 'to engender creativity, first we must value it!' (p. 614) Modelling, or mentoring, creativity, is one clear way in which this is evidenced to pupils (Sternberg and Lubart, 1991b).

The role of the mentor in fostering creativity has been documented by many in the literature (Beetlestone, 1998; Craft, 2000; Fryer, 1996; Shagoury-Hubbard, 1996; Torrance, 1984). Essentially, the research suggests that the provision of a role-model who can provide a learner with an apprenticeship approach to developing creativity is a powerful aid to fostering their creativity. The mentor may be an adult (for example, a teacher or someone from beyond the school itself), or indeed another pupil. In *The Very Hungry Caterpillar* story above, the teacher acted as mentor to the children, but also encouraged the children to mentor adult and child visitors to their classroom, too. The lifewide aspects of little c creativity mean that mentoring it is a particularly powerful means of encouraging it. It seems a reasonable assumption to propose that children surrounded by parents and early years educators who in their own lives exercise little c creativity, rather than allowing the stumbling blocks they come across to limit their ideas and activities, are more likely to manifest little c creativity in their own lives.

### SUMMARY

Having briefly explored the NACCCE distinction between teaching creatively and teaching for creativity, I have suggested that teaching for creativity does not necessarily involve creative teaching, although it may do. Research on teaching for creativity suggests that teacher values and characteristics influence the effectiveness of teaching strategies which encourage creativity, and that mentoring, or an apprenticeship model of learning, is a powerful way of stimulating children's creativity. I have suggested that mentoring or apprenticeship may be particularly appropriate in fostering little c creativity.

In the next part of this chapter, I explore pedagogical strategies for fostering little c creativity specifically as defined earlier in the book, drawing on a general (and international) creativity literature from a range of education phases, including, but much broader than, the early years. However, I want to add a caveat. As discussed in Chapter 8, little c creativity may be culturally and possibly social-class specific (embodying future-oriented values, individualism, and problem-solving): thus, drawing from a diverse literature could be problematic, in that these values may not be reflected universally in the populations drawn upon for the empirical studies. In addition, the methodologies used in the empirical studies include both qualitative and quantitative, and very from very small-scale to the much more substantial, and embody, inevitably, a variety of models of how we may 'build knowledge'. Further, some of the literature, being philosophical, does not draw on systematically gathered empirical work except by reference to examples, many of which may be fictional. However, insofar as little c creativity is an attempt to draw another part to the creativity map, the points of reference which exist are not specific to little c creativity but come from a broader territory. It therefore seems to me reasonable to draw upon the wider literature, and to explore the possible relevance of other empirical and conceptual work on creativity, to teaching and assessing little c creativity in particular.

## Pedagogical strategies for creativity

Practical pedagogical strategies depend, of course, on an underpinning theory of what it is to be creative, which may or may not be explicit. Examples which are currently prevalent in the international community as regards the creativity of the ordinary person, may be grouped into five areas: those emphasizing a creative cycle, single strategy approaches, multi-strategy approaches, system approaches and those emphasizing overall pedagogic criteria. Some dominant approaches within these categories are described below.

### 'Creative cycle' approaches

Examples of 'creative cycle' approaches are those based on the processes of creativity originally proposed by Wallas (1926), but then developed by others such as Storr (1972), Guildford (1973), and much more recently by Kessler (2000). These researchers describe the stages as preparation, incubation, inspiration or illumination, and verification. All but the last stage were proposed in the original thinking of Wallas (1926). Preparation involves the gathering of skills, principles and data; a time of discipline and focus. Incubation by contrast involves the doing of nothing – 'letting go'; a kind of essential, fallow period, of receptivity and openness – sometimes even chaos or muddle (and thus offering a potential challenge in the classroom). Inspiration, or illumination, comes directly out of the incubation space. Finally, verification (the part of the cycle added by theorists building on the original work of Wallas (1926) involves the refining of the outcome. Craft (2000) adds to this sequence the start of the next cycle at the end of the last one. Such process approaches, when developed in the classroom, may involve offering pupils specific kinds of experience.

Both Kessler and Craft, though, suggest the need, in a teaching situation, to foster in learners and in oneself:

- being open to possibility, the unknown and the unexpected
- bridging differences – making connections between apparently unconnected ideas and integrating different ways of knowing (for example, physical, feeling, imagining)
- holding the paradox of form and freedom
- holding the tension between safety and risk
- being willing to give and receive criticism
- awareness of the individual

### Single-strategy approaches

One well-known single strategy approach is De Bono's 'Six Hats' method (1993). Some schools already use this and it is used in other organizational contexts. Based on his view that creative thinking is essentially 'lateral thinking', this is a method developed to encourage the viewing of any issue from a number of different perspectives. The idea is that when 'wearing' any one of six possible fictional coloured hats imbued with certain qualities, the thinker emphasizes certain approaches to thinking.

'Possibility thinking' (Craft, 2000) could be seen as another single-strategy approach. As described in Chapter 7, above, essentially pupils are encouraged to approach learning across the curriculum, with a 'what if?' attitude. In other words, with a questioning approach that wonders about possibilities and is both prepared to follow, and be supported in, seeing the questions through to an outcome.

A further, broad, strategy, is play, and since play forms a significant focus in the experience of very young children, I devote a little more space to examining this strategy. Balke (1997) suggests that, in early childhood and primary education, play is essential in the development of creativity. This is a perspective which is quite dominant in the early years literature, perhaps because of the diversity of what play can mean (and therefore be seen as promoting), as documented by many (Fisher, 1992, Meek, 1985, Moyles, 1989, 1994). The application of social constructivist learning framework arising from the work of Bruner (1978) and Vygotsky (1978) respectively can also be seen as having contributed to the association of play with creativity. Wood and Atfield (1996) emphasize the interaction of logic and reasoning with children's play, enabling them to construct 'as if' and 'what if' scenarios in a creative way. The teacher's role as careful observer and thoughtful facilitator of such play is also well-documented in the literature.

The association of play with creative development can be misleading, however. For play is necessary to creativity, but not all play is necessarily creative (Craft, 2000), as discussed in Chapter 1 and Chapter 8. A number of theorists have developed play-frameworks, including the philosopher, Dearden (1968). Dearden offers a classification of play, noting that 'play' covers a wide variety of activities – including:

(i) gross physical activities, such as running and climbing, (ii) manipulative activities with sand, water and bricks, (iii) impersonation, either by the children themselves, as in 'mothers and fathers', or by their toys; (iv) quite strictly rule-governed games, both for the table and for outside, such as Piaget's classic case of marbles and a range of increasingly elaborate games leading up to those of adults (Piaget, 1932, ch. 1); (v) verbal catches and teasings, such as the Opies described (Opie and Opie, 1959);

(vi) ... unseemlinesses which children may get up to in their play (Dearden, 1968, pp. 95–6).

All of these categories of play involve, I would suggest, openness to 'possibilities'; although play involving impersonation must by definition involve the manifestation of less inventive possibility options than, say, manipulative activities with sand, water, and bricks.

What seems to be missing in Dearden's classification is imaginative play, which may not necessarily involve impersonation. For example, 'travelling to the moon' may not involve the taking on of a persona, although it may involve the imagination of a variety of kinds of possibilities. It seems to me that this category of play necessarily involves particularly inventive possibility options.

Many writers, including Moyles (1994), have suggested that through play children first explore, then use knowledge, then recognize, and subsequently solve, problems, using it. Later they practise and revise the knowledge and skill involved, for future use. Play, even that which is imitative or fantasy-based, therefore builds the child's confidence in being able to learn about their world. Making mistakes is an important part of this process: mistakes can be viewed as positive learning rather than errors never to be repeated. Thus, play can be seen as *encompassing* possibility thinking in that the positing of possibilities for the way in which play may unfold may be a necessary part of children's play – but this is not the same as saying that play is essential for (i.e. leads to), possibility thinking.

Play, then, may involve the consideration and exploration of possibilities.

Other play-frameworks can help tease out the connections between play and creativity. Take Hutt's (1979) well-used framework for analysing the play of children under five. She divides play into 'epistemic play' (where children explore the properties of materials, and develop knowledge and skills which then underpin later learning), 'ludic play' (which includes socio-dramatic play, language play, and creativity and practice/rehearsal) and 'games-play' (which includes social games, number games, riddles, etc.). Some epistemic play may foster creativity, in helping children to explore possibilities through play with, and deepening their knowledge of, materials for example. Griffiths (1994) recounts a number of case studies demonstrating children developing mathematical understanding through play; some of her examples also show mathematical creativity. Similarly some ludic play will be creative. On the other hand some will not, so a child mimicking a role they already have some first-hand experience of (such as a parenting role), would not be creative, but going beyond that to exploring a 'new' role, such as being an astronaut, or exploring the 'olden days' (McCaldon, 1991) might.

Likewise in games-play, snakes-and-ladders would not be creative, being based purely on chance and the throw of the dice, whereas hide-and-seek could well be. Bruce (1991, 1994) contends that her notion of free-flow play (which combines wallowing in ideas, feelings and relationships, with application of competence and technical prowess) forms a fundamental part of fostering a child's creativity and wider learning; for a feature of Bruce's free-form play is that it involves 'supposing' alternative or possible worlds, which involves 'being ima-ginative, original, innovative and creative' (1991, p. 64). Certainly this can be so, and as Beetlestone notes (1998), 'Play provides a safe opportunity for imaginative risk-taking and testing out of ideas' (p. 79), which are fundamental to creativity.

Einon (1986) offers many practical play suggestions which provide such opportunities. However, it remains the case that creativity and play are not synonymous in that not all play involves creativity.

In addition, the potential for play is not always taken up as fully as it might be, as Bennett *et al.*'s (1997) study of play in reception class-rooms highlighted.

Finally, it is interesting to speculate, briefly, on some cultural and historical aspects of play, for as an artefact it is not universal either across different cultures or time. For example, in earlier historical periods when 'fate' had a larger role to play than it does currently, in the precariousness of people's everyday lives, it is possible that 'pre-determined' forms of play (i.e. published games with a range of set outcomes) were more in evidence than they are today, and were perhaps more common than other forms of play. It is possible that in the twenty-first century in the capitalist world we shall require and produce play activities and objects for children that are more intended to exercise and to foster autonomy and individuality. Although having said this, a large number of toys are now mechanized, and may even include voices; and others which are marketed as specifically designed to foster exploration and individuality, also manifest all sorts of pre-determined cultural values within them. For instance, the Barbie doll is sold with many outfits and environments from skiing to cooking. It is possible to build up an entire pink plastic Barbie world. However, she is presented as an archetypal woman, dependent on Ken, her boyfriend, for rides in the car and good times. She also has an hour-glass figure and long blonde hair (although there are now some multicultural versions of Barbie). The cultural assumptions built into Barbie's appearance, her relationship with others, her occupations and hobbies, are very particular. Thus, although she is marketed as a toy for whom

children can create a whole play world, thus mimicking adult autonomy, this is constrained within a definite set of values.

### Multi-strategy approaches

Shallcross (1981) identified a range of strategies important in pedagogical approaches to creativity. These include having adequate space
and time for developing a creative response to any given situation. She
suggests that teachers often intervene too early in a child's thinking
process, preventing pupils from working out ideas for themselves. In
addition, she suggests that it is essential to provide an overt 'mental
climate' in the classroom, which includes fostering self-esteem and self-
worth and the valuing of achievability (i.e. setting tasks for children
that are achievable, in order to build their confidence). The emotional
climate of the classroom should enable each child to grow in security
and personal confidence without constant scrutiny. As Shallcross puts
it: 'the ground rules are personal guarantees that allow [pupils] to grow
at their own rate, retain the privacy of their work until they are ready
to share it, and prize their possible differences (1981, p. 19).

### System approaches

Edwards and Springate (1995), writing of the Reggio Emilia approach
to fostering creativity in the Italian pre-school, suggest a range of
teaching system strategies which enable the modification of classrooms
to support children's creativity. Although they are discussing mainly
artistic creativity, there may be relevance in some or all of these
strategies for other curriculum areas. The pedagogical strategies which
they name are listed below.

- *Space*: i.e. offering children the physical space to leave classroom
  work from one day to the next without it being destroyed; also by
  the provision of a bright working space with harmonious colours,
  furnished with child-sized areas and examples of their own and
  others' work including that of known artists, and the provision of
  both appropriate and inviting materials
- *Time*: i.e. enabling children adequate time to finish their work,
  and not be artificially rotated or asked to move on before being
  ready to
- *Climate*. The atmosphere in the classroom, they propose, should
  encourage risk taking, making mistakes, innovation and
  uniqueness, alongside mess, noise, and freedom, whilst in an
  overall environment of order. Teachers themselves should be
  encouraged to experiment alongside the children.

- *Occasions*. Teachers should provide a variety of exciting and intense encounters for the children between their outer and inner worlds. The stimulus of field trips, visitors to the classroom, the introduction of specific artefacts, animals or plants to the learning environment, and so on, can be intensified, they suggest, by representations both before and afterwards.
- *Offering rich resource materials*. Particularly useful when the children themselves have helped to select them. Resource materials may be bought, found or recycled; and, they suggest, may include paper goods of many kinds, tools for writing and drawing, construction and collage materials, including buttons, shells, beads, seeds and stones, as well as sculpting materials such as shaving cream, clay, and play dough.

These pedagogic strategies reflect studies done beyond schools, such as that by Greenberg (1992) investigating the creativity of fashion design students at college in the USA, in which she discovered that those students who were more creative had been given more choice in identifying which problems they were going to work on, and took more time over completing their task. She also found that such students expressed more positive feelings about their work, an important point for school teachers. For it could be argued that fostering a positive attitude to one's own creativity is an essential starting point.

Sternberg and Lubart (1991a) propose an 'investment theory' of creativity which is influential in creativity research internationally. They suggest that it is possible to create, or foster, creativity in children and adults and that this involves teaching them to use the following six resources:

- *Intelligence*. By this they mean problem definition and re-definition, and the ability to think insightfully, i.e. either 'seeing things in a stream of inputs that most people would not see' (p. 609), or 'seeing how to combine disparate pieces of information whose connection is usually non-obvious and usually elusive' (p. 609). Most school situations set up problems as obvious. But encouraging children to identify problems in the first place is an important role of provision in education.
- *Knowledge*. Knowledge of a field is essential in order to be creative within it. It is essential that the knowledge is usable for the pupil. Pupils also need to know *why* they are learning particular knowledge, if they are to use it.
- *Intellectual style*. Here they suggest that the creative individual enjoys seeing things in new ways as well as having the ability to

do so. They call this having a 'legislative proclivity' in 'mental self-government' (p. 611).

- *Personality.* Personality attributes include tolerance for ambiguity, willingness to surmount obstacles and persevere, willingness to grow, willingness to take risks, courage of one's convictions and belief in oneself.
- *Motivation.* Intrinsic motivation is, they propose, important. Extrinsic motivation can even undermine creativity. The motivation to excel is also important.
- *Environmental context.* They suggest that the environment (or classroom) needs to spark creative ideas, encourage follow-up of creative ideas, evaluate and reward creative ideas.

## Overall pedagogic criteria approaches

Based on qualitative research in primary school classrooms, Woods (1990, 1993, 1995) identified four features at work for both pupils and teachers, where creativity was successfully fostered:

- relevance
- ownership
- control
- innovation

Interpreting these, Jeffrey (1997) has suggested that any given situation may offer or demand all or some of these features. For creativity to be fostered, he suggests, there must be 'an innovative idea or approach, some ownership and control over the process by the teacher and the pupil, and the event must be relevant to both teacher and pupil'. From a more philosophical perspective, Sisk (1989) suggests that the overall employment by the teacher of novel strategies, techniques and approaches will enhance creative behaviour in the classroom. The NACCCE Report (1999), suggests that teaching for creativity will encourage:

- autonomy on both sides (here they refer to the work of Woods, discussed above)
- authenticity in iniatives and responses, making decisions for oneself based on one's own judgements
- openness to new ideas and possibilities, including methods and approaches
- respect for others and for their ideas
- fulfilment (for teacher and learner)
- trust, in fostering self-esteem and self-confidence
- independent thought

Faced with this wide variety of approaches to fostering creativity in the classroom, the advice of Perkins (1999) is perhaps apposite. He suggests that teachers need to adopt a pragmatic approach to enabling pupils to construct their own understanding of knowledge which further enables them to express creativity. He urges teachers to consider their repertoire of skills as a 'toolbox', given that no one situation in teaching is ever identical to the next. His advice reminds us of the complex artistry involved in teaching, which has been well documented (Dadds, 1993, 1995; Woods and Jeffrey, 1996; Halliwell, 1993).

It is also worth noting that the emphases in different settings for the early years may vary. As Fontana and Edwards (1985) found, early years practitioners (in this case nursery school teachers) tend to set social expectations for children above other aspects of learning (on the basis that being able to take turns, give and take, and be aware of others is an essential foundation for learning anything else) and to provide a strong physical curriculum. Although the social expectations remain through primary school, certainly that early emphasis on socialization and physical development and exploration does diminish. Clearly the teaching strategies which practitioners use will reflect these different emphases and the extent to which little c creativity, as opposed to a broader view of creativity, is what is being fostered.

## SUMMARY

In this part of the chapter, I have explored some major approaches to stimulating the creativity of the ordinary person in the classroom, which in turn may influence the actual pedagogical approaches used. Drawing on Perkins (1999) I have suggested that the tool-box could be a useful metaphor in adopting strategies in any specific situation or setting. I have also noted the documented contrast in emphasis between pre-school and later school settings.

The discussion in this last section has focused on the creativity of the ordinary person, and drawn on the literature associated with this, but it has not been specifically focused on little c creativity. Perhaps the following four mini-case studies drawn from fieldwork will capture some of the complex pedagogical strategies which could come into play in teaching for little c creativity.

## Case Study 1: Manouella and the hoops

Manouella is leading a music and dance session, with a group of children aged three and four, in a nursery school. She uses hoops during the session, for a number of different imaginary things, including puddles, trays of cakes, and handbags. Using music and song as the backdrop, the children jump into the 'puddles', hold the 'trays' and carry the 'bags'. They do all these things as children, as an old person, and so on, again listening to the mood of the music to help them determine how to move. Later in the morning, Manouella notices some of the same children are playing with their hoop play objects in exactly the same way, in the outdoor play area. Going over to them and bending down, she engages with their play, acknowledging their choice of imaginary object and again using her voice to encourage them to experiment further with direction (high pitch signifying 'up' and low pitch signifying 'down', etc.), tempo, and so on.

## Case Study 2: Rowan and the computer game

Four-year-old Rowan is playing on the computer, whilst his teacher works on the play mat nearby, helping some other boys do some drawing for their personal record books. Rowan completes the game which was on the screen, which is a teddy bear with 'clothes' which need to be placed over the correct part of his body. He looks around at his teacher, and then seeing him occupied, deftly finds the menu screen to select a new game. He seems to be concentrating hard on his task. After a few seconds he succeeds in bringing up a new game, this time involving sorting. His teacher notices what he is doing at this point and comes over. 'Did you manage it all by yourself, Rowan?' he asks, appreciatively. Rowan nods and smiles. But this is a game he is unfamiliar with and he then seems puzzled about what to do next. His teacher asks, 'What do you think you might need to do for this game?' Rowan is unsure, and meanwhile another child from the carpeted area notices and calls out a suggestion. His teacher warmly acknowledges the suggestion, whilst at the same time encouraging Rowan to consider what the game might require. Rowan eventually decides on his own rules for the game which involve putting all of the pieces into the 'rubbish bin'. Although this is not 'officially' the way the game works, Rowan in fact sorts each of the fruits verbally, as he puts them into the bin (i.e. he does each fruit-type in groups). Rather than criticizing this, his teacher praises his idea and his grouping and encourages him to continue to think about how this game works.

## Case study 3: Possibilities and thinking thumbs

A small group of six-year-olds are working with a disparate selection of materials that their teacher has introduced to them. The materials include bread, glue, tissue paper, scissors, water, and card. During the discussion before they start on their own individual projects, their teacher encourages them to explore the properties of each resource, showing that they are thinking by waggling their 'thinking thumbs'. She talks both gently but purposively with the children, trying to maintain a relationship with each as an individual. As the children come up with ideas of how the materials could be used, she uses language carefully to hint that each person will make up their own mind about how to use these materials. 'You might be going to do that' she mentions several times in response to ideas.

## Case Study 4: Stacey's news sheet

Eight-year-old Stacey decides to start a club with her friends, in the playground. Within a few days they have decided that one of their roles is to write up the local news for their school. They go first to their class teacher and then to the head, with their idea, which is encouraged by both. With the help of some external printing resources donated by a parent of another child in their class, the girls create a monthly school news sheet, which they write and edit and distribute to all members of their school community.

I return to some of these mini case studies later in the chapter. For now, I hope that they will have illustrated the importance of close observation of children's engagement with their curriculum. This is a point made by Sheridan (1999) despite, as Hurst (1994) notes, the increasing pressure on time and therefore difficulty in doing so.

They have also, I hope, underlined the importance of relationship and of conversation. This is eloquently portrayed in Tizard and Hughes' ethnographic study of four-year-olds in nursery school and at home (1984), in Paley's study of five-year-old kindergarten children (1981), and emphasized in practical guides such as that by Hughes (2000). The studies by Tizard and Hughes and by Paley focused on children making sense of the world generally and were not specifically exploring the development of children's creativity. However, they highlighted the importance of learner and teacher being in a relationship of some depth, to enable children to bring ideas and knowledge from one context to another, essential in the fostering of creativity.

I would argue that knowing the children and caring about their individuality and agency is an essential foundation for pedagogical strategies which enhance the child's agency.

## Assessing creativity

In the literature very little is written about assessing creativity, although as mentioned earlier, in the field of psychometrics creativity tests, for example, those developed by Torrance (Torrance, 1966, 1974), were historically used. Torrance described four components by which individual creativity could be assessed.

- *fluency*: the ability to produce a large number of ideas
- *flexibility*: the ability to produce a large variety of ideas
- *elaboration*: the ability to develop, embellish, or fill out an idea
- *originality*: the ability to produce ideas that are unusual, statistically infrequent, not banal or obvious

More recently, however, teachers have preferred to use a variety of means to assess creativity, i.e. monitoring pupils' work, behaviour, and what they say (Fryer, 1996).

Some attempts have been made to identify the criteria relevant to the assessment of creativity. Besemer and Treffinger (1981), for example, group these into:

- *novelty*: how new the product is in terms of techniques, processes, concepts; also the capacity of a product to spark further creative products inspired by it; the potential of a product to 'transform', or create a radical shift in approach
- *resolution*: the extent to which a product meets a need, or resolves a situation
- *synthesis*: the extent to which a product combines elements which are unlike, into a coherent whole; thus encompassing criteria such as complexity, elegance, attractiveness, expressiveness, completeness and the quality of its crafting

Others (for example, Jackson and Messick, 1965 and Kneller, 1965) propose 'relevance' or 'appropriateness' as an additional and essential area of criteria. It could be argued that this set of criteria is implicit in the three groups of Besemer and Treffinger, as it would be difficult to imagine how a product could be novel without also being appropriate or relevant.

However, as Fryer (1996) notes, when applying such criteria to the creativity of school pupils, there are some problems with taxonomies. For example, how is novelty to be understood in the context of school pupils? In Fryer's study of 1000 teachers, many suggested they preferred judging pupil's work against each individual's past performance. Thus, something might be deemed to be original for a particular pupil. This is a position which the NACCCE Report also adopted, as discussed earlier (NACCCE, 1999). It raises the question, too, of the locus of judgement. Who is to decide whether something is creative?

Earlier, in Chapter 5, I suggested that for something to be creative, it must demonstrate some sort of originality; but I acknowledged that, in theory, the 'field of judgement' on that originality, could be provided by the agent themselves (and by their peers). So, a child's proposal that the school uniform be abandoned for a day in order to raise money for charity, may be original to them, but not the first time anyone had ever proposed that idea. Are we to say this is original, if to the child and their peers it may be original, but to the world, it is not? And yet, to exclude the child from the assessment of originality would be inconsistent with the concept of little c creativity built up so far, where their awareness of whether something departs from previous expectations is, I have suggested, a necessary part of little c creativity.

Even where the child has an input, however, to the assessment of their own creativity, the purpose of the assessment will determine who else has, and the balance of the adult–child roles. And ultimately, it seems to me that it is the teacher who assumes responsibility for the global assessment of a child's creativity.

Another area of difficulty concerns how comprehensive all criteria for assessing creativity must be. For work which succeeded in satisfying all or most of the criteria would be of a very high standard, with a potential for damaging pupil self-esteem. Fryer recommends that in the case of school pupils' creativity, much less stringent criteria are required, and that self-assessment should be encouraged. I have argued (Craft, 2000), following the same line of less stringent criteria, that the teacher's role is very important too – particularly in the observation and recording of the behaviour of young children, as this helps to highlight what is then novel for the individual child as meaning maker.

A further area of difficulty highlighted by Fryer's study concerns teachers, in terms of the approach which they bring to the definition of creativity as a whole. For example, there are gender differences: female teachers seem to value the personal aspects of creativity more than male teachers who place higher value on the elegance of an outcome, and this affects their judgements of pupil creativity (Fryer, 1996). This finding was also borne out by Stoycheyva's work (1996). In addition, the teacher's subject area has an impact on their confidence as an assessor, for it seems that staff teaching art and design feel most confident about assessing creativity and other teachers are much less so. Stoycheva also found that primary teachers were reluctant to nominate children of either gender as non-original.

The puzzle of how to assess creativity, then, is a taxing one. Another dimension is a concern that where self-expression is involved in creativity (and I have argued in Chapter 6 that it is a significant part of little c creativity), assessment of this for a summative purpose could have an impact on self-esteem. Ultimately, however, whether the assessment is for a formative purpose (i.e. to inform next steps in learning) or a summative one (to assess progress at the end of a specified period) or both, is less significant than the criteria adopted to judge creativity – and the extent to which the pupil shares any understanding of these. Certainly the increased transparency to pupils as to the criteria by which learning outcomes are judged, and the very existence of learning outcomes (in the form of the Early Learning Goals and National Curriculum), provide, in theory, a framework for judging creativity. However, the actual criteria for judging Creative Development are tied to a different definition of creativity from little c creativity, and there are no explicit criteria for assessing creative thinking skills in the National Curriculum, so there is still much work to be done to clarify and develop these.

From the literature, there is some evidence (Spiel and von Korff, 1998) that females mostly associate 'ideas' with creativity, whilst males mainly focus on the aspect of 'novelty'. In addition, males regard the concept of 'fantasy' as important in creativity, and females frequently describe creativity by what it is not. Fryer's (1996) large-scale study of teachers in primary, secondary, and further education suggested that male teachers were far more inclined to view creativity in terms of the product's 'elegance', as noted above, and by the critical thinking involved in its conception and evolution, assessing a product's creativity *per se*, rather than seeing it as a product of experience. By contrast, women teachers were far more likely to see creativity in terms of depth of thought, depth of feeling, originality, and experience. To what extent these findings are directly relevant to teachers and other practitioners in the early years is not clear; but this gender difference, which has been identified in the literature, highlights the need for careful attention to be given to the development of criteria for judging creativity.

On the other hand, assessment can become over-burdensome. It has been argued that the relationship between bureaucratic arrangements for the quality assurance of teaching and learning, including subject-centred level grading of achievements of both teachers and pupils, and the fostering of creativity, needs examination. Some have argued (Jeffrey and Woods, 1998; Woods et al., 1997; Woods and Jeffrey, 1996) through the use of empirical studies, that such arrangements have led to the diminution of creativity in education.

Ultimately, though, if we are keen to encourage young children's little c creativity, their agency, and their possibility thinking, we need to identify manageable and transparent criteria for assessing this. For, as Drummond and Nutbrown (1996) argue, about assessing young children's learning: 'Through assessment we can distinguish what is unique and particular about a particular child: this distinction will make it possible for us to support each child's individual growth, as a learner and as a person' (p. 106).

I want to suggest that assessing young children's little c creativity must stem from a foundation of understanding of what children can understand and do, and how, since observing children carefully provides a foundation for knowing each child better. As Drummond and Nutbrown (1996) note, observation and assessment are very close. They reveal the uniqueness of each individual child and enable us to support next stages in learning, as long as we know what it is we are observing.

I want to illustrate the importance of relationship and observation in assessment by returning briefly to two of the case studies introduced earlier.

### Manouella and the hoops

Manouella engaged in many small conversations with individuals in her group of three-and four-year-olds, as they pretended the hoops were different everyday objects. She connected the children's responses with her knowledge of them, their interests and their lives, in a warm and acknowledging way. The children each visibly glowed each time she engaged in one of these conversations. Therefore she knew that for one child, discussing the fragile nature of the cakes on his 'tray' and altering the tone of the tune she played on her accordian would inspire him to step more carefully and with more awareness of the sound around him, as he held it. By contrast, she also knew that for another, visualizing the cakes and comparing them to those she had baked for a family birthday party a few days previously, combined with a quiet 'happy birthday' tune, would help her to enter the imaginary world. In both cases, Manouella succeeded in bringing the children through imagination and listening to an awareness of rhythm and melody. She brought in what she knew of the children previously, and drew on this knowledge with her observations of their behaviours during the lesson to inform her interventions – and whilst making it clear to the children that she was wanting them to match their body movements with the sounds that she was playing.

**Rowan and the computer**

In the case of Rowan and the computer, his teacher judged what was new for Rowan (i.e. finding his way to a new game and then working out what it might involve), on the basis of his past knowledge and existing relationship with him. He noted that Rowan had worked out how to find a new game and engaged with him from there. His interventions made explicit that he was assessing, or evaluating, Rowan's ability to try out his own ideas about how the computer game worked. He gave Rowan adequate space to try the ideas out himself, as Rowan chose not to take up offers from the other boys around him or from his teacher. He joined him towards the end of the first game to point out that what Rowan had done was to sort the fruits in groups, which was the aim of the game, although he had done it in a different way to that intended. His feedback to Rowan offered explicit acknowledgement and appreciation of his creative action.

These two case studies may also serve to illustrate the significance of seeing the child's perspective, too.

## CONCLUSION

In this chapter I have explored the interaction between creative teaching and teaching for creativity, suggesting the former is not necessary for the latter but may be involved in it. I have discussed a range of pedagogical strategies for fostering creativity, which are associated with specific underpinning theoretical positions, and have given case-studies of these. Finally, I have explored issues in assessing creativity, noting that the locus of assessment must involve child and teacher dimensions, and that the definition of criteria, is both challenging and essential. I discussed some gender issues in the development of criteria but nevertheless proposed that observation and assessment are necessary to fostering the little c creativity of each individual learner.

In the next chapter, the perspective shifts to the sorts of continuing professional development which may be appropriate to supporting early years practitioners in enabling children's creativity.

## References

Angeloska-Galevska, N. (1996) 'Children's creativity in the preschool institutions in Macedonia', in *Childhood Education: International Perspectives* (Research Report). New Zealand.

Bachelor, P. A. and Michael, W. B. (1997) 'The structure-of-intellect model revisited', in M. A. Runco (ed.), *The Creativity Research Handbook* vol. 1. Cresskill, NJ: Hampton Press.

Balke, E. (1997) 'Play and the arts: the importance of the "unimportant"'. *Childhood Education*, 73(6), 355–60.

Beetlestone, F. (1998) *Learning in the Early Years: Creative Development*. Leamington Spa: Scholastic.

Bennett, N. Wood, L. and Rogers, S. (1997) *Teaching Through Play: Teachers' Thinking and Classroom Practice*. Buckingham: Open University Press.

Besemer, S. P. and Treffinger, D. J. (1981) 'Analysis of creative products: review and synthesis'. *The Journal of Creative Behavior*, 15(3), 158–77.

Bruce, T. (1991) *Time to Play in Early Childhood Education*. London: Hodder & Stoughton.

Bruce, T. (1994) 'Play, the Universe and Everything!' in J. R. Moyles (ed.) (1994), *The Excellence of Play*. Buckingham: Open University Press.

Bruner, J. (1978) *The Process of Education*. Cambridge, MA: Harvard University Press.

Craft, A. (2000) *Creativity Across the Primary Curriculum*. London: Routledge.

Dadds, M. (1993) 'The feeling of thinking in professional self-study' *Educational Action Research*, 1(2), 287–303.

Dadds, M. (1995) 'Continuing professional development: nurturing the expert within'. *Cambridge Institute of Education Newsletter*, 30, Autumn/Winter.

Dearden, R. F. (1968) *The Philosophy of Primary Education*. London: Routledge & Kegan Paul.

De Bono, E. (1993) *Six Thinking Hats*. London: Penguin.

Drummond, M. J. and Nutbrown, C. (1996) 'Observing and assessing young children', in G. Pugh (ed.), *Contemporary Issues in the Early Years: Working Collaboratively for Children*, 2nd edn. London: Paul Chapman Publishing Ltd.

Edwards, C. P. Springate, K. W. (1995) *Encouraging Creativity in Early Childhood Classrooms*, ERIC Digest. Washington, D. C: Office of Educational Research and Improvement (ED).

Einon, D. (1986) *Creative Play*. London: Penguin Books.

Fisher, E. P. (1992), 'The impact of play on development: a meta-analysis', *Play and Culture*, 5(2), 159–81.

Fontana, D. and Edwards, A. (1985) 'Teachers' perceptions of socio-economic development in nursery school children'. *The Durham and Newcastle Research Review*, October, 239–42.

Fryer, M. (1996), *Creative Teaching and Learning*. London: Paul Chapman Publishing Ltd.

Greenberg, E. (1992) 'Creativity, autonomy and evaluation of creative work: artistic workers in organizations'. *Journal of Creative Behavior*, 26(2), 75–80.

Griffiths, R. (1994) 'Mathematics and play', in J. R. Moyles (ed.) (1994) *The Excellence of Play*. Buckingham: Open University Press.

Guilford, J. P. (1973) *Characteristics of Creativity*. Springfield, IL: Illinois State Office of the Superintendent of Public Instruction, Gifted Children Section.

Halliwell, S. (1993), 'Teacher creativity and teacher education', in D. Bridges and T. Kerry (eds) (1993) *Developing Teachers Professionally*. London and New York: Routledge.

Hughes, P. (2000) *Principles of Primary Education Study Guide*. London: David Fulton Publishers Ltd.

Hurst, V. (1994) 'Observing play in early childhood', in J. R. Moyles (ed.) (1994), *The Excellence of Play*. Buckingham: Open University Press.

Hutt, C. (1979) 'Play in the under 5s; form, development and function,' in J. G. Howells (ed.), *Modern Perspectives in the Psychiatry of Infancy*. New York: Brunner/Marcel.

Jackson, P. W. and Messick, S. (1965) 'The person, the product and the response: conceptual problems in the assessment of creativity'. *Journal of Personality*, **33**, 1–19.

Jeffrey, B. (1997) 'Framing creativity in primary classrooms', in A. Craft, with J. Dugal, G. Dyer, B. Jeffrey and T. Lyons, *Can You Teach Creativity?* Nottingham: Education Now.

Jeffrey, B. and Woods, P. (1998) *Testing Teacher: The Effect of School Inspections on Primary Teachers*. London: Falmer.

Kessler, R. (2000) *The Soul of Education: Helping Students Find Connection, Compassion and Character at School*. Alexandria, Virginia: Association for Supervision and Curriculum Development.

Kneller, G. F. (1965) *The Art and Science of Creativity*. New York: Holt, Rinehart and Winston.

McCaldon, S. (1991) *In the Olden Days, in Play in the Primary Curriculum*. London: Hodder & Stoughton.

Meek, M. (1985) 'Play and paradoxes: some considerations of imagination and language', in G. Wells and J. Nicholls (eds), *Language and Learning: An Interactional Perspective*. Lewes: Falmer Press.

Moyles, J. R. (1989) *Just Playing? The Role and Status of Play in Early Childhood Education*. Buckingham: Open University Press.

Moyles, J. R. (ed.), (1994) *The Excellence of Play*. Buckingham: Open University Press.

National Advisory Committee on Creative and Cultural Education (NACCCE) (1999) *All Our Futures: Creativity, Culture and Education*. London: Department for Education and Employment.

Opie, I. and Opie. P. (1959) *The Lore and Language of Schoolchildren*. Oxford: Clarendon Press.

Paley, V. G. (1981) *Wally's Stories: Conversations in the Kindergarten*. Cambridge, MA: Harvard University Press.

Perkins, D. (1999) 'The many faces of constructivism'. *Educational Leadership*, **57**(3), 6–11.

Shagoury-Hubbard, R. (1996) *Workshop of the Possible: Nurturing Children's Creative Development*. York, Maine: Stenhouse Publishers.

Shallcross, D. J. (1981) *Teaching Creative Behaviour: How to Teach Creativity in Children of All Ages*. Englewood Cliffs, NJ: Prentice-Hall.

Sheridan, M. D. (1999) *Play in Early Childhood: from Birth to Six Years*. 2nd edn. London and New York: Routledge (Revised and updated by Jackie Harding and Liz Meldon Smith).

Sisk, D. A. (1989) 'Creativity: potential and progress'. Paper presented at the Suncoast Music Education Forum, Florida.

Spiel, C. and von Korff (1998) 'Implicit theories of creativity: the conceptions of politicians, scientists, artists and school teachers'. *Journal of High Ability Studies*. **9**(1), 43–58.

Sternberg, R. J. and Lubart, T. L. (1991a) 'An investment theory of creativity and its development'. *Human Development*, **34**, 1–31.

Sternberg, R. J. and Lubart, T. L. (1991b) 'Creating Creative Minds', in *Phi Delta Kappan*, April, 608–614.

Storr, A. (1972) *The Dynamics of Creation*. London: Secker and Warburg.

Stoycheva, K. (1996) 'The school: a place for children's creativity?' Paper Presented at the 5th ECHA (European Council for High Ability) Conference (Vienna, Austria, October 19–22).

Tizard, B and Hughes, M (1984) *Young Children Learning: Talking and Thinking at Home and at School*. London: Fontana Paperbacks.

Torrance, E. P. (1966) *Torrance Tests of Creativity*. Princeton: Personnel Press.

Torrance, E. P. (1974) *Torrance Tests of Creative Thinking*. Lexington, MA: Ginn & Company (Xerox Corporation).

Torrance, E. P. (1984) *Mentor Relationships: How they Aid Creative Achievement, Endure, Change and Die*. Buffalo, NY: Bearly.

Vygotsky, L. (1978) *Mind in Society*, trans. and ed. M. Cole, C. John-Steiner, S. Scribner and E. Souberman. Cambridge, MA: Harvard University Press.

Wallas, G. (1926) *The Art of Thought*. New York, NY: Hartcourt Brace.

Warnock, M. (1994) *Imagination and Time*. Oxford: Blackwell.

Wood, E. and Atfield, J. (1996) *Play, Learning and the Early Childhood Curriculum*. London: Paul Chapman Publishing.

Woods, P. (1990) *Teacher Skills and Strategies*. Lewes: Falmer.

Woods, P. (1993) *Critical Events in Teaching and Learning*. London: Falmer Press.

Woods, P. (1995) *Creative Teachers in Primary Schools*. Buckingham: The Open University Press.

Woods, P. and Jeffrey, B. (1996) *Teachable Moments: The Art of Teaching in Primary Schools*. Buckingham: Open University Press.

Woods, P., Jeffrey, B., Troman, G. and Boyle, M. (1997) *Restructuring Schools, Restructuring Teachers: Responding to Change in the Primary School*. Buckinghamshire: Open University Press.

# CHAPTER 11

## Nourishing the early years practitioner

*In this chapter, I focus on the nourishment of the educator as a facilitator of creativity in children. Reviewing research on teacher identity, I discuss some features of continuing professional development (CPD) for creativity. Drawing on an earlier research project (Craft, 1996, 1997), I propose principles for nourishing the early years practitioner with respect to little c creativity.*

### Introduction

People who work with young children traditionally have a strong social/caring orientation, as observational studies of teachers in particular have demonstrated (Acker, 1995; Woods, 1990, 1993, 1995; Woods and Jeffrey, 1996; Pollard, 1987, 1990; Nias, 1989). Studies demonstrate that teachers are often very hard working and very busy (Nias, 1989, Fryer and Collings, 1991, Craft, 1996), and the feeling of 'being there' for the children, of the teacher's own needs as irrelevant except insofar as they directly relate to the perceived needs of the children, is very common and can sometimes manifest itself as feelings of guilt (Hargreaves and Tucker, 1991). The professional identity of early years teachers has been described by Siraj-Blatchford (drawing on Cowley, 1991, Bruce, 1987, DES, 1990, Grieve and Hughes, 1990), as being strongly rooted in a concern for the social, emotional, and physical development of children, 'as children's cognitive development is seen in a holistic context' (Siraj-Blatchford, 1993). This may have been eroded to some extent by the curriculum reforms affecting infant and junior education at the start of the 1990s, when teachers were found to be under severe pressure with working hours increasing, a reduction in the amount of time spent with pupils and a wider variation in teacher commitment or alleged 'conscientiousness' (Campbell, et al. 1992). However, despite further and massive reforms during the

1990s and at the start of the twenty-first century, the professional identity of early years practitioners has probably continued intact.

Knowing oneself as a professional educator can be challenging. It can mean acknowledging personal feelings in professional life and development, and allowing a connection between self-study and self-esteem. As Marian Dadds (1993, 1995) notes of teacher development, exploring professional work may mean close scrutiny of aspects of daily life which run close to one's heart. Her contention is that the more closely identified a teacher is with their work, the more likely it is that their feelings will be deeply implicated. Teachers involved in a small, recent study of teachers and teacher advisers in London and the Home Counties (Craft, 1996) said they felt that knowing oneself was difficult, since their role as a teacher was to provide, and they tended to think of their own needs as unimportant in that situation.

I would argue that knowing and nourishing oneself as an educator in any domain is critical to being able to provide for others. This is because genuine relationship, with oneself and with others, is at the heart of the teaching and learning process. Choosing continuing professional (and personal) development which does nourish us as people, then, I suggest, is fundamental to nourishing learning in others (including, of course, the fostering of learner creativity), and it applies whether the practitioner is a childminder, a nursery worker, a teaching assistant, a teacher, a playgroup leader, parent or other carer.

## Nourishing the practitioner

Teaching creatively can often be nourishing in itself. In *The Very Hungry Caterpillar* example given in Chapter 10, this was one of a number of interactive displays in the teacher's classroom, on which she prided herself. She was clearly as stimulated by the planning and creating of the display as she was by observing the ways in which children then engaged with it. The processes involved in making, learning, stimulating, and generating interest and excitement may harness a life-giving energy for the teacher as well as for pupils, in part through the dynamic interaction of the relationships between children, children and teacher, and children and resources such as this one.

Nevertheless, creative teaching can also be exhausting for the teacher. As Selleck and Griffin (1996) have said, 'Educators must ... be responsible for their own psychological welfare ... The demands of children and of parents can drain the emotional and physical resources of the [teachers]' (p. 168) The practitioner needs nourishment in order to both teach for creativity and to teach creatively; and nourishment will ideally include both personal and professional development, which in practice often overlap, although the focus in this chapter is on the professional practice end and continuing professional development (CPD).

As argued elsewhere (Craft, 2000), it seems to me that on one level, there is no reason why forms of CPD that are likely to foster creativity should be any different from other forms of CPD. In a different book, I note that conventional methods include:

- action-research
- self-directed study
- using distance learning materials
- receiving on the job coaching, mentoring, or tutoring
- school-based and off-site courses of various lengths
- job-shadowing and rotation
- membership of a working party or task group
- teacher placement
- personal reflection
- experiential 'assignments'
- collaborative learning
- information-technology mediated learning (e.g. through e-mail discussion groups, or self-study using multi-media resources) (Craft, 2001, pp. 10–11)

However, one may also argue that CPD, which is specially designed to nourish teachers' creativity as practitioners, and their ability to stimulate learner creativity, will be distinct from other CPD in three major ways:

1. Feedback will play a major part, meaning that the teacher is in relationship with others, giving and receiving feedback, exploring the interpersonal dynamics of encouraging or limiting creativity in others.
2. Opportunities for accessing the non-conscious for both teachers and learners will be both encouraged and stimulated.
3. The CPD needs to be positively chosen by the individual concerned – constructing the appropriate and unique profile of CPD to meet their particular needs and interests. As I have argued elsewhere (Craft, 2001), individuals are each attracted to their own unique profile of forms of CPD. There is no 'correct' CPD profile, just as there is no one 'right way' to teach; professional artistry and personal style are influential and necessary elements in the mix, affecting the shape of the outcome.

Early years practitioners have long recognized the need for CPD in general, supporting the principles of child-centred learning practices which are built on child development foundations, as documented by Siraj-Blatchford (1993), although there may sometimes be obstacles to professional growth, as Ebbeck (1990) has noted. These may include:

- job security
- support from the employing body
- stability and continuity in the practitioner's work situation
- sufficient time to do the job satisfactorily
- adequate autonomy in carrying out the job

Given the wide diversity in context and staffing for the education of children aged two-and-a-half to eight, it is difficult to generalize, although I attempt to do so in this chapter. In terms of creativity in first and primary schools specifically, Woods (1995) has documented similar practical questions about teachers being sufficiently nourished to foster pupil creativity, and his ethnographic studies have highlighted practitioners' concerns about:

- legitimation (within the curriculum structure)
- resourcing (time, materials, equipment, energy)
- support (colleagues, critical agent, critical others, receptive pupil culture)

But as suggested above, there are exceptions, such as the teachers involved in the recent project focusing on creativity and teacher development mentioned earlier (Craft, 1996, 1997). The educators in that study (including those working in the early years) began instead from a position of belief in 'creativity as a good thing', regardless of these contextual influences.

But as indicated in the introduction, taking time for personal nourishment does not come easily to teachers as a group. Hard-working, caring, conscientious, and self-effacing in many ways, teachers and carers tend to put the needs of learners ahead of their own wants. In the CPD study by Craft (1996, 1997), there was much evidence of personal and/or professional change having moved individuals to take this particular course on creativity; over half of the group of eighteen had experienced some kind of 'critical incident' which had influenced their choice to be part of the study and to emphasize creativity in their practice. These critical incidents included negative professional experiences such as:

- bad experiences of OFSTED
- a desire to increase personal creativity through initiating specific events or projects or through peer supervision and feedback

- reaching a critical point of frustration with the declining emphasis on teaching as artistry in favour of a technician approach

Critical incidents also included personal events, such as changes in home circumstances, or the recent and sudden recognition of long-lost dreams or hobbies.

The project, which involved the teachers concerned in the study of a Master's level course on creativity, investigated what those teachers found nourishing in the course. First, understandably, was the experience of being involved in the project itself, which offered teachers emotional support, being part of a student network, getting feedback on their skills and general personal presentation (written and oral) away from but linked with their normal teaching and learning situation, and the challenge of studying at MA level. But there were other findings, too. For some, working in a supportive atmosphere was central. For others, it was out-of-school activities which nourished them; these included travelling, dressmaking, going to the theatre, listening to live and recorded music, seeing friends, sport, reading.

For these educators, discovering what they felt would be nourishing to their professional role often involved taking some risks. For example, risking unexpected discoveries which might prove challenging to accommodate. Engagement with risk was both challenging and nourishing for this group, perhaps because through risk comes inevitable change, and change is, it could be argued, at the core of growth and development – indeed of creativity itself.

## Possible principles for CPD to foster creativity

In the study briefly referred to above (Craft, 1996, 1997), some themes emerged around how creativity was understood and experienced by the group. These could perhaps be seen as principles relevant to the in-service education of all early years practitioners, or indeed, of CPD generally. There were five broad themes, as follows:

### 1. Openness

This is the belief that creativity involves a personal 'receptivity' or 'openness' to a wide range of influences, including spiritual and intuitive ones. This belief echoes points made by Fritz (1943) about having vision and then allowing ideas to 'germinate' and 'assimilate', and by Gardner (1993b, 1999) about valuing creativity across the different intelligences. It also echoes the writing of Csikszentmihalyi (1994) in which he reports that artists with whom he worked demonstrated openness to experiences and impulses, and Gardner's (1993a) discussion of great creators.

Personal nourishment involves the same quality of openness, or receptivity. An infant teacher in the study (Craft, 1996, 1997) described how at the time in his life when he got married, he was somehow able to be receptive to lots of impulses and ideas. This led to a huge class-based project with the infant children he was teaching. The act of being open, which originated in his personal life, nourished his unconsious self in enabling a new idea to grow and be implemented in school.

## 2. Releasing the unconscious
Several practical strategies emerged from the study, in relation to 'releasing the unconscious', for the educators concerned. They included:

- *looking at their 'reflection'*, i.e. noticing what they valued in their pedagogy as regards creativity, for it usually reflected what they themselves valued, wanted or needed
- *giving themselves space*, i.e. enabling both conscious and non-conscious ideas to be synthesized by 'listening' to dreams and daydreams
- *remembering dreams*, i.e. noticing how the unconscious likes to be nourished, by interpreting the symbolic messages in dreams.
- *imaging and visualization*, i.e. drawing on the metaphors which the unconscious constructs. As Jung observed (1995), the symbolic forms of dreams are generally drawn from waking life.

## 3. Self-esteem and vision
This is the belief that self-esteem and self-confidence must be nourished, in teachers as well as learners, in order to be creative. Concern with esteem reflects the social and caring orientation typical of educators, as others have documented (Collings, 1978, Fryer and Collings, 1991, Acker, 1995, Hargreaves and Tucker, 1991, Hargreaves 1994).

## 4. Working with others, but with some professional autonomy
This refers the need to feel comfortable with one's own professional artistry, to be able to be oneself rather than playing a role ascribed by others. However, this needs to be balanced with working with others, for collaboration is a key aspect of teaching, at every level in education. Relating, and relationship, with colleagues and with children, are central to all that happens. The need for adequate professional space to do the job was also cited by Ebbeck (1990) as highly valued by early

years practitioners. Some early years teachers are faced with the particular challenge of isolation from others (Selleck and Griffin, 1996), and thus for some, opportunities to connect with colleagues can be a significant aspect of self-nourishment.

## 5. Relationship
Many referred to creativity as 'being in relationship', suggesting that dynamic interaction, with oneself or others or both, is essential to creativity. Implicit in all of the references to 'relationship' was this sentiment expressed by one of the group: 'through the right kind of relationships that teachers have with people, they will liberate the creativity that their students have'. This emphasis reflects the focus and findings of much literature researching teachers' work (Woods, 1990, Woods, 1995, Woods and Jeffrey, 1996, Cooper and McIntyre, 1996a, 1996b). The importance of 'relationship' to learners is also well documented, both in terms of relationships between learners and in their relationships with educators (Cleave et al., 1982, Cullingford, 1991, Delamont and Galton, 1987, Jackson, 1987, Pollard, 1987, Sluckin, 1987). Recent work exploring the perspectives of children also bears this out (Jeffrey and Woods, 1997, Jeffrey, 2001).

The particular study from which these early years CPD principles for creativity are drawn was not purely focused on early years practitioners, and it centred on a particular MA course of study, for which the practitioners had enrolled. So the positive attitude towards self-nourishment and the emphasis on the non-conscious that emerged from it may not be replicated elsewhere, although there is some consonance with others' work (e.g. Gardner, 1993a). It was also a small study which may also militate against replication. However, it focused on the development of little c creativity and is cited as an example of some of the possible principles around which CPD in this area could perhaps be structured. A significant challenge in CPD for little c creativity, lies in addressing what it means to be little c creative, in both one's own life and in terms of young children's learning, given the distinct positioning of little c creativity as a concept.

## CONCLUSION
The importance of nourishing the educator appropriately has been proposed as fundamental to the fostering of children's little c creativity. Positioned within a literature on educator identity which suggests a caring orientation and perhaps resistance to nourishing the self (certainly an unfamiliarity with what one might need for oneself), it has examined some of the potential

barriers to nourishing the educator. These include particular factors relevant to the working conditions of the diverse body of early years practitioners (Ebbeck, 1990), including job security, support from the employing body, stability and continuity in the practitioner's work situation, and sufficient time to do the job satisfactorily. The chapter has laid out some methods of CPD, and some proposed features of CPD for fostering little c creativity, i.e. the need for feedback, accessing the non-conscious, and the exercise of individual choice in opting-in to the CPD. Drawing on themes identified in an earlier study which explored educator nourishment for fostering little c creativity (Craft, 1996, 1997), the chapter laid out (tentatively, given a number of limitations to the earlier study), several possible principles for nourishing early years practitioners in fostering little c creativity. These principles offer a possible framework for understanding the nature of little c creativity as well as strategies for putting it into practice, given that the concept is distinct from other concepts of creativity, and involve openness, releasing the unconscious, self-esteem, and vision, working with others but with autonomy, and relationship.

The final chapter of this book examines organizational and systemic issues, asking what kinds of wider systems would be most effective in the fostering of little c creativity in the early years.

## References

Acker, S. (1995) 'Carry on caring: the work of women teachers'. *British Journal of Sociology of Education*, **16**(1), 21–36.

Bruce, T. (1987) *Early Childhood Education*. London: Hodder & Stoughton.

Campbell, R. J., Evans, L., Neill, S. and Packwood, A. (1992) 'The Changing Work of Infant Teachers: Some Policy Issues'. *British Journal of Educational Studies*.

Cleave, S. Jowett, S. and Bate, M. (1982) *And So To School: A Study of Continuity from Pre-school to Infant School*. Windsor, Berks: NFER-Nelson.

Collings, J. A. (1978) 'A Psychological study of female specialists in the sixth form'. Unpublished PhD thesis, University of Bradford.

Cooper, P. and McIntyre, D. (1996a) *Effective Teaching and Learning: Teachers' and Pupils Perspectives*. Buckingham: Open University Press.

Cooper, P. and McIntyre, D. (1996b) 'The importance of power sharing in classroom learning', in Hughes, M. (ed.), *Teaching and Learning in Changing Times*, pp. 88–108. Oxford: Blackwell.

Cowley, L. (1991) *Young Children in Group Daycare: Guidelines for Good Practice*. London: National Children's Bureau.

Craft, A. (1996) 'Nourishing educator creativity: a holistic approach to CPD'. *British Journal of Inservice Education*, **22**(3), 309–22.

Craft, A. (1997) 'Identity and creativity: educating teachers for post-modernism?' *Teacher Development: An International Journal of Teachers' Professional Development*, May **1**, 83–96.

Craft, A. (2000) *Creativity Across the Primary Curriculum*. London: Routledge.

Craft, A. (2001) *Continuing Professional Development: A Practical Guide for Teachers and Schools*. London: Routledge.

Cullingford, C. (1991) *The Inner World of the School*. London: Cassell Educational Ltd.

Csikszentmihalyi, M. (1994) 'The Domain of Creativity', in D. H. Feldman, M. Csikszentmihalyi, and H. Gardner, *Changing the World: A Framework for the Study of Creativity*. Westport, CT: Praeger Publishers.

Dadds, M. (1993) 'The feeling of thinking in professional self-study'. *Educational Action Research*, **1**(2), 287–303.

Dadds, M. (1995) 'Continuing professional development: nurturing the expert within'. *Cambridge Institute of Education Newsletter*, **30** (Autumn/Winter).

Delamont, S. and Galton, M. (1987) 'Anxieties and anticipations – pupils' views of transfer to secondary school', in A. Pollard (ed.), *Children and Their Primary Schools*. P. London: Falmer Press.

Department of Education and Science (1990) *Starting with Quality (Rumbold Report)*. London: HMSO.

Ebbeck, M. (1990) 'Professional Development of Early Years Teachers'. *Early Child Development and Care*, **58**.

Fritz, R. (1943) *The Path of Least Resistance*. Salem, MA: Stillpoint.

Fryer, M. and Collings, J. A. (1991) 'Teachers' views about creativity'. *British Journal of Educational Psychology*, **61**, 207–19.

Gardner, H. (1993a) *Creating Minds: An Anatomy of Creativity seen through the Lives of Freud, Einstein, Picasso, Stravinsky, Eliot, Graham and Gandhi*. New York: Harper-Collins Inc.

Gardner, H. (1993b) *Multiple Intelligences: the Theory in Practice*. New York: Harper-Collins Inc.

Gardner, H. (1999) *Intelligence Reframed: Multiple Intelligences for the 21st Century*. New York: Basic Books.

Grieve, R. and Hughes, M. (eds.) (1990) *Understanding Children*. Oxford: Basil Blackwell.

Hargreaves, A. (1994) *Changing Teachers, Changing Times: Teachers' Work in the Post-modern Age*. London: Cassell.

Hargreaves, A. and Tucker, E. (1991) 'Teaching and guilt: exploring the feelings of teaching'. *Teaching and Teacher Education*, **7**(5/6), 491–505.

Jackson, M. (1987) 'Making sense of school', in A. Pollard (ed.), *Children and Their Primary Schools*. London: Falmer Press.

Jeffrey, B. (2001) 'Primary Pupils' Perspectives and Creative Learning', *Encyclopaideia Volume 9*, Spring 2001 (Italian Journal).

Jeffrey, B. and Woods, P. (1997) 'The relevance of creative teaching: pupils' views' in A. Pollard, D. Thiessen, and A. Filer (eds) (1997) *Children and their Curriculum: The Perspectives of Primary and Elementary School Children*. London: Falmer.

Jung, C. J. (1995) *Memories, Dreams and Reflections* (recorded and edited by Aniela Jaffe, trans. from the German by Richard and Clara Winston). London: Fontana Press. (Originally published in German under the title of *Erinnerungen, Tauma, Gedanken*, copyright held by Random House Inc. 1961.)

Nias, J. (1989) *Primary Teachers Talking*. London: Routledge & Kegan Paul.

Pollard, A. (1987) 'Goodies, jokers and gangs', in A. Pollard (1987) *Children and Their Primary Schools*. London: Falmer Press.

Pollard, A. (1990) *Learning in Primary Schools*. London: Cassell.

Selleck, D. and Griffin, S. (1996) 'Quality for the under threes', in S. Pugh (ed.) (1996) *Contemporary Issues in the Early Years: Working Collaboratively for Children*, 2nd edn. London: Paul Chapman Press (in association with the National Children's Bureau).

Siraj-Blatchford, I. (1993) 'Professional identity of early years teachers', in P. Gammage, and J. Meighan (eds) (1993) *Early Childhood Education: Taking Stock*. Nottingham: Education Now.

Sluckin, A. (1987) 'The culture of the primary school playground', in A. Pollard (ed.) *Children and their Primary Schools*. London: Falmer.

Woods, P. (1990) *Teacher Skills and Strategies*. Basingstoke: The Falmer Press.

Woods, P. (1993) *Critical Events in Teaching and Learning*. London: Falmer Press.

Woods, P. (1995) *Creative Teachers in Primary Schools*. Buckingham: The Open University Press.

Woods, P. and Jeffrey, R. (1996) *Teachable Moments*. Buckingham: Open University Press.

# CHAPTER 12

# Overall provision in early years education and the fostering of little c creativity

*This chapter briefly sums up the overall argument of the book, and explores some principles for designing educational and care systems which value the nurturing of children's little c creativity.*

## Introduction

Throughout this book as a whole, I have argued for the development of little c creativity as a desirable aspect of learning in early childhood. I have positioned the concept as distinct from the Plowden notion of creativity, and also distinct from the pushes towards creativity in the formal curricula applied to children from three to eight, from the end of the 1990s onward. I have suggested that it involves intelligence, imagination, and aspects of self-creation and self-expression. These are combined together into what I have called 'possibility thinking' which sits at the core of little c creativity. In Part Three, I have explored curriculum, pedagogy, and assessment issues in relation to little c creativity, and also the professional development of the practitioner. In this final chapter, I look more globally at early years provision and ask what sorts of systems might best foster little c creativity.

At the time of writing (November, 2001), children from age three to rising five can experience an enormous range of possible pre-school provision. This includes being cared for by parents, close relatives or friends, nannies, or childminders; and being looked after in daycare, or attending a playgroup, nursery school, or a nursery class in a school. Integrated care, health and education centres – early excellence centres – are in the process of being introduced in some places, but these are still relatively few and far between. Most children from the age of rising five will be in either infant, first school, or junior and infant mixed, school-based provision. The continuities of care and education are being developed for the under-fives, but not in any sort of coherent way for those of five and over.

The questions underlying this final chapter are.

- What are the implications of these forms of provision for fostering little c creativity in young children?
- What forms of provision could be appropriate to fostering little c creativity in the early years?

## The current provision: implications for little c creativity

A central feature of the current mix of educare provision for the pre-school child is its patchiness in emphasis, quality and style, and this was one of the foci of the Rumbold enquiry into education provision for three to four year olds (DES, 1990). There is a huge variety, as the RSA's *Start Right* project noted (Ball, 1994), in the physical premises and equipment utilized, in lines of responsibility, in planning, assessment and recordkeeping, in forms of partnership with parents, in getting the 'high-challenge, low-threat' equation right, in the training of providers, and in many other aspects of early childhood educare. The following case study drawn from my experience may illustrate what this varied provision means, early in the twenty-first century, over ten years on from the publication of the Rumbold Report, for the development of little c creativity.

Jamie, Joshua, Claire and Sam were all born on the same day and lived initially within half-a-mile of one another. Their mothers became friends through ante-natal classes and have remained so until now (the children are each now three-and-a-half). Each mother, having had a career before becoming a parent, and anxious to retain their work identity alongside motherhood, returned to work, each of them part-time. They each chose different forms of care. From two and a half, the children were in a mix of care and education, each one unique, and by the age of three, the children were in the following contexts.

Jamie: went to a private daycare nursery, a short drive away from his home, for three days a week, 8 a.m. – 6 p.m., with his little sister. He was withdrawn for short periods each day for pre-school activities around the Early Learning Goals, with other children of his age. For the other four days of the week, he was looked after at home with his sister, by his parents, although as his father worked very long hours, he generally saw more of his mother.

Joshua: was looked after four days a week with his little sister, by a nanny, 8.30 a.m.–7 p.m. He also attended a morning playgroup from 9.30–12.00 five days a week. In the upstairs room of a church, the playgroup offered play opportunities and daily structured activities around the Early Learning Goals. The rest of the week, his parents cared for him and his little sister.

Claire: attended a highly structured private nursery school for one full day (9.30–4 p.m.) and three afternoons a week (1.15–4 p.m.), and at three-and-a-half is on the verge of reading and writing. She also attended a private daycare nursery near her mother's office, one full day per week. She was one of two older children in that nursery, and the two girls were withdrawn for part of the day for extension activities, including French.

Sam: attended a childminder three days a week, 8 a.m.–6 p.m., along with three other children, and at age three and three quarters he was scheduled to start at a nursery attached to an infant school, five afternoons a week (1.15–3.15). For the other four days of the week, his parents shared his care. There were no 'formal' curricula in either setting.

In terms of little c creativity, these contexts each offered different opportunities for the children. Thus, whereas Jamie's daycare nursery offered him plenty of possibilities for exploring his own agency through play and particularly through messy play, the time spent at home excluded any opportunities to make a mess indoors. His mother valued the development of his social skills and made much of visiting other families and having other children to play, but laid little emphasis on Jamie starting to make his own choices, preferring to circumscribe these herself.

Joshua by contrast was offered many opportunities in his playgroup to develop little c creativity, in many contexts. The staff prided themselves on knowing the children personally and in supporting their development and their interests. When Joshua became very interested in space, the planets and stars, the staff found ways of helping him to learn more about these using resources available in the playgroup. His love of the cartoon character 'Buzz Lightyear', became a context for exploring materials and physical resources in the room. The sand tray became a space scene, and the playdough provided a means for making aliens for Buzz's adventures. For Joshua there was little difference in the valuing of little c creativity when he was being looked after by his nanny or his parents, as all of these other adults valued highly his interests and opinions. Each one, in their different way, encouraged him to find out, to make choices and to exercise agency. Perhaps as a consequence, he was sensitive to many aspects of the adult environment. For example, he contributed to drawing up the weekly shopping list and was alert to the needs of adults around him (when his nanny was ill, wanting to ring her to send her some 'magic dust' down the wire).

Claire's private nursery school was extremely formal. It emphasized conformity and adherence to certain behavioural and cognitive expectations. Her daycare nursery by contrast encouraged self-expression in all contexts, even where the older children were withdrawn to work on the Early Learning Goals. At home, her mother encouraged confidence and capability in all matters, always assuming that Claire would be able to achieve anything that she chose to, and then modelling it for her (showing her how to do it both overtly and implicitly). In many ways, what she experienced at home and at the daycare nursery overlapped. Although the daycare setting provided no overt modelling of competence, it encouraged 'having a go' in attitude and action, and both the daycare setting and home fostered Claire's little c creativity, although the most powerful expression of that was at home where Claire was encouraged to believe that she could make anything happen.

Sam was cared for by a childminder looking after three children in all, of which he was the middle one. Each day's routine was fixed around the school day for the older child (aged six), and utilized local facilities such as the library, the indoor soft play centre, the park, music and movement groups and the '2 o'clock clubs'. The children usually took packed lunches and were out for the day until school pick-up time, meeting up with other local children and their minders. Having been taken into the play environment with other children, Sam's carer tended to socialize with the other adults, while Sam got on with playing with other children. He was encouraged to make choices in that he was left largely to his own devices, but he was not engaged with deeply in terms of his interests. This context seemed to offer Sam many opportunities to be little c creative, but with little adult feedback, encouragement or modelling to help him to do so. Sam was being cared for competently, but not engaged with in any deep way.

The differences between what these several children appear to have experienced are striking. And, of course, many questions can be begged in respect of this case-study: for example, the extent to which it matters that there are discontinuities in each child's experience.

Case-studies do, also, have limitations. They inevitably capture and relate only a part of each life history, so the complexities of each child's experience are, of course, simplified. For example, each child has experienced a range of models and contexts since birth and will do across their childhood. Joshua, for example, has had eight different nannies in his three and a half years, each with different styles of working with him. Claire was in the daycare nursery for two full days a week and the rest of the time with her mother, until she was three, when she started attending the nursery school.

## Visions of future possibilities

In this next part of this chapter, I want to consider the notion of futures education expounded by the Australian writer, Page (2000), where she talks about reshaping the early years curriculum, in order to introduce far more futures-oriented issues to children. Just as Watts (1987) emphasizes the need for early years practitioners to understand child development and growth in a wider social context, so that their knowledge has what she calls 'contemporary validity', and just as Halliwell (1992) and MacLean (1992) emphasize the need for early childhood educators to be future oriented in terms of what they consider it appropriate for young children to learn, so I propose a need for systemic future orientation in early years provision.

Although the learning of young children is in some ways timeless, in other ways it is very closely related to the future, because of the increasing pace of change which forms the context for their learning. Being a new generation, the children also symbolize and embody the future. And because their development occurs in a much faster-moving world, which holds fewer certainties than it probably did for previous generations, my observation is that the future becomes the present more quickly, even for small children. Fostering children's little c creativity can be viewed as a way of encouraging a future-orientation in the children themselves, lifewide, in order to lay the foundation for children to become flexible experts rather than rule-bound specialists, to adopt Abbott's (1999) distinction. Doing this through the systematic provision of opportunities throughout the myriad forms of provision for children aged three to eight, and building on the strong early years traditions of the past, would be desirable. One aspect of this would be the integration of educare, both in child provision and also in the initial training and continuing professional development of what Ball (1999) calls the 'teacher-carers' (p. 44).

As Moylett and Abbott (1999) observe, many of the changes in early childhood education have been reforms, (as they put it, 'making new shapes out of the same plasticine, now brown and dull through over-use'; or as Peacocke, 1999 has written in the same volume, dispensing old wine in new bottles) rather than vision-making. Vision, by contrast, aims to break 'out of the box'; it does not necessarily accept the status quo, it attempts to take risks, and it encompasses reflection and divergent thinking. It involves treating children as agents with an active role in making their future happen. This is not to say that they are 'hot-housed', but rather encouraged to exercise little c creativity, in the here-and-now.

These ideas can be seen as representing a logical and natural progression from the recommendations of the Rumbold Report (DES, 1990) on three- and four-year-olds, which advocated greater coherence and flexibility in education and care for the under-fives. The suggestions in this chapter clearly expand the age-span under consideration, up to the age of 8, and reframe curriculum priorities to place ordinary, or little c, creativity, in a far more central place.

Clearly, any vision for alternative possibilities carries with it important practical consequences such as those to do with funding, organization, and lines of responsibility, which are all beyond the scope of this book to explore in detail. One of the challenges, though, of extending vision-making beyond the pre-school years, is what Gillian Pugh (1996) calls the dilemma of 'horizontal' co-ordination versus 'vertical' (p. 4). By this, Pugh is referring to the potential for overlooking the need for continuity from pre-school to school based provision for children. As she puts it, 'If the pull towards co-ordination of all under-fives services becomes too great, is there a corresponding weakening of the continuity between education before five and education after five?' (*op. cit.*, p. 4).

In the attempt to co-ordinate under-fives services which at least at policy level started in the early 1990s, continuity between what happens to children before and after the age of five (i.e. 'vertical co-ordination') may be weakened. There has been a plethora of initiatives over the years since the early 1990s, to improve some of the discontinuities of access and provision illustrated by the case-studies at the start of this chapter – as well as those resulting from economic, social, linguistic, or cultural disadvantage. Although the aims of policy makers have been to improve horizontal continuity, the initiatives have been insufficient – both horizontally and vertically – to provide consistency of educational opportunity. This is true of the whole educare experience for children, including the nurturing of little c creativity.

There is a need for a co-ordinated attempt to provide continuity both horizontally and vertically across the years of childhood from three to eight, in a way which holds at its heart, in its aims and in its enactment, children's creativity. The formal and informal curriculum for children aged five and over needs review at the levels of both policy and practice, but particularly at the policy level, to ensure that opportunities exist to nurture children's little c creativity. One example of a policy step that could be taken is the reduction of curriculum content, to enable a little more time for the exercise of creative teaching and of teaching for creativity. The shift, since the last years of the 1990s (which includes the NACCCE Report on creativity and culture, the Early Learning Goals, and the changes in the National Curriculum, all of which have been discussed earlier) to place creativity and innovation more at the heart of policy making, is encouraging. The Education Bill for secondary schools which was introduced to Parliament in November 2001, for example, sought in a variety of ways to promote innovation and autonomy in schools, by encouraging the power to innovate, and by supporting deregulation and giving schools greater autonomy, in order to 'support the best schools in leading the next wave in educational reform' (DfES, 2001, para. 1.2). Creative approaches to teaching and learning systems in secondary education appear in the Education Bill to have the potential to raise pupil achievement. The Bill seeks to create a much more flexible education law, and to 'free schools to develop the ideas that will raise standards' (DfES, 2001, para. 2.2). Specifically, it introduces the notion of the 'power to innovate' (*op. cit.*, para. 2.4) for up to three years, where schools or Local Education Authorities have 'good ideas to raise standards which do not fit the rules as they stand' (*op. cit.*, para. 2.4). The Bill aims to encourage new forms of collaboration, between education providers, to enable schools to offer a much broader range of services to the wider community, and to encourage the creation of new all-age schools ('City Academies') through private-public-voluntary and faith-based partnerships. It aims to enable successful schools to vary elements of the National Curriculum, to lead the way in developing the curriculum for fourteen- to sixteen year-olds and even to make changes to teachers' pay and conditions. Encouragingly, the Bill seems to use the language of transformation – alongside the language of reform.

There remains, however, much to be done to give a fuller role to both creative systems and valuing pupil creativity all the way through from the early years. A part of what needs to be done, I would argue, is to transform, rather than to reform and I return to this idea later in the chapter.

## Looking at the big picture

Setting a vision necessitates standing back from the status quo, from the detail, and getting an overall feel for direction. It can also mean critically evaluating assumptions. One of the underpinning themes and justifications for little c creativity in this book has been that the individual and collective empowerment which is fostered by the development of creative skill, is a good thing at the social and economic level. These justifications have been discussed elsewhere

(Jeffrey and Craft, 2001). But it is important to ask how desirable are the cultural norms of continual change and innovation in wider Western society. For it could well be argued that there are socially and environmentally destructive aspects to fostering a culture of innovation through the education system. To what extent do we already, in the marketplace at any rate, encourage innovation for innovation's sake and not in response to genuine need? How desirable is it to encourage those values which present, via the market, 'wants' as 'needs'? It could be said that a culture of 'make do and mend' might be something to be fostered, rather than looking always for ways to change what may be working perfectly well already, whether that be a system, a relationship, a service or a product.

Related to this is the question, addressed in Chapter 8, of how culturally specific the notion of little c creativity may be, and the implications of advocating a model of creativity with its associated value-set, as if it were of universal validity. The issues raised by the shocking terrorist responses to some aspects of globalization and US policies in the latter part of 2001, and the subsequent response in going to war with terrorism, brought into focus some of the problems which the advocacy and spread of Western values may have. For it would appear that for some of the alleged terrorists who planned and carried out those actions on September 11th 2001, the United States is a powerful source of 'cultural imperialism', pursuing its economic and other interests in the global context, as if Western values were of obvious universal validity. Hence, for those responsible for the destruction of the World Trade Center and a part of the Pentagon, the US posed a legitimate target for a massive terrorist response. It could be argued that Western 'creativity' formed a part of the value-set perceived to have been imposed worldwide.

Then we might ask other questions about the limits of little c creativity, for creativity has a darker side. The human imagination is capable of immense destruction as well as of almost infinitely constructive possibilities. So, a further challenge in generating systems which could stimulate and celebrate creativity, in encouraging individual and collective agency, is to construct opportunities within a profoundly humane framework. In other words, to actively encourage the critical examination of the values inherent in creative ideas and action. The role of educators is perhaps to encourage children to examine the possible effect of their ideas on others, and to evaluate their choices in the light of this.

## A social system for creativity

Although recent studies of creativity have in fact tended to utilize systems approaches which explore creativity in a social setting, there is nevertheless evidence (Spiel and von Korff, 1998) that researchers tend to focus more on the person and the process, than on the social context in which the creativity occurs, or on the outcome. Given the social contexts of the classroom and school, and the wider environment in which pupils will exercise their little c creativity, the development of strategies which encourage creativity in the context of a social system needs further investigation. This is particularly the case within the education system, for creativity is often cast as not being relevant to conventional education.

However, it has been argued that, creating the climate and the skills for fostering creativity is essential in educating a generation of young people who can visualize new solutions to the problems of today and tomorrow's work force, social fabric, and wider environment (Kessler, 2000).

The organizational provision for the lower age-range of early childhood education and care have, over the last years of the twentieth century and the start of the twenty-first, gone through a creative transformation, in moving strongly towards the establishment of community-focused educare centres, combining health, education, and care in a single place. In Britain in 2001, these centres are known as early excellence centres, and at the time of writing there are approaching thirty in the country. Enabling parents (particularly women) to work whilst their children are both cared for and also educated, under the same roof, and providing many community functions including some health provision, is a creative response to a set of early childhood issues for families. It may also be seen as a precursor to the sorts of creative connectivity where the community, the workplace, and education come together to both foster creative and individually tailored learning which, for example, the independent think-tank, Demos, and in particular Tom Bentley have recently written about (Jupp et al., 2001). Such ideas were foreshadowed by others in the past (for example, by Adcock, 1994, National Commission on Education, 1995, Barber and Brighouse, 1992, Barber, 1996, Craft et al., 1997).

It may be that early excellence centres will blaze a trail into primary education too, and that a system which better fosters little c creativity for all within it will involve something quite different. Rather than reforming, we need to transform.

As to how all this may be achieved, it is perhaps worth reflecting on the words of Albert Einstein, who reputedly once said:

The significant problems we face *cannot* be solved at the same level of thinking we were at when we created them.

## References

Abbott, J. (1999) 'The search for expertise: the importance of the early years', in L. Abbott and H. Moylett *Early Education Transformed*. London: Falmer.

Adcock, J. (1994) *In Place of Schools: A Novel Plan for the 21st Century*. London: New Education Press.

Ball, C. (1994) *Start Right: The Importance of Early Learning*. London: Royal Society for the Encouragement of the Arts, Manufacturers and Commerce.

Ball, C. (1999) 'Quality and professionalism in early childhood', in L. Abbott and H. Moylett *Early Education Transformed*. London: Falmer.

Barber, M. (1996) *The Learning Game: Arguments for an Education Revolution*. London: Cassell.

Barber, M. and Brighouse, T. (1992) *Partners in Change: Enhancing the Teaching Profession*. London: IPPR.

Craft, A. with Dugal, J. Dyer, G. Jeffrey, B. and Lyons, T. (1997) *Can You Teach Creativity?* Nottingham: Education Now.

Department of Education and Science (1990) (DES) *Starting with Quality* (The Rumbold Report of the Committee of Enquiry into the Quality of the Educational Experiences offered to three- and four-year olds). London: HMSO (The Rumbold Report).

Department for Education and Skills (2001) (DfES) *Education Bill 2001: A Summary*. London: HMSO.

Halliwell, G. (1992) 'Practical curriculum theory: describing, informing and improving early childhood education', in B. Lambert (ed.), *Changing Faces: The Early Childhood Profession in Australia*. Watson: Australian Early Childhood Association.

Jeffrey, B. and Craft, A. (2001) 'The universalization of creativity', in A. Craft, B. Jeffrey and M. Leibling (eds), *Creativity in Education*. London: Continuum.

Jupp, R. Fairly, C. and Bentley, T. (2001) *What Learning Needs*. London: Design Council & DEMOS.

Kessler, R. (2000) *The Soul of Education: Helping Students Find Connection, Compassion and Character at School*. Alexandria, VA: Association for Supervision and Curriculum Development.

MacLean, S. V. (1992) 'Early childhood education and perceptions of "Curriculum"'. *Curriculum Perspectives*, **12**(3), 42–6.

Moylett, H. and Abbott, L. (1999) (eds) 'A vision for the future – reforming or transforming?' in L. Abbott and H. Moylett, *Early Education Transformed*, London: Falmer.

National Commission on Education (1995) *Learning to Succeed: A Radical Look at Education Today and a Strategy for the Future – a Follow-up Report*. London: NCE.

Page, J. M. (2000) *Reframing the Early Childhood Curriculum: Educational Imperatives for the Future*. London: Routledge.

Peacocke, R. (1999) 'Inspecting the future', in L. Abbott and H. Moylett *Early Education Transformed*. London: Falmer.

Pugh, G. (1996) Introduction, in G. Pugh (ed.), *Contemporary Issues in the Early Years: Working Collaboratively for Children*, London: Paul Chapman Publishing Ltd in association with National Children's Bureau Early Childhood Unit.

Spiel, C. and von Korff, C. (1998) 'Implicit theories of creativity: the conceptions of politicians, scientists, artists and school teachers', *High Ability Studies*, **9**(1), 43–58.

Watts, B. (1987) 'Changing families, changing children's services: where are the children going? Are kindergarten teachers ready to go too?' *Australian Journal of Early Childhood*, **12**(2), 4–12.

# Index